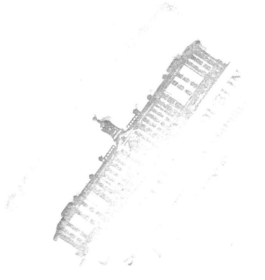

070. 4
HOR

BROADCASTING AND PUBLIC LIFE

BROADCASTING AND IRISH SOCIETY SERIES

Edited by Richard Pine

Broadcasting and Public Life

RTÉ news and current affairs, 1926-1997

John Horgan

FOUR COURTS PRESS

Set in 10 on 13 point Janson for
FOUR COURTS PRESS LTD
7 Malpas Street, Dublin 8, Ireland
email: info@four-courts-press.ie
http://www.four-courts-press.ie
and in North America by
FOUR COURTS PRESS
c/o ISBS, 920 N.E. 58th Avenue, Suite 300, Portland, OR 97213.

ISBN 1–85182–838–9 hardback
ISBN 1–85182–839–7 paperback

A catalogue record for this title
is available from the British Library.

Printed in England
by MPG Books Ltd, Bodmin, Cornwall.

Contents

Foreword

This series of 'Broadcasting and Irish Society' would not be complete without a searching, and frank, analysis of RTÉ's output in the areas of news and current affairs, and of the relationship between those areas within the broadcasting service. As series editor, I was therefore delighted when John Horgan, already the author of an authoritative study of the Irish media, accepted our invitation to undertake this volume. As a former working journalist (the visionary founder-editor of *Education Times*), as a former politician (a Senator and a TD) and, today, as a highly respected academic, he is no doubt more highly qualified than almost anyone else in Ireland to meet the challenges of such a work.

Although the advent of television in the 1960s pointed Irish households towards a new era of investigation, it emerges very strongly from this book that radio, especially in the success of *Morning Ireland* and *This Week*, continues to play a central role in the shaping of Irish public opinion. Indeed, Horgan mentions the day when many listeners awoke to hear RTÉ, on *Morning Ireland*, publishing a profuse apology to an unnamed company – later revealed to have been the Goodman Group – for having broadcast allegations of an unspecified nature, which must have left them even more in the dark than they had been before waking. It would require months of in-depth and controversial reportage of the so-called 'Beef Tribunal' on investigative programmes such as *Today Tonight* to eventually unravel the factual strands which underpinned the original allegations.

It is clear from this book that broadcasting can be a very dangerous occupation and the newsroom and the television studio can be dangerous places. Horgan reminds us graphically of the careers of such prominent broadcasters as Eoghan Harris, Muiris MacConghail, Seán Ó Mordha and Patrick Gallagher, whose passion for representative broadcasting often brought them to the edge of (and beyond) what was considered acceptable or appropriate. The relation of broadcasters to their line management, and of management to the directorate-general, to the RTÉ Authority and to government, constantly raises issues which permeate the organisation, whether through the medium of canteen gossip or the higher levels of demarcation, dispute and disciplinary action.

News and current affairs programmes, on radio and television, are highly audible and highly visible: they tell us – sometimes by way of straight reportage, sometimes by debate and even drama-documentary – stories about the society in which we live. For the most part, these stories are true. But there is an affinity between this genre of programming and another which also receives due attention in 'Broadcasting and Irish Society': television drama. Often the two genres seem to work together, or at least complementarily, to affect the way we perceive our society. The often turbulent and always challenging personalities who populate the newsrooms and the studios might not be out of place in a soap opera such as *Fair City*; dramatic disclosures and the cut-and-thrust of public debate are frequently the matter evoked by generations of broadcasters such as Brian Farrell, David Hanly, Proinsías MacAonghusa, Olivia O'Leary, Miriam O'Callaghan and Mark Little. We are in John Horgan's debt for having recreated many of these 'dramas' of public service broadcasting in an informative and incisive fashion.

Richard Pine
Series Editor

Introduction

To write a book about news and current affairs in RTÉ is an undertaking that tempts fate. At one level, it is an impossibility: the output of the station on radio and television since 1961 (let alone the decades preceding the introduction of television) is so voluminous that any attempt at selection would of itself be doomed to failure: whole books have been written about the television coverage of a small number of issues over a restricted period of time.[1] This work is therefore necessarily primarily an overview, in which various programmes, events and personalities will bulk larger than others: it does not claim to be comprehensive, because it cannot. At the same time, it attempts to convey not only the flavour, but occasionally the significant detail, of episodes, trends and developments in the history of Irish broadcasting in a way that will be recognisable to many of those who participated in them, as well as offering the general reader an appreciation of some of the issues involved, and the academic reader a benchmark and a source of ideas for future research.

Selection is not the only problematic area. Definition is another. News is news, and has traditionally been organised in RTÉ and in other media on closely defined lines. But current affairs is a chimera, despite the existence of organisational units which are called 'Current Affairs'. As it happens, there was no Current Affairs department in the early days of RTÉ television and radio: it was 'Public Affairs'. But 'Current Affairs', even after it had been created and designated, never contained more than a variable proportion of the programming that could legitimately be so described. Some current affairs programmes went out under the Features rubric, especially on radio. Some went out as Information Programming. Some went out as Irish language programming. Some went out as part of the output of the Religious Broadcasting section. Some went out as Light Entertainment (who could exclude the *Late Late Show*?). And is satire current affairs? The ministers who privately fulminated against *Hall's Pictorial Weekly* during the embattled days of the 1973–77 coalition government could have been forgiven for assuming, on occasion, that it was. Everybody will make a different selection: this is mine.

Writing this book has also underlined one central fact, often forgotten in an era of fragmented audiences, satellites, multiplexes and de-regulation. This is that listening to radio and watching television in the early years, and even to an extent right up to our own day, has always been not just a private or domestic activity,

---

1 Greg Philo, *Really Bad News*.

but one with an important communal and indeed political dimension. Watching or listening to the programme has always been only part of the experience: the balance, in terms of the social impact of media, is contributed by the discussions, arguments and disagreements with those of us who were part of the same audience elsewhere, or even with those of us who were not part of the audience on any particular occasion but who do not experience this as a disqualification from commentary.

This is in turn related to the fact that broadcasting in general, and public service broadcasting of news and current affairs in particular, lives in permanent and dangerous proximity to the political process. There is always the risk that this close and sometimes almost symbiotic relationship would take over; regardless of how the task is approached, it is impossible to prevent it bulking large in the narrative.

The question of sources also needs to be addressed. RTÉ gave me unparalleled access to internal documentation at any and every level within the organisation, and without that degree of access this book simply could not have been written at all. But in an area as fluid as broadcasting, paper alone cannot ever tell the full story, and sometimes distorts it. Programmes and programme-makers who feature in the documentary sources frequently do so because they gave rise to controversy, or were criticised by powerful vested interests. I suspect that much excellent programming did not come under notice simply because it was good.

This problem of sources is compounded by the fact that although the narrative ends with the appointment of Bob Collins as Director-General in 1997, much of it deals with events of comparatively recent memory, and with individuals who are still active in their professional and journalistic fields. Although I have discussed one or other of the topics covered in this book with many of them, the sensitivities are such that they remain for the most part in the background. It should, in this context, be emphasised that the views and judgements expressed are entirely my own. Some individuals, however, were central to this work, and should be publicly acknowledged. They include Bob Collins's personal assistant, Ms Beverly Hanly, who beat many pathways for me through the thick undergrowth of RTÉ documentation; Brian Lynch of RTÉ's Print Archives, who presides over an Aladdin's cave of paper; Malachy Moran of the RTÉ Reference Library, which is a vital part of the whole RTÉ system; Dr David Craig and the staff of the National Archives; and Dr David Sheehy of the Dublin Diocesan Archives. Thanks are also due to Tom O'Dea, who lent me cuttings of his television columns written for the *Irish Press* over a period of almost twenty years, and which provide a fascinating counterpoint to the history of broadcasting generally in that period.

At the same time, I have attempted to balance this account of news and current affairs in RTÉ by placing as much emphasis as is possible, given these inevitable limitations, on programmes and programme-makers, whether journalists, presenters, producers or directors. At the end of the day, it is difficult to avoid the conclusion that paper and ink alone are an inadequate medium in which to convey the sheer excitement of broadcast journalism, the multifarious skills involved, the innumerable moments of high drama, and the practised professionalism which assembles sound and vision, people and events, emotions and insights, into a dramatic and yet coherent and authentic version of social reality hour after hour, day after day, week after week, and to the most exacting deadlines. Its public nature ensures that the version of social reality which broadcasting presents will never go unchallenged for long by its audiences, and indeed many of the challenges come from within the organisation, from broadcasters themselves. And it is to these broadcasters in news and current affairs – all of them, irrespective of organisational designation or function, trade union affiliation, or political views – that this work is affectionately dedicated.

CHAPTER 1

The inheritance

Broadcasting in Ireland generally, in the first half of the twentieth century, was shaped primarily by a whole range of social and political circumstances that hampered, where they did not simply frustrate, the emergence and growth of a culture of public service broadcasting in the areas of news and current affairs. Ironically in view of recent events, finance was not primarily an issue. It was an issue of sorts, simply for the reason that the Department of Finance was always niggardly in its disbursement of State resources. But Finance had less reason to be niggardly with 2RN or Radio Éireann, as it later became, if only because, for much of its early existence, broadcasting actually made a profit for the State: including customs revenue from the duties on imported radio equipment, there was a consistent surplus from 1926 until the early 1940s.[1] In the late 1920s, as the country struggled through the reconstruction process in the wake of the civil war, any services dependent on the State were run with minimal funding, even (and perhaps especially) when they themselves generated a profit. As the Postmaster-General, J.J. Walsh, told the Seanad in December 1926:

> The position is that we have little money for broadcasting purposes. Our resources have never been what we desired, and the Exchequer is slow to part with its finances for that particular purpose, a purpose concerned with the amusement of the people.[2]

In the 1930s, the economic war with Britain exercised much the same effect. And, even if these influences had not been so powerful, the growth and development of broadcasting remained conditioned by other factors: a centralised system of government and public administration, including education; the top-down view of radio as primarily a medium for instruction, education and entertainment, and only secondarily (if at all) as a medium of information, commentary or criticism; and one-party government from 1932 to 1948.

Early news broadcasts were for the most part re-broadcasts of material taken (with permission) from the BBC, and from other stations. Not least for the latter reason, the broadcasts were restricted to late in the evenings: to broadcast the

1 Richard Pine, *2RN and the origins of Irish radio* (2002), p. 133.   2 Seanad Debates, 16 December 1926.
3 Dáil Debates, 20 November 1926; quoted in John Horgan, *Irish media: a critical history since 1922*, p. 20.

4

bulletins earlier would have risked offending the powerful newspaper interests, and indeed this practice was effectively copied from the BBC, which was similarly restrained. The bulletins were delivered by an official known as the Station Announcer. This was initially a part-time post, but by November 1926 he had become full-time, and the Postmaster-General told the Dáil that he would have a part-time assistant who would be expected to record the proceedings of Dáil and Senate, to obtain reports from police and fire brigades of 'important or sensational happenings', to obtain particulars of outstanding events from national cultural organisations, to prepare a bulletin of foreign news, stock market reports, provincial news and market prices. In addition to all of this, and on a part-time salary of £4 per week, he would be required

> to furnish a guarantee that there will be no infringement of copyright, and shall provide a bond for £1,000 to be obtained from an approved insurance society or company indemnifying the Minister for Posts and Telegraphs as representative of the State against any action, claims or expenses caused ... by any infringement or alleged infringement of copyright.[3]

By December 1926 the time of the evening news bulletin had been advanced from its original time slot of 10.30 p.m. (which was effectively the close of broadcasting) to 7.30 p.m. Part of the problem was that the only readily available sources of news, apart from the BBC, were other foreign stations: 2RN was precluded by copyright legislation from broadcasting items from the morning and evening newspapers, although this restriction was apparently not always observed to the letter.[4] This ensured, in turn, that the news was strongly biased towards international events, which were not only inexpensive but less potentially controversial than accounts of domestic controversies. Walsh explained:

> The news we are now issuing is of an international character, news taken up by a strong wireless receiver which is located in the Central Telegraph Office. All that news is taken from the air. It emanates from stations in Moscow, Rome, Berlin, Paris and England. We pay nobody for it. It is a little bit behind time, but later on we hope to extend this foreign news series and bring it up to time. It is a venture which no other broadcasting station has embarked upon. We are not quite satisfied that foreign news is sufficient for our station, and we have taken the necessary steps to build up a Press section here. Already one Pressman has been appointed; at

4 Maurice Gorham, *Forty years of Irish broadcasting* (1967), p. 46. Gorham suggests that Irish radio 'continued to lift its news without acknowledgement or payment for its first twenty years' (ibid., p. 63).

least authority has been given for an appointment. In all probability we will find another later on, and possibly a third, and eventually there may be quite a number of Press correspondents not only attached to our station here in Dublin but correspondents in the country. Our general policy is to use broadcasting as a means of disseminating news, irrespective of any other agency.[5]

Despite such good intentions, the news service continued to attract criticism. The question was addressed intermittently by the Government's Broadcasting Advisory Committee, which operated under the chairmanship of P.S. O'Hegarty, Secretary of the Department of Posts and Telegraphs (as the Postmaster-General's fiefdom had been renamed). In April 1929 *Irish Radio News* complained that the bulk of 2RN's news coverage was 'British propaganda as broadcast by Rugby station amplified by what local news the News Editor can obtain.'[6] Two months later this criticism found a ready echo on the committee, as one of its members, J.J. Halpin, complained that the 2RN news service was 'most unsatisfactory.' The assistant secretary of the Department sought to deflect the criticism by disclosing that 'negotiations with the associated newspapers for a joint service had failed, and alternative proposals were now being considered'. The matter came up again in September, when the committee was told that 'negotiations with the press Agencies for supplies of British and foreign news had … been abandoned owing to prohibitive cost.'[7] For the most part, however, the committee devoted its proceedings to lengthy disagreement about the use of Irish on the new station and, by the time it expired in June 1933, it had signally failed to oversee any significant improvement in the news service.

Until the 1930s, indeed, controversy was conspicuous by its absence. There was no such area as current affairs, for example, and the provision of a news service was bedevilled by the parsimony of the Department of Finance. In this context, the brief flurry occasioned on 18 June 1926, when the station carried a lightly coded but anonymous report indicating that Cumann na nGaedheal was unwilling to enter a coalition arrangement with any other party or parties, was less a foretaste of things to come than a reminder of the quasi-paralysis which was the station's defining characteristic in this sensitive area. The fact that this evidently Government-inspired leak (the Postmaster-General, J.J. Walsh, is assumed to have been the culprit) was followed a week later by an officially authorised broadcast by Mr de Valera, whose party was at that stage not even in the Dáil, was patently a sop to the opposition. Even at this early stage, the concept of balance was finding hesitant expression in the emerging culture of public service

5 Seanad Debates, 16 December 1926.   6 Muiris Mac Conghail, 'Politics by Wireless: News and Current Affairs on Radio, 1926–2000' (2001), pp. 74–5.   7 NAI, 2001/78/74. Minutes of Broadcasting Advisory Committee for 25 June 1929 and 24 September 1929.

broadcasting.[8] The corollary, however, was also clear: if controversial political statements by or on behalf of government spokesmen had to be balanced by statements from the Opposition, the absence of controversial statements by the Government would have the beneficial effect of keeping the opposition away from the microphone. And this, for quite some time, seems to have been part of the rationale for the editorial decision, conscious or otherwise, to afford news a generally low priority. No doubt chafing at the bit, one of Fianna Fáil's up-and-coming young men, Seán Lemass, complained from the Opposition benches that 'the policy of the Department in respect to programmes is too timorous. They avoid very carefully anything which might be considered controversial in any way. I think that is a mistake.'[9] His proposed remedy for this state of affairs – a suggestion that the Advisory Committee should be re-constituted to incorporate all shades of political opinion, and should vet controversial discussions or lectures in advance – was one which was to lie fallow for many years.

Fianna Fáil's accession to power in 1932 saw a continuing modest expansion in the station's resources. There is some evidence, indeed, that Fianna Fáil were more pro-active in their use of this new medium and that – not least in consequence of this – allegations of pro-Government bias, and censorship of Opposition views, became more frequent. In 1934, a number of Opposition deputies alleged that, in the words of Frank MacDermot TD, 'addresses are being broadcast which are distinctly political in their tendency.'[10] The Minister, Gerry Boland, was dismissive: 'I do not admit that there have been any political addresses at all. There have been broadcasts by different Ministers on matters relating to their respective Departments, which concern the whole country'.[11]

The under-resourcing of the news service led to the extraordinary situation in which, on occasion, listeners would be told, as the broadcast moved from international to Irish news, that there was no Irish news. Deputy J. Morrissey, who raised this in the Dáil in May 1935, noted that it was a frequent occurrence on Sunday nights.[12] Additions were made to the news staff in 1935 which allowed for extensions to the news bulletins at 6.45 p.m. and 10.30 p.m. and which allowed the Minister to announce, the following year, that such lacunae would no longer occur.[13] This was the year in which statistics first became available on programme output, revealing that news was responsible for a total of 169 hours in all.[14]

The same year also saw an important innovation with the first of a series of what were described as 'debates' – in this case, a discussion between the writer, Frank O'Connor, and the editor of the *Irish Times*, Robert Maire Smyllie, on 'The Press and the Nation.'[15] This, coupled with increasing use by ministers of

8 Pine, op. cit., pp. 170, 177; Muiris Mac Conghail, 'Wireless', pp. 74–5.   9 Dáil Debates, 23 April 1931.
10 Dáil Debates, 12 April 1934.   11 Ibid.   12 Dáil Debates, 15 May 1935.   13 Dáil Debates, 26 March 1936.   14 Alacoque Kealy, *Irish radio data, 1926–1980* (1981), p. 31.   15 *2RN Report*, 1935 (RTÉ Writ-

the facility for ministerial broadcasts, led to a distinct increase in the political temperature. Interestingly, however, there was no unanimity in the Oireachtas about the advisability or otherwise of allowing political debates on the radio. James Dillon TD was against it, 'on mature reflection', as he put it, 'because the people do not want that kind of thing, and because I believe that it would give rise, at the present time in any case, to endless practical difficulties which, in theory, it would be very hard to define clearly.'[16] Both Frank MacDermot TD and the Minister disagreed. Boland, in particular, said that he would have no objection personally if a political debate could be arranged from time between the accredited speakers of political parties. However, he gave in the same speech a defence of government use of the airwaves in terms which echoed down through the years that followed, and in particular in Seán Lemass's answer to a Dáil question in November 1966.[17] Boland's view, redolent of a kind of democratic centralism, and infused with a belief in the centrality of the Dáil which must have brought a wry smile to the countenances of his political opponents, was that

> the Government has not taken sufficient advantage of the broadcasting station to try to put across legislation concerning the agricultural and the economic policy which has passed into law. Once that has happened these things are above Party ... My complaint is that Ministers have not availed of the broadcasting station sufficiently to impress upon the people the necessity of giving effect to the legislation that has been passed and of co-operating with the Government in that legislation.[18]

The Spanish civil war gave rise to accusations that the station was broadcasting news 'somewhat tainted with a pink outlook.'[19] But such brief passages of arms were shortly to be overshadowed by the outbreak of World War II, in the course of which the censorship of all the news media, and not least of Radio Éireann, became an openly acknowledged element of government policy. Where Radio Éireann was concerned, a task which had never been exceptionally difficult was further facilitated by the fact that the director of the Government Information Bureau was Frank Gallagher, a Republican journalist who had been prominent in the IRA's propaganda campaign during the War of Independence, who had served briefly as founding editor of the *Irish Press* from 1932 to 1934 and who had been Deputy Director of 2RN from 1936 to 1938. This informal self-censorship, however, had its embarrassing moments, as on occasions when the station inadvertently broadcast items which had been censored from the print media.[20] This led to a tightening of the structures, and of the policy itself,

ten Archives), quoted in Mac Conghail, 'Wireless', p. 76   16 Dáil Debates, 26 March 1936.   17 Cf. below, pp. 41–2.   18 Dáil Debates, 26 March 1936.   19 Deputy Minch, Dáil Debates, 22 April 1937. 20 Dónal Ó Drisceoil, *Censorship in Ireland, 1939–45* (1996), p. 99.

in relation to broadcasting. Dáil deputies complained particularly at the fact that ministerial speeches were more generously reported than those of the Opposition, and W.T. Cosgrave on one occasion expressed his wonderment at the fact that on one particular day, the BBC news had reported two speeches from the Dáil in its 6 p.m. news while Radio Éireann, 40 minutes later, had reported only one.[21] Séamus Ó Braonáin, in a series of articles published in *The Leader* after the war, spoke frankly about the organisation's difficulties:

> Purely because of Radio Éireann being Government-controlled, anything which might be regarded as contentious, or as critical of our own Government or institutions or the governments or institutions of other countries had to be cut out or handled with great caution.[22]

One of the victims was Frank O'Connor, who had been a participant in the first 'debate' on radio in 1935. His critical broadcasts for the BBC led to him being unofficially banned from appearing on Radio Éireann as a talker from February 1942, and even the facility of using the Radio Éireann studios to record his BBC talks was withdrawn.[23] The Labour TD Jim Larkin was another casualty: after having been invited to give a talk, he was told to take a particular passage out of his script, declined, and refused to deliver the censored version.[24] Throughout the war, Opposition deputies generally were not slow to allege that the radio coverage of Dáil debates, in particular, was slanted in favour of the government – in the words of James Dillon TD, 'insidious ... dishonest ... time-serving'.[25] The high-risk aspect of domestic political news, and the continual criticism of it in the Dáil, may in turn have been partly responsible for the additional resources devoted to domestic news-gathering in 1944, including the appointment of eight local correspondents in different parts of the country.[26] Foreign news was next: an agreement with the British service provided by the Press Association–Reuters–Exchange telegraph network began on 16 September 1946, to be followed two years later on 10 December 1948 by a similar service from the American news agency, United Press International.

News coverage of political speeches was not the only area in which controversy arose. The popular programme 'Question Time', arranged by the Irish Tourist Association, had been in trouble during the war when, in a special programme broadcast from Belfast, one panellist had given 'Winston Churchill' as the answer to the question 'Who is the world's greatest story-teller?' No further visits to Belfast were arranged for the duration of hostilities. Not long after the war ended, however, the same programme was again involved in political con-

---

21 Dáil Debates, 6 February 1941. 22 Seamus Ó Braonáin, 'Seven Years of Irish Radio: (iii)', *The Leader*, 15 January 1949, 19–20. 23 Ibid., p. 212. 24 J. Larkin TD, Dáil Debates, 9 November 1943. 25 Dáil Debates, 9 November 1943. 26 Gorham, op. cit., p. 147.

troversy, although this time indirectly. The ITA had chosen as the presenter of the programme the young barrister Noel Hartnett, who had long been associated with Fianna Fáil and whose organisational skills for that party were legendary: he was reputed to have been one of the few people who could walk into Éamon de Valera's office without knocking. His strong Republican sympathies had, however, been inflamed during the war by de Valera's policy of interning IRA men in the Curragh, and he had drifted out of the party. He had even appeared as a junior barrister at an inquest on one IRA prisoner who had been shot while attempting to escape. The senior barrister on that occasion was Seán MacBride, a former IRA Chief of Staff, with whom Hartnett was shortly to found the Clann na Poblachta political party.

At a protest meeting in Dublin about internment, Hartnett described his former political associates in Fianna Fáil as 'Belsen camp gaolers'. P.J. Little, the Minister for Posts and Telegraphs, immediately informed the ITA that if they continued to employ Hartnett as their compere, the programme would not be allowed on air.

The issue immediately exploded into the Dáil, where it was raised by Richard Mulcahy and James Dillon. Mulcahy wanted to know whether the Government had made any regulations 'as to the standard of political conduct to be required of persons before they will be permitted to broadcast from Radio Éireann'. Dillon, who underlined the fact that he 'detested' Hartnett's political convictions, argued that the sacking had been a breach of Hartnett's civil liberties, because there was no evidence that Hartnett had ever said anything on air which was of an improper character or a contravention of the station's rules.

Little's defence was two-fold. In the first place, he had not sacked Hartnett; he had merely told the ITA that if Hartnett presented the programme, his Department would refuse to broadcast it and the ITA, not the Department, was Hartnett's employer. Conscious of the fact that this sinuous explanation might not, of itself, be enough, he cut to the chase. His detailed explanation exposed the political elements of the case without any ambiguity.

> Mr Hartnett, speaking at a recent political meeting, defamed the Government of his own country by calling them 'Belsen camp gaolers.' If Mr Hartnett were retained as compere, that defamation could be circulated abroad as having the authority of the Irish Tourist Association. It is a well-known rule in the Civil Service that state employees shall not participate in political activities. As regards comperes and lecturers, the same rules do not, of course, apply. But is obvious that if Radio Éireann is to serve the interests of the country and its listening public, persons engaging in violent controversy likely to arouse widespread hostility should not

be employed. Mr Hartnett's defamatory and subversive remarks have aroused bitter and widespread resentment.[27]

It was not long, of course, before the shoe was on the other foot. Although Hartnett himself failed to secure a Dáil seat in the 1948 election, his party leader, Seán MacBride, went into government as Minister for External Affairs. The ink was hardly dry on the deputies' signatures on the roll of Dáil Éireann when Little was accusing his replacement as Minister for Posts and Telegraphs, the National Labour deputy Jim Everett, of allowing Radio Éireann to be used through its news bulletins for 'direct political attacks against the Opposition party'. Everett, in a reply which might have been scripted for Little himself a few months earlier, retorted:

> I have assured the Deputy that the broadcasting service will not be used in the interests of any party. If, however, Ministers are doing a certain service to the country, they will get a broadcast which other deputies who are not giving any such service will not get,'[28]

The question of the political *bona fides* of certain broadcasters, however, resurfaced in a somewhat rancorous way as two Fianna Fáil speakers in particular – Little and Seán MacEntee – referred to the extra-mural activities of the Director of Broadcasting in Radio Éireann, C.E. Kelly. The context demonstrated not only the sensitivity with which Fianna Fáil was reacting to the loss of office after sixteen continuous years, but to its readiness to apportion blame elsewhere for its defeat. Kelly (although he was not directly named in the debate) was the editor of *Dublin Opinion*, which Little described with considerable unfairness as a paper 'which has taken sides in politics'. Unfairly, because it would have been difficult for even a gently satirical paper like *Dublin Opinion* to operate in isolation from the context in which one party was almost continuously in power. Seán MacEntee, as was his style, went even further, describing it as 'a certain Party partisan journal published monthly in this country which has been consistently anti-Fianna Fáil.' It was left to the Clann na Poblachta deputy, Con Lehane, to remind Fianna Fáil of the Noel Hartnett case, and to pointedly urge Everett to 'resist the temptation, no matter from what quarter it comes, to impose political tests such as were imposed by his predecessor in order to prevent a very popular and capable broadcasting artist from reaching the Irish public on the air'.[29]

Undeterred, Fianna Fáil wasted no time in dealing with the irritant as soon as they returned to office. Kelly was moved to be Director of Savings in the

27 Dáil Debates, 5 June 1946. **28** Dáil Debates, 22 June 1948. **29** Dáil Debates, 20 July 1948.

Department of Posts and Telegraphs, a move that the new Minister, Erskine Childers, described without blushing, as a 'promotion'.[30]

Masked by the partisan charges and counter-charges about the content of broadcasting during the war years and immediately afterwards, another event had taken place which, if it was not to shape the direction of news and current affairs broadcasting as much as politics and journalism did, nonetheless introduced into Irish public life a new and powerful figure who was under no illusions about the power of the mass media. This was the appointment, in 1940, of Dr J.C. McQuaid, as Catholic archbishop of Dublin. Although the broadcasting station for Radio Éireann was in Athlone, and therefore technically outside his jurisdiction, the signals emanated from the studios in Henry Street, which unarguably were. In ecclesiastical jurisdiction, territory is everything, and the new archbishop – an energetic and exceptionally able moderniser, in sharp contrast to his predecessor – lost no time in establishing his control of important areas of turf. He wrote to the Minister for Posts and Telegraphs, P.J. Little, in December 1940 requesting that anyone who wanted to broadcast from 'the Dublin station' would have to submit their manuscript to ecclesiastical censorship 'if they purport to give the Catholic viewpoint'.[31] Little replied by return that he was 'happy to arrange to have your proposals for the ecclesiastical supervision of these talks put into operation'.[32] At McQuaid's instigation, the possibility of having 'lectures on practical questions from a Catholic viewpoint' were discussed at a meeting of the Catholic hierarchy in May 1943: the archbishop told a correspondent that he had 'long advocated such a series of broadcasts'.[33]

McQuaid's approach to broadcasting was, however, not only pro-active but pre-emptive. By 1948, an informal vetting system had apparently already been set in place, operated on McQuaid's behalf by Monsignor J.C. Boylan, the parish priest of Dun Laoghaire, whose well-deserved reputation as a Biblical scholar may not have enhanced, but certainly did not impede, his ventures in this area. Boylan, evidently by virtue of a prior arrangement, was sent scripts of topical talks for vetting by the Radio Éireann officer, Francis MacManus, himself a noted writer of novels and short stories. One such series of scripts, on adoption, prompted Boylan to write to McQuaid with the warning that they were 'full of potential trouble for us.'[34] McQuaid short-circuited the process by writing directly to MacManus: 'I consider the issue treated to be so complex and contentious that it would be inadvisable to allow the State broadcasting system to be used by a private group for propaganda.'[35]

---

30 Dáil Debates, 5 November 1952. **31** McQuaid to Little, 1 December 1940 (hand-written draft), DDAAB8/B/XXVI (a) **32** Little to McQuaid, 2 December 1940, ibid. **33** McQuaid to John Fitzpatrick, 7 May 1943, ibid. **34** Boylan to McQuaid, 17 July 1948, ibid. **35** McQuaid to MacManus, 21 July 1948, ibid.

Other forms of propaganda were regarded as more legitimate. In 1948, McQuaid secured permission to give a talk on Radio Éireann in which he appealed for funds for the Italian Christian Democrat party, then fighting a crucial election. No doubt largely as a result of this appeal, a total of some £20,000[36] was raised and despatched to help Dr McQuaid's co-religionists carry on the fight against godless Communism. It is difficult – although it is of course arguable – to imagine that he would have been permitted to do so under the immediately preceding Fianna Fáil Government, which had lost office in the January of that year.

By now McQuaid had another important ally in the Secretary of the Department of Posts and Telegraphs, León Ó Broin. Ó Broin, a distinguished historian in his own right and a defender of the concept of public service broadcasting (he was largely instrumental in preventing the State's television service from being farmed out to private contractors in 1957–61), was also a devout Catholic and a member of the Legion of Mary. He was appointed Secretary of the Department on 16 April 1948. In August 1948, when the new inter-party government were wondering what to do with the short-wave station which had been bequeathed to them by Mr de Valera, Ó Broin and de Valera privately discussed the possibility of this facility being used for Catholic broadcasts, but this plan, to which the Minister was apparently not averse, foundered on the element of cost: the State would not subsidise it, and it would have cost the Church a minimum of £36,500 for two hours broadcast time a day.[37]

By 1955, the 'Topical Talks' series on Radio Éireann, which was the successor of the 'debates' launched in 1935, and still the closest approximation to a current affairs output that the station could provide, was evoking discernible vibrations in the ecclesiastical antennae. In February of that year, McQuaid sent an unnamed cleric to see Ó Broin to enquire about the possibility of facilitating 'cultured Catholic laymen' on some of these talks. Dr McQuaid's emissary reported:

> Mr Ó Broin said that he was disturbed at some talks given on Radio Éireann recently by Liam Mac Gabhann – a fellow-traveller in his opinion, including one 'Topical Talk'. He had intervened to express disapproval. Steps were taken to avoid a recurrence.[38]

Ó Broin went further, outlining the system by which speakers were selected for these talks, and intimating that the man in charge, Mr M.J. Lawlor, the News

---

36 Approximately €375,000 in today's terms.   **37** McQuaid to Ó Broin, 26 August 1948, ibid.   **38** Unsigned memorandum, 11 February 1955, ibid. Liam Mac Gabhann, a journalist with strong republican and socialist sympathies, was for many years a valued member of the staffs of a number of Dublin newspapers, including the *Irish Press* (for which he wrote a long-remembered account of Big Jim Larkin's funeral in 1947) and, in the 1960s, the *Irish Times*.

Editor, was 'an excellent Catholic, and a Legionary'. Ó Broin demurred at the suggestion that those chosen to give the talks should be chosen from a panel of legionaries – 'the RE Comhairle would have to refuse talks supplied by a group' – but assured his interlocutor that 'negatively, talks by "Liberals" and fellow-travellers would be excluded as far as possible.'[39]

By now, of course, the system was beginning to change and, as Ó Broin put it to Dr McQuaid's informant, 'Radio Éireann was at present enjoying more independence from the Department.' Even the powerful hand of McQuaid on the tiller was not, of itself, enough to deflect the course of broadcasting history. News and current affairs, in particular, remained the focus of much of the controversies that were increasingly to bedevil the work of professional broadcasters, and inflame the imaginations of sensitive churchmen and politicians.

The institutional and structural changes of the 1950s in Radio Éireann had been set in motion by an experiment which failed – the short-wave radio station through which Mr de Valera's government had hoped to broadcast to the Irish diaspora, and to create a distinctive Irish voice which would, among other things, impress on the international community the iniquities of Partition. The experiment had been shelved during the war, when the equipment required was to all intents and purposes unobtainable, but was revived immediately afterwards, and in 1947 a huge increase in the estimates for the Department of Posts and Telegraphs envisaged a substantial expansion of the station's news service as well as the development of outside broadcast facilities and the recruitment of an orchestra. The Inter-Party government which took office in February 1948 regarded de Valera's ideas with suspicion, and put the short-wave station back on the shelf: but the money was spent, and Radio Éireann underwent a sea-change.

Two 'descriptive news-writers', P.P. O'Reilly and Brian Durnin, joined the station on 22 March 1948, and became known as 'observers', involved with the new outside broadcast unit, as announcers, as scriptwriters and as reporters. In their first year at work, the station proudly reported, they had delivered 106 'news talks' (excluding records used in the straight news) and had travelled no less than 8,200 miles 'by train and bus, plane and ship, mobile unit and railway, and in an assortment of official and other cars'.[40] Seán Mac Réamoinn, one of the two Outside Broadcast Officers who took up duty at the same time, and a migrant from the Department of External Affairs, hailed the mobile unit as the answer to the charge of over-centralisation which, he noted, had 'long been one of the favourite poisoned arrows of the critic of Radio Éireann.'[41] Their first recording session was in the bar of the Royal Hotel on Valentia Island in November 1947; the artistes a group of visiting Spanish sailors. O'Reilly, in a talk broadcast many years later on RTÉ, described the newsroom to which he

39 Ibid. **40** *Radio Éireann Annual Report, 1948*, p. 12. **41** Ibid., p. 13.

had become attached. There was the news officer, Michael Lawlor, with an assistant news editor, 'two professional reporters, two clerks, and, lo and behold!, at last a teleprinter service linking us to the world service of Reuters-Press Association ... we had reached the end of the beginning.'[42]

Michael J. Lawlor, now re-titled news editor, recorded two years later that deadlines were sometimes extremely close:

> When Count Bernadotte was assassinated, the news started to come in after twenty past six, just barely in time for our six-thirty bulletin, on which the news was first given to this part of the world.[43]

In the same year, news in English accounted for 11.3% of the 2,740 broadcast hours, news in Irish 1.9%, and the 'talks Department' (effectively current affairs, but of an overwhelmingly non-contentious character) for 16.8%.[44] Writing some ten years later, John Ross, a veteran of the old days in the Henry Street newsroom, recalled no more than 'a few sub-editors, two reporters, no mike-bearing rovers such as myself.'[45]

The half-way mark in the century also marked, more or less, the first quarter-century of public service broadcasting. It also coincided with the development – at first almost imperceptible – of a new regime in relation to Radio Éireann. Government was still watchful – even wary. But windows and doors were being opened, however cautiously, to allow for the introduction of new practices, standards and expectations. Erskine Childers, who was appointed Minister for Posts and Telegraphs in the new Fianna Fáil government in 1951, has generally been given credit for the modernisation process that was now being put in train, but it was discernible even earlier. In his first estimates speech as Minister in June 1948, Jim Everett had touched on a policy question which he described as 'perhaps the most fundamental of them all – the question of whether the present system of control and operation of the broadcasting services is the best one'.[46] He had, just prior to this, reconstituted the Broadcasting Advisory Committee which had been allowed to wither away in 1933, and he was now talking for the first time about the possibility of delegation. Praising the 'most competent staff' who had been hired by the station, he now expressed his belief that the broadcasters were quite capable of doing everything that broadcasting required if they could be made to feel that they were free to do so without all the inhibitions associated with the more normal type of Civil Service department.

> To give an adequate trial to the present broadcasting set-up I feel that one desirable step is the creation for these people of an atmosphere in which

42 RTÉ Written Archives; quoted in Mac Conghail, 'Wireless', p. 77.   **43** *Radio Éireann Year Book, 1950*, p. 18.   **44** Ibid., p. 54.   **45** John Ross, 'Looking Back' (1961).   **46** Dáil Debates, 20 July 1948.

they can give of their best. A form of encouragement I believe in is to tell the staffs responsible for the programmes, as I do now, that I have every confidence in them and that apart from laying down policy for them in general terms I propose to give them the widest measure of freedom possible to do their job. This will help towards the provision of better programmes and will give us the opportunity of judging, at our leisure, under the better conditions created, whether a Civil Service organisation is capable of catering adequately for this most unusual type of State service. I am sure that in this task the Broadcasting Service will continue to benefit from the advice tendered by the advisory committee which is being reconstituted with an enlarged membership.[47]

Everett was, to put it mildly, not widely regarded as a political mould-breaker or an administrative innovator. To find an explanation for this abrupt change of policy, therefore, one has to look further – but not much further. Leon Ó Broin, who had been a career civil servant in the Department of Finance since 1925 and whose role has already been mentioned in connection with Dr McQuaid, had become secretary of the Department three months earlier. The conservative nature of his Catholicism did not obscure or qualify a mind that was administratively innovative and intellectually rigorous. Indeed, if it is correct to assume that he was directly responsible for this initiative, the roots of his opposition to over-centralised control of media could perhaps be found in his experience during the war years, when he was the editor of *Maria Legionis*, a journal published by the Legion of Mary, of which he was a prominent member. The censors were at first unwilling to move against the magazine because of it association with 'a very laudable religious movement'. Eventually they took action in January 1945, when the Minister himself, Frank Aiken, ripped out, from page proofs, photographs of individuals in British military uniforms, and banned the serialised story of Stalag 383, 'the POW camp which introduced the Legion to Germany'.[48]

Four years after Everett had – presumably – been used to fly this particular kite, the pace of change was to be accelerated under a new government. Now, in Childers, Ó Broin had an articulate, highly-educated minister who was fascinated by media generally and who wanted to make his mark. Childers told the Dáil of his pleasure at the success of a new broadcasting development – the introduction of unscripted political discussions – and announced that he was taking steps to inaugurate party political broadcasts, as Radio Éireann was now one of the few stations in Western Europe that did not afford their political parties this facility. He went even further, declaring that although having broadcasting controlled by an independent corporation would be 'too extreme a measure in a

---

47 Ibid.   48 Dónal Ó Drisceoil, *Censorship*, p. 232.

small country such as our own', he was setting up a new advisory council which would, 'broadly speaking [...] take the place of the Department of Posts and Telegraphs in assisting the Minister in the framing of policy and the carrying on of the administration of broadcasting.'[49]

Within a few short years, Radio Éireann had moved up several gears. The 40–minute Wednesday night unscripted discussions referred to by Childers – *Talking It Out* – were now an established feature. They had been supplemented by programmes such as *What's on Your Mind?* and *In Reply to Yours*. In December 1953 there was an abortive attempt to persuade TDs and senators to take part in discussions on radio, but 'when the speakers turned out to be less than impressive, their party HQs instructed them not to take part'.[50] March 1954 saw the first appointment of a full-time staff journalist in Belfast.[51] The same year saw the introduction not only of party political broadcasts (before the election in that year) but of the monthly *Round Table on World Affairs*, which Francis MacManus inaugurated, and whose anchor was Jack White, then deputy editor of the *Irish Times* and later to move into RTÉ as head of Public (i.e. Current) Affairs. Brian Farrell was among the broadcasters who cut their teeth on that programme: others involved included Professor Desmond Williams of UCD, Dr Garret FitzGerald, and Dr Donal O'Sullivan, the historian, musicologist and former Clerk of the Seanad. These initiatives, however, did not presage a more general introduction of politicians to the airwaves: only one member of the Oireachtas participated in radio programmes in 1954, five in 1955, none in 1956, three in 1957, five in 1958, and six in 1959.[52]

What White described as 'the most notable event on Irish radio in 1954,' however, was a debate on partition. This took place in Kilkenny under the chairmanship of the Celtic scholar, Dr Myles Dillon, with two Unionists – Col. William Topping and Mr William Douglas – and two irredentists, the former Minister for External Affairs, Seán MacBride, and the historian and genealogist, Eoin O'Mahony. An edited version of the proceedings was broadcast. As White commented:

> It is only within the last few years that Radio Éireann has had real freedom to import controversy into its programmes. Experience has shown that the Irish people will accept and enjoy controversy with at least as much toleration as most other civilised peoples.[53]

In the years between 1955 and the introduction of television at the end of 1961, progress in news broadcasting was incremental rather than spectacular.

49 Dáil Debates, 5 November 1952. **50** Colm McCaffrey, 'Political communication and broadcasting: theory, practice and reform' (1991), p. 222. **51** Kealy, *Data*, p 32. **52** Dáil Debates, 26 November 1959. **53** Jack White, 'Controversy on the air', *Radio Éireann Handbook: 1955*, p. 60.

This involved an extension of the range of events which would be covered – particularly abroad. These included most notably the participation of Irish troops in the UN operations in the Congo (which was also the first major foreign story to be covered intensively by the print media). There were echoes of radio's historic coverage of the 1932 Eucharistic Congress in the decision to send broadcasting staff to report on the Eucharistic Congress in Munich in 1960 and, in the same period, the Passion Play at Oberammergau: some of the new bottles were always available for old wine. But there was also a weekly discussion programme on the United Nations, again in 1960, which underlined the perhaps still somewhat solemn, but genuine attempt to maintain a Reithian tradition. Nonetheless, the assertion that until the advent of television there was an 'almost total absence of current affairs broadcasting'[54] seems a trifle harsh, especially in the light of the constraints under which the service operated, and the fact that similar restrictions were commonplace in other, better-developed broadcasting systems.

There were, nonetheless, brief but significant controversies which prefigured the sort of intense scrutiny which would, in the future, be applied to news and current affairs on television. A Dáil question in 1958, for example, queried the lack of publicity given to a protest which occurred during one of Mr de Valera's visits to London as Taoiseach, when he had been heckled outside a church on his way to Mass. The background note for the Minister observed:

> It would of course have been possible to stress the unusual incident, as some of the newspapers tend to do, and given it more prominence than the facts warranted, but the practice in RÉ news is to try to avoid giving a false impression of what actually occurred.[55]

The file for a withdrawn Dáil question a year later gives a more direct insight into the sensitivities involved on major political issues, particularly in relation to the IRA Border campaign which was then in progress. The questioner, Kieran Egan TD, had wanted to evoke a government statement on the withdrawal, by the BBC in Northern Ireland, of a television programme by Ed Murrow in which Siobhán McKenna had controversially described the IRA as idealists. The civil service background note warned:

> The minister will no doubt consider that it would be unwise to involve the Irish broadcasting service by transmitting a programme, not on its broadcasting merits, but which would be regarded entirely as a political gesture against the Six-County government, the BBC, the British Prime

---

54 Pine, op. cit., p. 169.   **55** NA, 2001/78/28. The question was put down by the Fine Gael TD Oliver J. Flanagan for answer on 23 May 1958; the note for the Minister is signed 'Peadar'.

Minister, and to some degree against the head of the Irish government in regard to the action that had to be taken against the IRA here.[56]

More significantly, there was a substantial dispute over a current affairs programme on civil defence prepared for radio by the free-lance broadcaster Proinsías Mac Aonghusa in August 1960. The Minister for Finance, Kevin Boland, was alerted by his officials to their concerns about the programme as it was being made. These concerns included alarm at the fact that the programme was to have opened with the sound of a hydrogen bomb exploding, and displeasure that the programme was being edited in such a way – the Department thought – as to minimise the usefulness of civil defence personnel and procedures. To top it all, no less a person than President de Valera, unaware of the storm-clouds that were gathering, had agreed to do an interview for the programme.

Boland insisted on a special meeting in Radio Éireann on 22 November to listen to the programme, and expressed, with the forcefulness which was his political trademark, his view that the inclusion of Mr de Valera would lead listeners to assume that the President 'agreed with the views and interpolations of Mr Mac Aonghusa.' The Acting Director of Radio Éireann, Matt Doherty, who was present for this event, then 'directed that the feature would not be broadcast.'[57] Technically, the programme had been withdrawn by the station rather than banned by the Minister, but the difference was, in the circumstances, purely academic. The incident is nonetheless of value, not only because it indicated the powerlessness of Radio Éireann executives in the face of Ministerial displeasure, but because within less than a year the same government was, by legislation, sharply to limit its own facility for similar interventions in the newer and reputedly far more powerful medium of television.

By 1960, before the passage of the Broadcasting Act which not only provided for the introduction of television but which established the governance of national public service broadcasting on a completely new basis under a new Authority, news programmes accounted for 21% of the 3,277 broadcast hours, and features 12%.[58] The relative importance of these two key components of the broadcasting schedule (music totalled only 26%) is a strong indication that the underlying ethos of the station was still, to a considerable extent, speech-driven. Given what was happening in radio in other countries at this time, it showed that Radio Éireann was, if not exactly swimming against the tide, at least swimming across it. It also puts a slightly different gloss on the image of the station within government in the pre-television era: on one occasion, Lemass described it, no doubt with a mixture of affection and irritation, as a 'hurdy-gurdy'.[59]

56 NA, 2001/78/28, note dated 12 May 1959. 57 NA, 2001/78/25; Department of Defence memorandum, 4 Deireadh Fomhair, 1960. 58 *Radio Éireann Year Book, 1960*, p. 20. 59 Roibeard Ó Faracháin,

The advent of television, however – and with it the danger that radio would be transmogrified from Cinderella into ugly sister without any intervening period of stardom – was the issue which dominated part of 1960 and most of 1961. Behind the scenes, civil servants were grappling with the thorny questions of censorship, which was the subject of exchanges involving Posts and Telegraphs, particularly on the question of films,[60] and also on the question of political balance. The Acting Director of Broadcasting pointed out in a letter to Maurice Moynihan, secretary to the government, in March 1959, that although Radio Éireann had often had to defend lack of balance by reference to the number of words and minutes devoted to each of the main parties, it was impossible to achieve that sort of arithmetical balance if there was to be any sense of values, because 'important political pronouncements do not balance themselves in time or in length.'[61] Later, he strengthened his case, noting that 'the former practice of keeping controversial matter off the radio has been completely abandoned in all broadcasting and television organisations and the policy is now to have these matters fully and impartially ventilated'.[62]

As the 1959 Broadcasting Bill, framed in the light of these and other deliberations, made its leisurely way through Dáil and Seanad, the focus was almost exclusively on the bright new medium, and on the implications of the new structures for the governance of the broadcasting station.

In the light of subsequent events, it is noteworthy that one of the main *foci* of these debates was not about news and current affairs in particular, much less about Section 31 and the powers reserved to government under that section, than about a presumed conflict of interest involving Eamonn Andrews, the Chairman-in-waiting of the new Authority. Because Andrews also controlled a company producing programmes for television, it was argued, he was not the right person for the job.

The debates on Section 31 in the Dáil and Seanad on this issue are interesting precisely because so few people adverted to the problems that would arise later. In the Seanad particularly, Opposition speakers (notably Senator Owen Sheehy Skeffington) expressed their alarm at the powers written into Section 31, but the points being scored were, for the most part, party political, and echoed to some extent the criticisms that were made by the then Opposition of the freedom of the press section in the 1937 Constitution. It is worth remembering that the country was still dealing with the IRA Border campaign that had been initiated in 1956 and was not finally to peter out until 1962. At the same time, the orthodoxy of Radio Éireann in its guise as part of a government department ensured that issues which were to arise dramatically in later years under the new Author-

interviewed on radio by John Bowman, January 1976.   **60** NA 2001/78/90, memorandum to Government from Department of Posts and Telegraphs, Nollaig 1959.   **61** NA, S 9908C/94, Ó Dochartaigh to Moynihan, 14 March 1960.   **62** Ibid., Ó Dochartaigh to Moynihan, 29 March 1960.

ity simply had not manifested themselves at all during the former dispensation.

The Minister responsible for the passage of the act, Michael Hilliard, argued that Section 31 did little more than replicate the power given to the British Postmaster-General under the equivalent UK legislation. He also suggested that it might be necessary to use the powers it contained 'to prevent the broadcast of morally objectionable programmes'.[63] Later, he admitted that there were other circumstances in which it might be invoked:

> A situation can develop here, as it can develop in any country, that when an Authority broadcasts a certain class of programme or a certain item, they may not be in a position to have the information that would be at the disposal of the Government in regard to the implications that the broadcast would have in respect of our relations with other countries or a crisis at home. Therefore, it is incumbent upon the Minister, acting for the public in the public interest, to have this authority.[64]

In this modest way did coming events cast their shadow before them.

---

63 Seanad Debates, 20 January 1960.   64 Seanad Debates, 10 February 1960.

CHAPTER 2

Testing the water

The new Radio Éireann Authority (later the Radio Telefís Éireann Authority), which was to oversee the establishment of the national television service and which, for the first time, established broadcasting under a semi-state body rather than under direct government control, was established on 1 June 1960. The Chairman of the Authority was the Irish broadcaster and entrepreneur, Eamonn Andrews. The first Director-General was an American, and former consultant to the NBC network in the USA, Edward J. Roth, but this was a temporary appointment and he was rapidly succeeded by Kevin McCourt, an able businessman who had been prominent in the Industrial Development Authority and who certainly had the confidence of the new (since 1959) Taoiseach, Seán Lemass. The first Controller of Programmes, initially Michael Barry, was also succeeded at an early date by Gunnar Rugheimer. Rugheimer, a Swedish national, had acquired much of his broadcasting experience in Canada, and could use the untouched canvas with which he was presented to develop some ideas – thematic programming, for example – which he had been unable to experiment with in Canada.

The broadcasting context within which the new Authority took power was one marked by heightened expectations. The BBC television broadcasts had already been available to about 40% of the population; these services were supplemented by the inauguration, in late 1959, of Ulster Television. Socially and politically, also, there were substantial changes in the offing. De Valera had resigned as Taoiseach in 1959 following his election as President, and his successor, Seán Lemass, was widely seen as a moderniser, anxious to get the economy moving again after it had languished in the doldrums of the 1950s, and looking to the creation of an export-led economy. The long flow of emigration throughout the 1940s and 1950s was weakening, and as the economy picked up in the 1960s former emigrants who returned to join the workforce brought less insular attitudes with them, not least in relation to the role of the Catholic Church in Irish society.

Despite its monopoly position, therefore, the new Authority immediately had to cope with competition in broadcasting, particularly in television. Although UTV had not yet become the powerful magnet for advertising from the Republic that it later became, it was an important competitor for audience share, and the new station had to fight for its audience, often with very much lower resources than its competitors, right from the beginning. Its television broadcasting hours, for example, immediately exceeded those of the new station in Denmark, despite the fact that Denmark had a noticeably larger population to serve. It was also under considerable pressure, both from its audience and politically, to maintain a high level of domestically-produced programming.

There was also a political context. De Valera's successor, Seán Lemass, had originally felt that the new television service could be entrusted to private entrepreneurs, but the majority of the cabinet he had inherited had opposed this course of action. He had won his first election as party leader in 1961. Although the 1950s had been marked by electoral volatility, following a sixteen-year period of Fianna Fáil single-party government which had ended in 1948, it was now looking to some degree as if that party's notable hegemony was in the process of being re-established. This was all the more believable in that the Labour Party, whose co-operation with Fine Gael and other parties had been essential in putting Fianna Fáil out of office in 1948 and 1954, had been so bruised by its experiences in government that it had adopted a policy of opposition to coalitions: in effect, this meant that there was no credible alternative government. This factor, combined with the social and other changes in the 1950s, helped to create an environment in which young people, in particular, who had radical views about society, were relatively unlikely to see any party they supported as having a role in government. In such circumstances, the media inevitably became part of the political battle-ground.

Finally, there was the new legislative context, which included not only Section 31 of the Broadcasting Act, dealt with in the preceding chapter, but Section 18 of that Act, which enjoined impartiality on the new station in respect of news and current affairs broadcasting in general. As one legal (and political) authority noted later, 'it was not intended to provide a service in which the only material in broadcasting programmes would be material which the government thought would be harmless to its policies on general governmental matters.'[1] A critical part of the legislative context, insofar as news and current affairs is concerned, was Section 18 (1) of the 1960 Act, which states:

> It shall be the duty of the Authority to secure that, when it broadcasts any information, news or feature which relates to matters of public controversy or is the subject of current public debate, the information, news or feature is presented objectively and impartially and without any expression of the Authority's own views.

---

1 J.M. Kelly, 'The constitutional position of RTÉ' (1967), p. 209.

The first thing to note about the definition is that it is, to a considerable extent, a definition that originated in print journalism, and arrived in television via radio. This tripartite division into information, news and features, however, was one that would rapidly be rendered obsolete, especially in television. Although 'current affairs' took some time to emerge as a category, and was not finally enshrined in the legislation until 1976, its forerunner, 'public affairs', actually accompanied the birth of the television service (although the phrase now stands for something quite different).

Secondly, the phrase 'objectively and impartially' bespeaks a cultural, political and ideological world-view firmly rooted in the 1950s. The drafters of the phrase, the politicians who introduced it, and the audience to which it was addressed, would have been in little doubt about what they thought it actually meant. Impartiality and objectivity were the Holy Grail of journalism; the idea that they might be difficult of attainment, or even problematic in themselves, was a hot topic only in the dim and distant recesses of the Frankfurt School.[2] Media research, although no longer in its infancy, was not far advanced into its adolescence.

Objectivity meant that journalists did not misrepresent the views of those they reported or the social reality they described. Impartiality meant that they did not take sides. But what was social reality? And who – and how many – were the protagonists among whom journalists had to maintain their studious neutrality?

Fair representation of the views of those you were reporting did not present much of a problem: journalists had been doing this in one way or another since the partisan press of the nineteenth century had to some extent been overtaken by the mass circulation media of the twentieth. Social reality, however, was a different matter: was it something ordained by fate, or subject to change? What were its abiding characteristics and values? What was to be protected, and could anything be challenged?

As the number of begged questions multiplied like flies, broadcasters generally were left to get on with it, to muddle through as best they could, dimly aware that there were unspecified boundaries which they should not cross, flying – as ever – by the seat of their pants. They would not have been encouraged by the only guidance (apart from the intermittent wrangles about alleged pro-Government bias in the old Radio Éireann days) available in the records of the legislature. The 1937 Irish Constitution included a defence of the freedom of the press but – as its principal progenitor, Éamon de Valera, enunciated this principle when the Constitution was being debated in the Dáil – this was hardly grounds

---

2 The Frankfurt School, founded in Germany in the 1920s, enjoyed considerable influence after World War II in the United States, to which some of its practitioners had fled. It was characterised by a close analysis of the role of media – initially cinema and radio – and by a pessimistic view of the relationship between capitalism and the cultural industries generally.

for optimism. In one of these debates Mr de Valera, evidently without fear of contradiction, solemnly declared that

> The right of citizens to express freely their opinion and convictions cannot, in fact, be permitted in any state. Are we going to have anarchical principles, for example, generally propagated here? I say no ... you should not give to the proponents of what is wrong and unnatural the same liberty as would be accorded to the proponents of what is right.[3]

On that occasion he had the full-blooded agreement of the future Fine Gael Taoiseach, John A. Costello, who was moved to declare bluntly that 'the dissemination of Communistic doctrine would be against public order and morality'.[4] More than a quarter of a century later, this was a somewhat inadequate route map for the television age.

The principle that de Valera was articulating, although he did it only indirectly, was that freedom of expression operated within a consensus – one more formally defined by the terms 'subject to public morality', but still necessarily vague. Objectivity, therefore, had its boundaries, which were fundamentally ideological. What about impartiality? Most of the legislators who debated the 1960 Broadcasting Act would have understood this as primarily related to the permanent struggle between government and opposition. Some more sophisticated commentators might have interpreted it as having a relevance to the amount of coverage given to different political parties whether in government or not. Nobody, it is safe to say, would have interpreted it as having a relevance to – for instance – a conflict of wills as between the Dáil and elements in civil society: farmers, or trade unionists, paramilitary groups or other illegal organisations.

The first few years of broadcasting under the new regime, which was inaugurated on 31 December 1961, were therefore characterised by a number of developments. The first – perhaps inevitable – consequence was the way in which television rapidly overshadowed radio. The print media's radio critics rapidly turned their attention to the glamorous new medium, and there was a hiatus between the end of 1961 and the late 1960s during which the national newspapers' media critics concentrated on television to the exclusion of radio. Secondly, it took time for the station to develop a distinctive voice. Not least because of the transatlantic influences in senior management, and because of the hot breath of competition, many of the initiatives in the early years were as much about scheduling as they were about programming – about developing (or buying in) the right kind of programme to trap the right kind of audience at the right kind of time. Thirdly, the new set of relationships between government in particular

3 Dáil Debates, 12 June 1937.　4 Ibid.

(although it affected the whole political class) and the new broadcasting structures was one which could be elaborated only by a process of trial and error.

It was all very well to enshrine the concept of impartiality in the statute: its working out in practice was to involve conflict, misunderstanding and an elaborate, if unstructured process of range-finding as each of the protagonists fought for territory. The new Head of Public Affairs, Jack White, expressed the confident opinion at the very beginning that 'in home affairs, I hope to see many of our political leaders before the cameras in the next twelve months'.[5] In the event, it was to be a question of hope deferred. Many of the programmes broadcast in this area were cautious, and some depended on bought-in material which created its own problems. Mike Burns, later prominent in the development of current affairs on radio, noted in an article for the *RTV Guide* that the *Wednesday Special* series, though excellently produced, often had scripts which sounded 'like a White House hand-out labelled "anti-Russian propaganda".'[6]

News and current affairs output in fact accounted for more than half of the home-produced programmes in the first three months of 1962 (68 hours of news and 62 hours of public affairs out of a total of 254 hours) and the newsroom, under its new News Editor, Pearse Kelly, was substantially resourced. New positions were advertised and filled, involving reporters as well as sub-editors; a contract was signed with United Press International for news film; free-lance news cameramen were identified in locations around the country; and a short programme called *Newsview*, after the 9 p.m. television news, dealt in greater depth with a single topic. 'At the outset', the new Authority affirmed proudly, 'the primary object of the News Division was to provide an objective, impartial summary, completely free of any editorial view, of the significant and interesting events in Ireland and abroad. The Authority believes that this has been achieved.'[7] Despite the new level of resources, the news bulletins were still occasionally a high-wire act. Charles Mitchel, the first and for many years principal newsreader, recalled occasions when telephones rang in the newsroom while the news was being broadcast live, and nobody dared to answer them; when word had to be sent around the building to stop workmen hammering during the broadcast; and when – in the wake of a technical breakdown – the news had to be read from the engineer's hut at the base of the transmission mast on Kippure in the Dublin mountains.[8] Mitchel's appointment in itself signalled the fact that a choice had been made by station management between two options. Mitchel was an actor, and the fact that he was chosen to front the national television news bulletins indicated that Telefís Éireann was, effectively, following the BBC model. The ITV model, on the other hand, went for journalists as presenters, and for a pacier presentation. Journalists were slow to colonise this important outpost in RTÉ.

---

5 *RTV Guide*, 12 January 1961. 6 *RTV Guide*, 23 March 1962. Burns was at the time television critic of the *Sunday Review*. 7 *Radio Éireann Annual Report 1962*, pp. 18–19. 8 Charles Mitchel, 'Stepping into the news' (1971).

It was not to be long, however, before Public Affairs became an area of contention. It was started on a shoe-string. Jack White, who moved from the *Irish Times* to be head of Public Affairs on 1 November 1961, was told that he would be responsible for an hour and a half of air time when the station went on air eight weeks later: in the event, he generated seven hours of programmes in the first week alone, as he set out to 'expand the range of enquiry, discussion, controversy'.[9] Looking back on it from the vantage point of almost half a century later, it is tempting to analyse the controversies that ebbed and flowed around the station's early current affairs output in terms of later questions of censorship and political interference. A closer study of the political and social context, however, suggests that, certainly on the part of some of the politicians involved, the primary emotion being expressed was less hostility than bafflement. Public affairs generally had been, up to then, conducted more or less in the spirit of Robert Browning's famous lines: 'It grew. I gave commands. Then all smiles stopped together.' There was, in effect, an absolutist and highly centralised culture of governance which was ill-equipped to come to terms with the desire of broadcasters to establish new parameters and, increasingly daringly, on occasion to tweak the lion's tail.

The new structure for the governance of broadcasting had, from the politicians' point of view, both advantages and disadvantages. Its chief advantage was that politicians, and in particular Ministers for Posts and Telegraphs, could no longer be made accountable in the Dáil for the day-to-day operations of the broadcasting service, as they had been when the service was under direct state control. The chief disadvantage was that they no longer had any input into these operations; worse, the structure did not provide any mechanism for such interventions, at any level. The Government had the right to appoint the Authority, and to veto the proposed appointment of any person as Director-General of whom they did not approve. These, however, were fail-safe mechanisms, not opportunities for influence or control, and there were political disadvantages to implementing them (e.g. by dismissing an unsatisfactory Authority) as later events were to make abundantly clear.

Initially, the system worked more or less as it had been supposed to work. Even as the new service went on the air, Lemass told one member of the public who wrote to him to complain about the tenor of a newspaper interview with the new Director-General, Ed Roth, that RTÉ would 'not be a political organ of the government of the day'.[10] For the most part, correspondents who wrote directly to him to express their displeasure at particular aspects of television programming were fobbed off with a template letter. Otherwise their complaints would be directed to the Minister for Posts and Telegraphs, Michael Hilliard, who in

9 Jack White, 'Inquiry, Discussion, Controversy' (1971).   **10** NA, S 14996 D, 12 January 1961

his turn would draft replies for Lemass stating typically that 'there is under the law no power of interference with [RTÉ's] programme arrangements given to any Minister'.[11]

This did not mean, on the other hand, that Lemass, in particular, would bottle up his own opinions indefinitely. He had already gone on record indirectly, in a speech he personally drafted for Hilliard to deliver at the opening of the new television service, about his concern that 'the pretext of objectivity should not be allowed to excuse the undue representation of our faults'.[12] He also set out an ideological brief for the station in a memorandum which his civil servants only just managed to dissuade him from incorporating in a specific directive to the new station under Section 31 of the Act. This would have required broadcasters to avoid 'stage-Irishisms' or 'playboyisms' and the 'God-help-us' approach to social and economic problems.[13] In his view – although he included a customary obeisance to the Irish language – he wanted the new television service to present, and perhaps even in part engender, an image of Ireland as a progressive, scientifically inclined, modern industrial nation. In this he was, to an extent, challenging a widespread image of Ireland as a kind of pre-Enlightenment oasis in which eternal verities counted for more than material progress, or even old-fashioned prosperity. The implementation of this vision was to be entrusted to a generation of young broadcasters who, paradoxically, might have shared his impatience with the Ireland of thatched cottages and tranquil rural landscapes, but who were also imbued with an anti-authoritarian ethos to which his generation of politicians had yet to become accustomed. The increasing asperity of his observations on programme content demonstrated a particular concern with a number of topics, particularly the economy and emigration. It can be noted, however, that the tenor of his interventions was generally aimed at what he perceived as a lack of balance, rather than objecting to the broadcasting of politically opposing viewpoints *per se*.

The chief object of his attention was the programme *Broadsheet*, produced on five nights a week by Jim FitzGerald and edited by the old Radio Éireann hand, P.P. O'Reilly. It was presented by 'a team full of what Kipling called "satiable curiosity"'[14] and was 'curious about the background to the big news, but concerned too about things that don't hit the headlines but still reflect the way we live in Ireland.'[15] The team included Brian Farrell, then on the administrative staff in University College Dublin, Brian Cleeve, and Des Moore.

The bewilderment of Lemass and other politicians at the *lèse-majesté* which was already beginning to characterise current affairs coverage was exemplified by

11 NA, S 14996 F/65, Lemass to Miss Maisie Dooley, 7 April 1964. **12** NA, S 14996 D, Lemass's rewriting of original draft by Maurice Moynihan, Secretary to the Government, Lemass to Moynihan, 4 May 1960. **13** Dermot Keogh, 'Ireland and "Emergency culture": between civil war and normalcy, 1922–1961' (1995), p. 32. **14** *RTV Guide*, 1 February 1961. **15** Ibid.

a number of incidents in its first year on air. *Broadsheet* was not the only programme in the firing line. As early as April 1962 Lemass wrote to Pádraig Ó hAnnracháin, head of the Government Information Bureau, asking him to seek 'formal' discussions with the station about a programme devoted to viewers' letters, and called *Pick of the Post*. His main criticism was lack of balance: and the main evidence he adduced was the presence on the programme, as a panellist, of Donal Nevin, then research officer for the Irish Congress of Trade Unions, and someone who had, as Lemass put it 'a strong Labour bias'.[16] He added:

> When important topics such as the Budget are dealt with on T.E. [i.e. Telefís Éireann] there should be some attempt at balancing of views and serious treatment, not a casual discussion comprising two men of similar political persuasion and two ladies [one was Miriam Hederman] who had little understanding of it. Either these topics should be kept off the programme altogether or the panel reconstituted to ensure proper treatment of them.[17]

In May 1962 Lemass complained to Ó hAnnracháin that Ministers were not being invited on *Broadsheet* sufficiently frequently to put the government's point of view.[18] In September he voiced his annoyance again to Ó hAnnracháin, complaining that the programme was becoming increasingly 'a medium for the uncritical presentation of the views of persons associated with various ramps and crank projects.'[19] Ó hAnnracháin, an enthusiastic critic of the station's output, advocated a total reorganisation of broadcasting and the creation of a 'Minister for Information'. Neither suggestion was acted on and, although Ó hAnnracháin had words with Roth about the matter, no disciplinary or other action seems to have ensued. Indeed, for the remainder of Lemass's period as Taoiseach, station executives generally seemed to succeed reasonably well in blunting the edge of governmental ire and protecting their broadcasters.

That ire, nonetheless, persisted. A further controversy in November had wider ramifications, and ended – paradoxically – by establishing an important broadcasting precedent. This was occasioned by a decision by the *Broadsheet* team to do a programme on the government's proposal to build a fertiliser project, to which farming interests were opposed. Late in the day, *Broadsheet* asked the Government Information bureau for a Government spokesman to defend the project, but the Minister concerned, George Colley, was on his way to the USA. Lemass was on an official visit to Germany and, when he got back, Ó hAnnracháin informed him of what had transpired. After consultations with the Department, he told Lemass, he rang Jack White at the station.

---

16 NA, S 9908 B/2, Lemass to Ó hAnnracháin 18 April 1962.   17 Ibid.   18 NA, S 3532 C/63, Lemass to Ó hAnnracháin, 4 May 1962.   19 Ibid., Lemass to Ó hAnnracháin, 13 September 1962. See also John Horgan, *Lemass: the pragmatic patriot* (1997), pp. 310–22.

Jack White said he knew nothing about the proposed programme and then proceeded to defend it. I put it to him that this proposal was not merely highly improper and unfair but could be construed as treating the Dáil with contempt since the required legislation had not yet come before the Dáil and the Minister was thereby debarred from presenting the detailed case 'for' until he did so in the Dáil first. Mr White retorted that it was odd if the matter could be discussed by them only when the matter had been decided by the Dáil. In reply I told him that it was Dáil Éireann which legislated for the people and, besides, there could scarcely be a balanced presentation of the facts when the only spokesman free to participate would be one viciously against the project. I also put it to Mr White, as my view that to proceed with the programme would be nothing short of sabotage of an important policy decision of the government.[20]

Ó hAnnracháin's objection was not entirely without foundation, albeit of a somewhat dated kind: there had been for many years in the BBC a convention that the broadcasting station did not discuss matters of Government policy which were the subject of legislation until Parliament had had sight of the legislation. This attempt to import a by now out-of-date British convention into the lively new world of Irish broadcasting was, however, doomed to failure. Lemass, although he agreed with Ó hAnnracháin, turned the matter over to his minister for Posts and Telegraphs, Michael Hilliard, for examination and action. Hilliard, whose eirenic approach contrasted strongly with that adopted by some of the more authoritarian members of that cabinet, suggested that it would not be appropriate to go after the broadcasters on this occasion, but merely to keep an eye on them. Lemass, his exasperation having by now subsided, agreed.[21]

If there were wars and rumours of wars, there were also conspiracies and rumours of conspiracies. Ó hAnnracháin at one stage was asked by Lemass for information about various broadcasters following a visit to Lemass by two Catholic archbishops who complained about the role of White (who was a member of the Church of Ireland, and in charge of religious programmes) and other named individuals. Ó hAnnracháin replied in scabrous terms, describing White as someone who

> has no great firm beliefs about anything and ... having no national outlook in the broadest sense of the word and has no loyalties (and) would think of Ireland as a place where those, like himself, who are 'liberal' in outlook must suffer as best they may.[22]

20 NA, S 9908 C/94, Ó hAnnracháin to Lemass, 29 November 1962. 21 Ibid., Lemass to Hilliard, 25 March 1963. When *Broadsheet* ended its run in mid-1963, *Hibernia* gave the whole of its cover page to the laments of the famous, under the title: 'Requiem for Broadsheet'. 22 Lemass papers, Ó hAnnracháin to

One of the chief movers in this was the Catholic archbishop of Dublin, Dr John Charles McQuaid, who had now been running the archdiocese for more than two decades, whose interest in broadcasting had been flagged as early as the 1940s, and who was possibly at the zenith of his power. The advent of television, however, acted to undermine this authority in a number of ways. The sheer size of the influx of new people into broadcasting with the introduction of television was a factor in itself. Many of them were coming into broadcasting from the universities, particularly University College, Dublin, where the archbishop's control of key appointments and of the actual content of courses in areas like history and philosophy was beginning, however slightly, to erode at the edges.[23] Anti-clericalism was on the increase, and an oppositional, irreverent quality was seeping into the hitherto staid world of national journalism, as exemplified, for instance, by the 'Backbencher' column in the tabloid *Sunday Review*. McQuaid did not lack for acolytes: there were always some sympathisers within RTÉ who were not slow to provide him with details of the actual or supposed political (and moral) shortcomings of some of their colleagues; and McQuaid himself took pains to cultivate senior personnel in the station. He entertained the station's first Director-General, Ed Roth, to dinner as early as January 1962: Roth was impressed by the 'excellent' quality of the archbishop's cigars.[24]

McQuaid continued a relationship at this level with Roth's successor, Kevin McCourt, although the development of the relationship was uneven. McCourt was not slow to apologise on occasion when he felt that the archbishop had been the object of unwarranted discourtesy or derision on the station. A flavour of the relationship can be gauged from an exchange of letters after the notorious 'Bishop and the Nightie' episode on the *Late Late Show* in February 1966. McQuaid – avoiding the temptation to go public on the issue for which Bishop Tom Ryan of Clonfert found himself held up to ridicule – wrote to McCourt in terms that were less outraged than sympathetic. 'The questions and answers in the case of a Mr and Mrs Fox were vulgar, even coarse and suggestive', he observed. 'You have not been fairly treated; for this type of thing is quite unlike what you have been so warmly thanked for.'[25] McCourt replied that the 'generosity and kindness' of the archbishop's letter had 'moved me to distress that you should have had cause at all to write on such a matter.' He added: 'Not infrequently to my frustration, I cannot be the policeman of all I want and still manage a large and complex organisation; but the mistakes, believe me, stem more from inexperience, enthusiasm and bad judgement rather than from malice or misery of outlook.'[26] McCourt also wrote to Dr McQuaid on another occasion in 1966, after

Lemass 5 October 1962. It is no doubt significant that this document is one of the few government papers that Lemass took home with him on his retirement in 1966. The archbishops were Dr Thomas Morris, archbishop of Cashel, and Dr John Charles McQuaid, archbishop of Dublin. **23** John Cooney, *John Charles McQuaid, ruler of Catholic Ireland* (1999), pp. 295–6. **24** DDA, AB8 XXVI (c), Roth to McQuaid. 20 January 1962. **25** Ibid., McQuaid to McCourt (at his home address), 12 February 1966. **26** Ibid., McCourt to McQuaid (from his home address), 15 February 1966.

one particular *Late Late Show* on which the archbishop had been the object of some disparaging comments, to express his 'great embarrassment and appreciable anger' at what had occurred.[27]

Nonetheless, the Director-General could also be steely if the occasion demanded. This was the case as early as 1963, and is perhaps emblematic of the way in which the media in general, and television in particular, were beginning to test the boundaries of spiritual, as well as of temporal authority. Pope John XXIII had inaugurated the Second Vatican Council in September of that year, and RTÉ, alone among national media organisations, had seen fit to send its staff abroad to report on the event. One aspect of this coverage – which was exciting considerable interest in Ireland – was an interview which took place in Dublin at the end of the Council's first session with one of the acknowledged new voices in Catholic theology, Fr. Gregory Baum, a Canadian scholar noted especially for his ground-breaking work in ecumenism. Baum was interviewed on *Newsview* on 11 December. The following morning, Dr McQuaid drafted a letter to McCourt to ask 'by whose authority the stranger-priest, the Rev. Gregory Baum, was invited to speak and did speak in my diocese on matters of faith and morals'.[28] McCourt stood his ground, which was an option more open to him because the letter had been signed by Dr McQuaid's secretary, Dr James A. MacMahon, rather than personally by the archbishop.

> Since Father Baum is a well known expert on the ecumenical movement and was attached to the Council, it was taken for granted that he was well qualified to comment on the proceedings there. The responsibility for using Dr Baum's services, of course, rests with Radio Éireann but we would assume that, if he required ecclesiastical clearance to participate in a programme of the kind involved, this would be a matter between him and the ecclesiastical authorities.[29]

Dr McQuaid also made sure to establish a personal relationship with McCourt's successor, T.P. Hardiman, although there is no suggestion that this relationship extended beyond the normal courtesies. The way in which he could continue to be involved in programme-making decisions, however, was demonstrated in 1965, when Brian Cleeve set out to make a programme on the industrial schools. The sensitivity of the issue, even at this early stage, is underlined by the fact that the religious orders were involved in three-way negotiations with RTÉ and with Dr McQuaid, conducted in part through the archbishop's personal intermediary, Monsignor Cecil Barrett, parish priest of Booterstown, Dublin. Both

---

27 Ibid., McCourt to McQuaid, 5 April 1966. It is noteworthy that Dr McQuaid, with his evident regard for strict accuracy, did not imply, as did his brother bishop, that the programme had been 'immoral'. **28** Ibid., McQuaid to McCourt (draft), 12 December 1963. As eventually sent, the letter substituted 'priest' for the offensive 'stranger-priest'. **29** Ibid., McCourt to McQuaid, 17 December 1963. A note on the letter in Dr McQuaid's handwriting reads: 'No answer sent.'

Artane and Goldenbridge were to feature in Cleeve's programme in the *Discovery* series. According to one of the archbishop's secretaries, Cleeve had told Osmond Dowling (the former journalist with the *Irish Independent* and now the archbishop's press officer), that the purpose of the film 'was to combat in some small way the recent and not so recent allegations made against what was being done for these children in Ireland.'[30] Barrett suggested to McQuaid that the Superior in Artane was 'shrewd enough and alive to the dangers', and would ask RTÉ for a guarantee that he would have prior approval of the script and prior approval of the finished film. The proposal to include Artane was eventually dropped, and McQuaid noted in a gloss on Barrett's letter, 'Glad Artane is out.'[31] McQuaid's reservations were also made clear in a comment he appended to a letter from one of the orders involved, a copy of which is kept in his archive. In this letter, Sister M. de Montfort of the Grange Convent in Kill-of-the-Grange, Dublin, the location of a small home which was to have been featured in the programme, wrote to her superior: 'I think we cannot afford to lose this chance.' Dr McQuaid underlined this phrase and added his own comment: 'It might well be useful to lose it.'[32] The archbishop maintained his interest in RTÉ. A 1967 *Seven Days* film report suggesting that Irish emigrants in Britain were losing their Catholic faith prompted a flurry of archiepiscopal activity designed to rebut the programme's conclusions.

He cannot have been pleased, either, by some other aspects of RTÉ's current affairs programming. The hot air generated in and around the *Late Late Show* could to an extent be disregarded – indeed, by putting RTÉ on the defensive, and by arousing popular conservative ire against the programme-makers, this to some extent played into clerical hands: letters to the *Irish Press* after the programme on which a TCD student, Brian Trevaskis, described Bishop Michael Browne of Galway as a 'moron' ran 60% against the station. It was less easy to dismiss more careful analyses, such as the programme on birth control presented by Michael Viney of the *Irish Times* in 1966, and entitled 'Too Many Children?' In this programme, a number of Dublin mothers were interviewed and were – by the standards and expectations of the times – astonishingly frank about their problems and attitudes towards family planning. Viney himself eschewed any obvious crusade, remarking at the end merely that 'any day now a pronouncement from the Pope may well take this big issue a whole step further'.[33] The same year saw an otherwise little-noticed Irish-language programme, *Caidreamh*, feature the same subject in a discussion involving Professor Daithi O hUaithne of TCD, Máire Nic Shiomóin, whose moral courage attracted praise from one reviewer, and Desmond Fennell.[34]

---

30 Ibid., Fr John Fitzpatrick to McQuaid, 4 June 1965.   **31** Ibid., Barrett to McQuaid, 1 June 1965.   **32** Ibid., copy letter Sister M. de Montfort, to Mother General, 24 May 1965.   **33** Louise Fuller, *Irish Catholicism since 1950: the undoing of a culture* (2002), p. 197.   **34** Tom O'Dea, *Irish Press*, 3 September 1966.

Taken together, these incidents demonstrate not only the degree to which television was changing the parameters for public discussion of contentious issues, but also the way in which current affairs, or 'public affairs' as it was still technically described within the broadcasting structures, was something which permeated many programmes, and could not in any sense be confined to those programme specifically produced under the 'Public Affairs' rubric. A case in point is provided by the *Radharc* series of documentaries. *Radharc* programmes were produced by Fr Joe Dunn, a young priest who, with others, had been sent to the USA for training in audiovisual media by Archbishop McQuaid, in the hope – which was to be frustrated by a certain independence of spirit on the part of RTÉ – that Dunn would be appointed as the new station's adviser on religious programmes.[35]

Deprived of direct influence at the station, McQuaid then set up Dunn and others as documentary film-makers. Ironically, McQuaid's loss was to be television's gain: from the outset, the *Radharc* team showed extraordinary inventiveness, imagination, and on occasion courage, in addressing new subjects in ways which helped to set a new agenda for the media generally. These included, for example, 'The Young Offender' dealing with life in St Patrick's Institution, Mountjoy (1963), 'Down and Out in Dublin (1964); 'The Boat Train to Euston', on the topic of emigration (1964); and a programme on prostitution in Cork city, 'Open Port' (1968). By the standards of the end of the twentieth century, these could be written down as modest enough in their scope and treatment of their topics, but by the standards of the 1960s they broke significant new ground.

The Late Late Show was only the most spectacular example of an entertainment programme which surreptitiously extended its brief to include current affairs, and indeed may have done so partly because of the high TAM[36] ratings which were being garnered by *Seven Days* and similar programmes. It was a number of years, though, before it actually succeeded in inveigling politicians onto its ample stage. Its first presenter and the man most associated with the *Late Late Show* as both presenter and producer for many years, Gay Byrne, expressed this succinctly when he observed that such a talk show 'is an opportunity to show how good an interviewer one is without having the strictures of the more formalised current-affairs programme situation'.[37] His long-term researcher, Pan Collins, put it even more directly, when she noted:

> Occasionally, at one of our Tuesday morning planning meetings, somebody may say, 'We've been a little bit bland lately – can't we think of something that would stir it up a little? What's been happening?' If nothing very exciting is going on in this island, one of us may say, 'Well, let's go back to the hardy perennials, there's always good mileage in sex, reli-

35 Horgan, *Lemass*, pp. 317–18.   36 i.e. Television Audience Measurement.   37 Gay Byrne, *To whom it concerns* (1972), pp. 20–1.

gion, politics and money. Now, which one can we find something fresh in?'[38]

By and large, the station's management tried to hold the ring as best it could when it came to adjudicating demarcation disputes between different programme areas. News, for example, would be upset if the *Late Late Show* had 'poached' a potential interviewee; television features or current affairs would be upset if radio, with its more adaptable technology, had 'scooped' some visiting celebrity or person in the news. It was, however, for the most part almost impossible to articulate a system which would prevent such turf wars breaking out from time to time, as was underlined by the fact that there continued to be intermittent post-mortems on such disagreements.

These internal disagreements, however, were relatively insignificant compared to the growing sense of frustration felt by politicians in general and in particular by government ministers, at their apparent inability to harness the creature they had created. No less a figure than Noel Browne TD, who had a year earlier criticised the government for taking excessive (as he termed it) powers under Section 31 of the Broadcasting Act, found the early run of programming so problematic that he wondered aloud whether the Government had not, in fact, given RTÉ too much freedom. It would, he argued,

> be wiser and safer that we here [i.e. in the Dáil] should try to retain some kind of over-riding control of the broadest general principles under which the machinery of television is operated (...) It would be much wiser if the Minister took responsibility for a very much wider level of broad, general policy, making decisions in regard to the general organisation and control of Telefís Éireann.[39]

In these circumstances, the role of Kevin McCourt assumes considerable significance. As has been noted, he had the confidence of the Taoiseach, Seán Lemass, and maintained a good personal relationship with him throughout his period in RTÉ. This was of critical importance in defusing Lemass's sometimes choleric outbursts, and maintaining the station's fledgling independence. A classic example of this was a special, once-off television discussion on Lemass's Second Programme for Economic Expansion, which was screened in July 1964. The Taoiseach took particular exception to comments made by the agricultural econimist J.B. Ruane, which he described as 'shallow, misleading and unconstructive'. He instructed the secretary of his department to get RTÉ to correct the 'criticisms and misrepresentations' and to warn the station that 'their function in this

38 Pan Collins, *It started on the Late Late Show* (1981), p. 42.   **39** Dáil Debates, 3 April 1962.

matter should be primarily to support the Programme rather than to facilitate criticism'.[40] On this occasion, and on at least one other, he was dissuaded by McCourt from insisting on the broadcast of a rebuttal programme, on the grounds that 'it would be all over Radio Éireann and outside that Government pressure had been put on him [McCourt]'.[41] All this tends to belie the observation by Dr Todd Andrews, whom Lemass appointed as second Chairman of the RTÉ Authority in 1966, that Lemass 'expressed very little interest in RTÉ except to say that some of the staff "appeared to be losing the run of themselves."'[42]

Throughout this early period, the question of actually getting politicians to appear on current affairs programmes in person was one which was approached extremely gingerly both by politicians and broadcasters. Probably the first programme on which they appeared on a formal, regular basis, was a programme called *Open House* which Bob Quinn produced in the autumn schedule of 1964. Billed as 'a series which invites members of rural communities to question a distinguished platform panel on subjects of their own choosing,'[43] it was an outside broadcast programme which ran back-to-back with *The School around the Corner*, i.e. editions of each programme were shot at the same location on each expedition. The up-and-coming young Fianna Fáil TD, Bobby Molloy, was the guest on one such programme recorded in Galway, at which one member of the audience asked a question – suggested by the programme's presenter, Michael Johnston – about the role of Galway as a university city. Many weeks later, Molloy confronted Johnston with an air of triumph, to tell him that he had found out why the question had been asked: 'You were staying at David Cabot's house!'[44]

The magazine programmes which supplemented the work of *Broadsheet* – *Sixty Four* and *Sixty Five* – were not the only other innovations in the field of current affairs. John O'Donoghue, for instance, presented *The Heart of Thy Neighbour*, a major documentary on Northern Ireland produced by Gerry Murray, in January 1965, and a counterpart documentary on the Republic, made by the Northern broadcaster John Hutchinson, was broadcast in April of the same year. However tentatively, the station was approaching the Northern question: few of those involved can have imagined how much that issue would dominate both national politics and broadcasting in the decade ahead.

This was also the period in which the nettle of political broadcasting was first grasped. For the first six years on RTÉ, as Muiris Mac Conghail once remarked, 'the politician on RTÉ, like the child, was seen but never heard, talked about but never talked to.'[45] R.J. Dowling, the station's first political correspondent, worked from the newsroom and had an independent but almost Edwardian rela-

40 NA, S 3532 D/95, Lemass to Moynihan, 10 July 1964.   **41** Ibid., Moynihan to Lemass, 14 July 1964.
42 C.S. Andrews, *Dublin made me* (1979), p. 270.   **43** *RTV Guide*, 2 October 1964.   **44** Information from Michael Johnston. Molloy's surmise was correct (Cabot was a lecturer at UCG at the time); what is intriguing is the length to which the politician had gone in order to discover the source of the question.   **45** *RTÉ Guide*, 31 November 1971.

tionship with the denizens of Leinster House.[46] John Healy, the *Irish Times* (and formerly *Sunday Review*) political columnist, was responsible for the first, wholly scripted programme, *Strictly Politics*. It did not feature any interviews with politicians. Nor did its successor, *Headlines and Deadlines*, also scripted by Healy. The latter programme was in turn succeeded by *The Hurler on the Ditch*, on which Healy and other political correspondents discussed some of the issues of the day, but only rarely with the participation of any of the politicians whose activities they were discussing (the first politician to appear on *The Hurler on the Ditch* was Senator W.A.W. Sheldon, who was a guest in February 1966). The political establishment, at this stage, was firmly under the impression that political broadcasting, when it eventually began, would be an extension of the system of party political broadcasts, i.e. it would to all purposes and effects be controlled by the politicians rather than by the broadcasters. From the summer of 1966 onwards, complicated negotiations took place between RTÉ, the Government Chief Whip, Michael Carty TD, and the whips of the other parties, in an attempt to find agreement on a suitable formula. Lemass, in a letter to Carty in July, agreed that RTÉ could choose the chairman for political discussion programmes, but warned that 'our participation will be continued only so long as we remain satisfied with his impartiality.'[47]

The other critical issue, at this stage, remained that of choosing the participants. Here Lemass adopted a considerably tougher line than his Minister for Posts and Telegraphs had some years earlier. Then, Michael Hilliard had told the Dáil that RTÉ 'should be free to invite any Minister of State or any politician or trade unionist or whoever else it wishes to appear before the cameras at any time'.[48] This freedom, it now appeared, did not extend to an area which was regarded as coming within the scope of party political broadcasts. Now, Lemass was telling Carty, 'we could not agree that the producer will select the Minister or deputy to speak for the government. He may make suggestions but the choice will be with you.'[49] The outcome of these discussions was *The Politicians*, first broadcast in the autumn of 1966. Although it involved representatives of all the political parties, this was formally classified as a party political broadcast rather than as a current affairs programme. In its first format, it involved a ratio of three Fianna Fáil speakers to two Fine Gael and one Labour, with Bunny Carr as Chairman.[50] This was hardly a success; 'six speakers guaranteed chaos; numerical advantage blunted the argumentative thrust, and the minority quite often gained emotional sympathy from the viewer. By mutual consent the loaded ratio was abandoned in favour of 1:1:1.'[51]

46 Dowling died in July 1967: his successor was Joe Fahy, who was succeeded in October 1973 by Arthur Noonan, political correspondent of the *Irish Independent*.   **47** NA 98/6/19, Lemass to Carty, 14 July 1966. **48** Dáil Debates, 3 April 1962.   **49** NA 98/6/19, Lemass to Carty, 14 July 1966.   **50** David Thornley, 'Television and politics' (1967), p 218.   **51** Ibid.

The chairmanship of Carr, who had achieved a certain reputation, in his own words, 'for gentle fairness',[52] combined with the unwillingness of the politicians to allow the chairman any real role – turned the whole thing into a self-defeating exercise. As Carr put it some years later:

> Week after week, I met three reasonable men in the conference room. They then went into a studio and 'performed' [...] They scored off each other like bold schoolboys. They displayed arrogance, shrewdness, rudeness and contempt in equal proportions. I asked them why they put on this charade in the studio and were so much more reasonable afterwards in the hospitality room. They told me, with a certain trace of contempt for their supporters, that 'the punter expected it'.[53]

Nonetheless, there was also concern among politicians about the shambles that the programme was becoming. Carr was succeeded as chairman of *The Politicians* by David Thornley, a young Trinity College politics lecturer who had already cut his teeth on a religious programme. Thornley's many qualities were, however, effectively submerged by the format. A programme in October 1967 was devoted, in line with a decision by the party whips, to the vexed question of housing, and Kevin Boland, the then Minister for Local Government, was a most reluctant debutant. Shortly afterwards, the Minister for Posts and Telegraphs phoned the Director-General to complain about the 'bad handling' of the programme, but McCourt stood his ground. He told the minister that the behaviour of the politicians involved had been 'appalling', and threatened to take it off the air completely if the station could not get an assurance from the politicians that they would behave reasonably. At the Programme Policy Committee meeting at which the whole issue was discussed, there was general agreement that, short of walking off the set, there was little that Thornley could have done.[54] After a Government meeting following this programme, the Whip, Michael Carty, was instructed to inform RTÉ that the programme should be suspended 'pending discussion as to its better and more edifying performance'.[55]

The politicians' view that this kind of rowdyism was what the public expected and enjoyed was wrong. The viewing ratings plummeted and the programme staggered on until it was eventually scrapped in February 1968, probably to the relief of all concerned. The gravediggers included a number of people in the print media, notably Arthur Noonan, political correspondent of the *Irish Independent*

---

52 Bunny Carr, *The instant tree* (1975), p. 73.   53 Ibid., p. 74.   54 PPC Minutes, 1 November 1967. The Programme Policy Committee, which was generally chaired by the Director-General and included all the station's divisional heads, was effectively the main editorial committee. It was later renamed the Editorial Committee, and later again the Editorial Board, as some of its functions became the preserve of a Management Committee. As the main policy-making body in RTÉ, its records have been drawn on extensively for the purposes of the present work.   55 NA, 98/6/19.

(and later to become political correspondent of RTÉ) and John Healy, Parliamentary Correspondent of the *Irish Times*. The fact that the regular television programme on which they had appeared – *The Hurler on the Ditch* – had been axed to make way for the new programme, undoubtedly served to sharpen their quills, and was generally acknowledged among broadcasters and executives to be at the root of the 'continuous barrage' to which they were subjecting the station at the time.[56]

RTÉ devised a 'code of practice' for political programmes, which it first supplied to the whips of the three parties in September 1966. Almost simultaneously, two new current affairs programmes were launched as part of the autumn schedules. One was *Division*, an independent features programme dealing with legislative, political and parliamentary affairs. The two chairmen chosen initially were David Thornley, and Patrick Gallagher, a more experienced journalist with interests that included literature as well as current affairs. Thornley had already written a pamphlet for the discussion group, Tuairim, in which he underlined the significance of television, and warned that 'in the next twenty years, we are going to have to overhaul the politics and sociology of this republic'.[57] For the next few years, he was to be at the epicentre of that process on television. The producer was Muiris Mac Conghail, and the programme's 'major innovation is that politicians themselves will regularly participate. This is something new in Irish television.'[58]

The second was *Seven Days*, which was an entirely different concept: a broad-ranging current affairs programme with a young and talented team of producers and journalists who were markedly unimpressed by traditional authority structures and despised officialese. The RTÉ Authority's report for 1967 introduced it with a very modest fanfare, as 'a revised form of "Sixty-Six" [the successor to *Sixty-Five and Sixty-Four*]'. The new programme's producer was Lelia Doolan, who had been with the station for five years. She had actually made her debut as the first ballad-singer to appear on a new traditional music programme in the summer of 1962, where she was billed as 'a brilliant comedienne, most at home in lampoon and satire. There is an edge to her comedy playing which gives it a raw, tangy flavour.'[59]

The team for the programme comprised two directors, Eoghan Harris and Dick Hill, and three reporters: John O'Donoghue, Brian Cleeve and Brian Farrell. Both the directors were from Cork – Harris from a Republican socialist background, and Hill from a comfortable, Protestant milieu. The breadth of the new programme was announced almost casually: 'Farrell is keeping an eye on family planning, US politics, comprehensive schools; Cleeve is watching world hunger, South Africa, and certain internal social problems; while O'Donoghue studies developments in the Communist world and the Common Market.'[60]

56 PPC Minutes, 1 November 1967.   **57** David Thornley, *Ireland – the end of an era?* (1965), p. 17.   **58** *RTV Guide*, 7 October 1966.   **59** *RTV Guide*, 29 June 1962.   **60** *RTV Guide*, 23 September 1966.

The menu they had set out for themselves was impressive by any standards; but, while *Seven Days* got under way, its first forays into current affairs journalism were overshadowed by a major series of incidents which embroiled government and broadcasters in bitter controversy, and led directly to the resignation of one of the station's senior executives.

The context was the growing dispute between the farming organisations and the government over agricultural prices. The smaller of the two farming organisations, the Irish Creamery Milk Suppliers' Association (representing on the whole smaller farmers) had picketed Leinster House, and picketers had been arrested under the Offences Against the State Act. Then, on 7 October 1966, members of the National Farmers' Association began a march from Bantry, Co. Cork, which was to conclude with a lengthy sit-in outside the offices of the Minister for Agriculture, Charles J. Haughey, in Dublin. As the march started, the eddies of the controversy seeped into the broadcasting station. The *Division* programme planned to interview both Mr Deasy of the NFA and the Minister for Agriculture. Mr Haughey, despite his ease with the medium – one critic observed that his 'virtuosity before the cameras was uncannily convincing and accomplished'[61] – objected strenuously to appearing in a format in which someone who was not an elected public representative would be given parity. This echoed the general government view that appearances on the programme should be confined to members of the Oireachtas, although this convention, if convention it was, had already been broken in January 1966 by the appearance of Proinsías Mac Aonghusa on *Division* in his capacity as the recently-expelled Deputy Chairman of the Labour Party.

In the event, Mac Conghail, after discussions with the Controller of Programmes, Gunnar Rugheimer, decided that the requirements of impartiality could be met if a journalist could be interviewed who would put the government's point of view in an authoritative way. MacConghail chose a journalist with whom he had previously worked on the agricultural programme *On the Land*, Ted Nealon. Nealon agreed with some reluctance, but did a competent professional job. There is a certain irony in the fact that Nealon, who had edited the *Sunday Review* and had been invited to become political correspondent for the *Irish Times*, later left a distinguished career in broadcasting to become a government press secretary, Fine Gael TD, and junior minister in a Fine Gael-led coalition. This device did not mollify the government: Carty now told RTÉ that Fianna Fáil were now withdrawing from any future participation in *Division* because of RTÉ's interpretation of the code of practice. 'We regard your decision to permit the participation in this programme of persons other than members of the Oireachtas as a flagrant breach of this code and, accordingly, have no option but to withdraw.'[62] He went further, warning the station that if it went

61 Tom O'Dea, *Irish Press*, 16 October 1965.   62 NA, 98/6/19, Carty to RTÉ, 10 October 1966.

ahead with its plans, he would have to lodge an objection under the terms of Section 18 (1) of the Act – the section which enjoins impartiality on RTÉ. The objection was never lodged: indeed, it is difficult to see with whom it might have been lodged, or to what effect.

The temperature had already been raised by the decision of the RTÉ news division to juxtapose a statement from Mr Haughey with another from the farmers' leader, Mr Rickard Deasy, on the 6 p.m. news on 7 October. The context for this controversy was the newsroom culture, of which McGuinness himself was a committed advocate, and which placed considerable emphasis on the recording and presentation of varied points of view. The style of television news, he wrote, had to be 'scrupulously correct' and should 'inform with accuracy and in depth that reflects the wealth and variety of modern progress.'[63]

Haughey rang the station to complain, and spoke initially to the duty editor, Rory O'Connor, who gave him little satisfaction. Shortly afterwards, O'Connor had a call from his superior, the Head of News, Pearse Kelly, (to whom Haughey had presumably spoken in the interim) who gave him an instruction that the Deasy statement was not to be broadcast on the next bulletin at 9 p.m. As soon as the newsroom staff, members of the National Union of Journalists, heard this, they became incensed. The union had some time previously formally objected to Kelly's handling of his responsibilities at a meeting with senior management attended by NUJ officials from London: there as a sense that what little confidence they had in him as Head of News had now evaporated.

The following day the Director-General, Kevin McCourt, attempted to justify the deletion of the NFA statement from the later news bulletin, but this succeeded only in evoking a statement from the NUJ challenging his version of events. Moves were then made to discipline the journalists for issuing this statement.

Less than a week later, the matter was raised in the Dáil by Opposition speakers, alleging that Mr Haughey's telephone call had been improper, and that the government was effectively trying to muzzle the station. This evoked, from the Taoiseach, a statement of government policy on broadcasting in terms which had certainly not been advanced in any sense during the passage of the Broadcasting Act or indeed at any time in the intervening six years.

> Radio Telefís Éireann was set up by legislation as an instrument of public policy and as such is responsible to the Government. The Government have overall responsibility for its conduct and especially the obligation to ensure that its programmes do not offend against the public interest or conflict with national policy as defined in legislation. To this extent the

---

63 James McGuinness, 'News broadcasting' (1967), pp. 200–1.

government reject the view that Radio Telefís Éireann should be, either generally or in regard to its current affairs programmes, completely independent of Government supervision.[64]

The carefulness of the language employed did not prevent some subsequent commentators from conflating 'public policy' with government policy, or even from accusing Lemass of having described RTÉ as a 'tool of government';[65] nor did it conceal the essentially minatory quality of the message. It could have been contrasted – had any of his critics been aware of the possibilities for comparison – with one of his earlier statements on the role of public service broadcasting, which was in a markedly different vein. This had been in 1949 when, languishing in opposition as managing director of the *Irish Press*, he had appeared in the witness box in the High Court to defend his paper against a libel action being brought by the then Minister for Social Welfare and leader of the Labour Party, William Norton. He used the occasion to contrast what he saw as the differing responsibilities of the broadcast and print media.

> I think news given by Radio Éireann, which is a public service, should be given without regard for its political effect. To lay down the same standard for a newspaper is ridiculous ... we [i.e. the *Irish Press*] try to give it objectively with due regard for its importance, and we have a close regard for its political effect.[66]

On this occasion the broadcasters decided to return fire with fire: *Seven Days* responded by devoting a week's programming to issues connected with freedom in broadcasting, including interviews with an impressive range of authorities such as Grace Wyndham Goldie of the BBC and Walter Cronkite of NBC. *Division*, under the editorship of Muiris Mac Conghail, ran a programme of its own on political interference in broadcasting, which degenerated into an unseemly squabble.[67]

It was a baptism of fire for, among others, the new Chairman of the Authority, Dr C.S. Andrews, a veteran of the War of Independence and the Civil War, who had previously served as a Fianna Fáil-appointed chairman of both Bord na Mona and Coras Iompar Éireann. Despite his political antecedents, Andrews – though critical of many aspects of RTÉ's operations – rapidly developed an empathy for broadcasters and their problems. In relation to this specific controversy, both he and Kevin McCourt were called to a private meeting in the Shelbourne Hotel with the Minister for Posts and Telegraphs, Erskine Childers, at

---

64 Dáil Debates, 12 October 1966.   **65** Bunny Carr, *Tree*, p. 54.   **66** *Irish Press*, 1 July 1949. Norton was awarded £1 in damages, earning him the soubriquet – from Seán MacEntee TD – of 'Billy the Quid'.   **67** 28 October 1966.

which the Cabinet's fury over the coverage given by television to the farmers' protests was communicated to the station's executives in no uncertain terms. Andrews, however, held firm, and pointed out to Childers that the government had, under the Act, an instrument at their disposal with which they could remedy the situation if they thought it sufficiently serious – the power to issue a directive under Section 31. Childers, and the government, backed off. Lemass resigned as Taoiseach shortly afterwards, to be succeeded by Jack Lynch. Childers, no doubt mindful of the NFA row, warned Lynch, in November 1966 that it was absolutely essential for about 10–20 government supporters, TDs and Ministers, to be trained for appearing on TV. 'There is', he told Lynch, 'a dearth of effective talent.'[68] But Childers was also at pains to allay the growing government fears that broadcasters were inherently biased against Fianna Fáil. He told Lynch: 'Andrews tells me that between the Board and the staff the idea that there is not sufficient Fianna Fáil support in RTÉ is ludicrous. McCourt has endless conflicts with Fine Gael and Labour.'[69] Anxious to avoid a repeat of the Haughey/NFA incident, he also argued strongly that no government minister should contact RTÉ at a level below that of Andrews, McCourt, or the Assistant Director-General, John Irvine.

From this point until 1971 government and the Authority circled each other warily in relation to Section 31: occasionally the Government would request time for a ministerial broadcast on some topic or other: RTÉ, when agreeing, would frequently indicate to the government its view that the request was tantamount to a direction under the section. Equally frequently, the government would dispute the Authority's interpretation.

The political outcome of this particular dispute was a decision by the government to boycott *Division*. The withdrawal from the programme lasted until Lynch's election as Taoiseach: this created a new situation, and Lynch broke the deadlock by agreeing to appear again on the programme at Mac Conghail's invitation. Administratively, however, the outcome was hardly the one that might have been anticipated. On 4 November McCourt recommended to Andrews that Pearse Kelly's appointment as Head of News should be ended, and that Jim McGuinness should be appointed as his successor. Kelly was allowed, instead, to resign.

McGuinness, coincidentally, shared a number of characteristics with his predecessor: both had been members of the IRA, and indeed, if rumour was to be believed, Kelly had at one point in their mutually stormy past 'court-martialled' McGuinness for some infraction of IRA discipline. Both were also Northerners: McGuinness had not only been deported on one occasion from Britain, but had been interned in Ireland during the war. He had subsequently worked as a news-

68 NA, 98/6/19, Childers to Lynch, 12 November 1966.   **69** Ibid., Childers to Lynch, 4 December 1966.

paperman in San Francisco, had been an unsuccessful applicant for the News Editor's position when Kelly had been appointed, but had then been brought over from the United States by Ed Roth in 1962 to act as the station's first public relations executive.

McGuinness took over a division that was still to some extent in the doldrums. News presentation was flat and story-driven. Like the newspapers on which so many of the news staff had trained, it viewed the news bulletins essentially as linear assemblages of stories, starting with the most important ending with the least important. The insights and techniques of programme-makers were to all intents and purposes absent. Production values had not improved much from the era described by Charles Mitchel at the beginning of the decade. With the exception of Des Greally, who had worked with ITN, none of the newsroom staff had prior broadcasting experience. 'We were all scribes.'[70]

McGuinness was a driven newsman, anxious to rescue his staff from the half-light in which they worked, but one of his earliest initiatives fell foul both of the government and of the Authority, in spite of the fact that he had had a friendship with Andrews which went back many years. The new Head of News planned to send a team from the newsroom to cover the Vietnam war: nothing unusual about that, perhaps, except for the expense involved. This, however, was to be a trip with a difference: it was to report from Communist North Vietnam. It is not hard to see elements of McGuinness's background in this: he felt it was important to get all sides of a story and, when he had been an employee of the *Irish Press*, he would have been imbued by that part of the culture of the organisation which was always suspicious of the Cold War propaganda regularly delivered to the foreign news desk by US-based international news agencies. Some commentators maintained[71] that the Vietnam trip had not only been approved by the Authority, but had been personally endorsed by McCourt and may even have been his own idea (although this, on the face of it, seems unlikely).

The controversy about the proposed Vietnam visit, coming as it did hard on the heels of the Haughey/NFA row and Lemass's tough line in the Dáil, underlined the fact that government was becoming more and more intrusive. The Taoiseach, Jack Lynch, heard about the proposed trip – possibly from his Minister for External Affairs, Frank Aiken – and telephoned Andrews to tell him that the trip was to be called off. Andrews wrote immediately to McCourt instructing him to see that this was done: there is no evidence that the Authority as a whole was consulted or took a decision on the matter – indeed, the first they heard of it was some days later, when it was presented to them as a *fait accompli*, and they issued a statement to the press indicating that the decision had been taken 'in the best interests of the nation' because the proposed trip would have

70 Mike Burns, interview, 5 April 2003.   **71** Lelia Doolan, Jack Dowling and Bob Quinn, *Sit down and be counted: the cultural evolution of a television station* (1969), p. 100.

been 'an embarrassment to the Government in relation to its foreign policy'.[72] Aiken defiantly told the Dáil, in terms which suggested that his attitude towards media had not greatly changed since he controlled Ireland's wartime censorship system:

> If anybody in this country does not know the issues in Vietnam, somebody should go at his own expense, or a group could go at the expense of people who send them out. They would be able to go out there, learn the language, live there for a couple of years, and describe it fully with their pens.[73]

Ironically, within two years Aiken, who had by then retired, gave an hour-long interview to *Seven Days* in which, although he justified the decision to ban RTÉ from sending a team to North Vietnam because 'we don't want to make enemies of anyone if we can help it', he also expressed the view that the United States had no right to be in Vietnam, and that sending US troops there had been a great error of judgement.[74]

A news team was sent to the Soviet Union in August of the same year, but that did little to damp down the fires of resentment and protest which were building up within the station. Indeed, September found the Authority taking the view that less detail of the Vietnam war should be shown in news bulletins: an element of micro-management was patently becoming part of the role of the Authority in addition to its more general, supervisory role.[75]

The curtailment of the activities of the news division underlined the perception that the glamour was elsewhere, in the programmes division. From the beginning, therefore, there was a tension between the two sectors, born in part of a difference in culture, and under-pinned by budgetary mechanisms. The difference in culture is easily explained. Newsroom staff, as already noted, came largely from the world of print journalism, and few enough of them, in the early days, would have had third level education. The young producers, directors and presenters in current affairs and features were drawn from the ranks of young university graduates, many of them politics graduates from UCD, UCC and Trinity. There was also an ideological dimension to the cultural gap: journalists had, by and large transferred into broadcasting from a milieu in which mainstream media relations were the norm: there was a consensus which, although it might be challenged, basically remained a consensus. The younger generation, on the other hand, embodied what Raymond Williams has described as 'new meanings and values, new practices, new significances and experiences.'[76]

---

72 RTÉ Authority, Minutes, 14 April 1967; NA 98/6/20; UCD, Andrews papers, P91/71. 73 Dáil Debates, 13 April 1967. 74 *Irish Times*, 1 November 1969. 75 RTÉ Authority, Minutes, 1 September 1967. 76 Raymond Williams, 'Base and superstructure in Marxist cultural theory' (1980), p. 41, quoted in Chris Atton, 'News cultures and new social movements: radical journalism and the mainstream media' (2002).

What was anomalous was the fact that – partly because Irish broadcasting had been created at this particular historical juncture – many young Irish people who were attracted to the media as a career, and who would have in other circumstances become attached to radical or alternative media, found themselves (and their ideologies) newly ensconced within the heart of the media establishment. Finally, there was a central organisational factor. Regardless of who controls the media, in a financial, political, or social sense, large media organisations are virtually impossible to micro-manage. Because their product is content, and to a degree abstract (insofar as it consists of ideas, criticisms, versions of reality and so on) it is all but impossible for managements to develop control systems of sufficient complexity to allow them to ideologically regulate this content at all times and in all places. Indeed, even though it might be technically possible to create such a supervisory system, it would militate dramatically against the degree of creative freedom and initiative without which all media organisations inevitably become stultified and inert. Pools of relative freedom, as it were, therefore develop within the mainstream. They can be stagnant pools, or invigorating eddies. But the degree to which they can be dammed or channelled is always problematic.

This did not necessarily mean, on the other hand, that all producers shared a common value system. In fact, there was a tension between different types of producer which was as real, although more subliminal, as the tension which existed between programme-makers and news staff. And that tension was, in part, worked out within the current affairs area, and more particularly in the varying approaches to the flagship current affairs programmes such as *Seven Days* and, later, *7 Days* and *Today Tonight*.

In its first incarnation under Doolan, *Seven Days* was organised out of a sometimes chaotic, semi-permanent seminar on politics, economics and current affairs conducted in a caravan parked beside the main building, which was home to the programme (it was replaced within the first ten years of the programme's existence, but only by a bigger caravan). The business of the programme was, first, to get to the root of whatever was going to be its subject and, secondly, to develop a broadcasting style hall-marked by clarity and spare, accurate prose. If, for example, the programme had to deal with the government's latest Programme for Economic Expansion, experts would be summoned to the caravan – Martin O'Donoghue among them on one occasion – to demystify the worlds of gross national product, deficit budgeting, savings ratios and God knows what else, so that the programme makers could put them into descriptive passages and links that everyone could understand. Lelia Doolan would preside over this ferment, chain-smoking and all but unconscious of the passage of time: sessions could last from 9 a.m. until 3 p.m. with little more than a coffee break. Brian Farrell, Harris, and reporters like Patrick Gallagher and Seán Egan crafted the prose.

What was also an essential part of this mission to explain was structural analysis: policies were analysed not so much in terms of what the government wanted people to think they meant, or what the opposition claimed they meant, but in terms of their impact on people in the real world. Who benefited, and why? Who was in charge of the mechanisms of change? For whose advantage were they being operated?

This approach plainly owed a great deal to Marxism: not only Harris, but other producers like Jack Dowling – a former Army officer and auto-didact who was older than many of the station's trainee intake and exercised a strong influence over some of them – had sharply focused political backgrounds which put them at a distinct advantage in dealing with other programme makers or reporters whose sensibilities were primarily journalistic. Dowling, in fact, operated on the basis of a declared belief – unusual, to put it mildly, in a producer of programmes which were intended to garner a mass audience in the face of competition from BBC and UTV – that any good television programme had to annoy up to 90% of the Irish people at any given time.[77] He may not have meant this to be taken literally, and indeed his practice sometimes contrasted with his precept, but he clearly enjoyed the role of *agent provocateur*.

One of the programmes with which he was chiefly involved at this stage, *Home Truths*, was basically a consumer affairs programme, but Dowling enlivened it with witty graphics, and enraged advertisers (and RTÉ advertising sales staff) by conducting forensic analyses of consumer products such as cosmetics to demonstrate how little they cost to produce. *Home Truths*, had, in September 1966, replaced a low-key family programme called *Home for Tea*. *Home Truths* had informal relationships with both *Seven Days* and *Division*, 'not only because of their material, which was social, political and economic, but because of the personal relationships of their Producers, Directors, reporters and research teams.'[78] From the beginning, it experienced sharp reaction from the retail and manufacturing interests whose activities it scrutinised: this was part of its brief, which included the right 'to discover and investigate any malpractices in administration or commercial practice […] and to right them as far as fair comment and publicity permit.'[79]

Dowling resigned from the programme in January 1967, alleging that pressures being brought to bear on him from the commercial side of RTÉ to modify the programme's often biting criticism of products and of the whole retail and distributive business. This was contradicted later, by McCourt's successor, T.P. Hardiman, who maintained that 'suggestions ... that the content of the *Home Truths* programme was subject to censorship by the Sales Division are untrue' although there had been 'advance advice to the Sales Division on the content of

77 Private source. **78** Doolan et al., *Sit Down*, p. 81. **79** Ibid., p. 94.

the *Home Truths* programme to avoid the placing of inappropriate advertising in adjoining slots.'[80] In a final rejoinder, not published until after McCourt's period as Director-General had ended, Dowling recounted that he had refused an instruction from the Controller of Programmes to get a graphic artist to change the name of a brand of toothpaste to a fictitious brand name, and that an item on Mr Charles Haughey had been 'taken out of the tape, without his knowledge, by means of a razor cut.'[81] These accusations, made in *Sit Down and Be Counted*, hardly amount to compelling evidence for the existence of a climate of ruthless, commercially-inspired censorship, although the climate generally, as RTÉ strove to establish its foothold in the advertising market, was hardly propitious for a Marxist-based analysis of the retail sector. On the other hand, it is striking how far – given that same climate – such an analysis could be pushed before meeting resistance.

Classical journalism, against which producers like Dowling would have seen themselves as reacting, was primarily about telling stories, about confrontation, putting spokesmen for competing interests onto the same stage and letting them fight it out. It involved recording and responding to the events of the day and, in appropriate modes, commenting on them, but only rarely initiating, revealing, or attempting to set a political agenda. It did not eschew analysis or the mission to explain, but it tended to be reactive and personality-driven, whereas programmes which attempted to identify and explain underlying structural issues tended to regard personalities as secondary, and to be more interested in the longer term implications of current events. The journalistic approach could be more vivid, and more exciting; the structural one could be more illuminating, but sometimes preachy.

The lines of journalism were, however, becoming blurred within broadcasting structures. This was because many of the younger producers and directors, and some presenters, were effectively broadcast journalists even though their job descriptions did not include the word. Many of them, in the programmes division, were not members of the journalists' trade union, the NUJ, but of Equity or the Workers' Union of Ireland. They found themselves in many respects rejecting the political consensus that had been established under older media systems, and challenging its basic tenets.

Like all dichotomies, this analysis of the tension between classic journalism and the new forms of broadcast journalism somewhat overstates the case, and part of the difficulty of current affairs programming on RTÉ in the early years, or at least up to about 1980, was that there was no single individual who could ride both horses at the same time: indeed, separately, each of them was a handful in itself. But the first incarnation of *Seven Days* was incontestably the ascen-

80 Ibid., Appendix III, p. xlvi.   **81** Ibid., Appendix III, p. l.

dancy of the structural analysis project. It was the first programme, for example, to analyse industrial unrest in semi-documentary style: a dispute at Ideal Weatherproofs in Cork, which had been simmering for months without any noticeable media interest, prompted the despatch of a film crew. When their car pulled up outside the plant and the crew emerged, camera already running, they were met by Gardaí with batons drawn. Television current affairs in Ireland had not been done like this before. On 19 March 1967 the programme was entirely devoted to unemployment, and used a studio audience for the first time; on 3 April it ran a programme on the Knights of St Columbanus, an oath-bound Catholic organisation whose members were reputed to exercise hidden influence in business and in other spheres, including RTÉ itself.[82]

Part of the problem, in the sense that one mis-step could have potentially serious consequences for programme-makers, was that, in 1966–67, the two largest potential targets for structural analysis and criticism were both very powerful, and dangerous if attacked. They were Fianna Fáil, which had been in government as a single party for the best part of ten years, and the Catholic Church, which had been around for rather longer. In its criticisms of industrial practice, and in particular of the high-handed entrepreneurial culture of the day, it was easy for the programme to fall foul of Fianna Fáil's friends in the world of business, and to earn a reputation for being over-friendly to the Labour Party or even to groupings further towards the political Left. E.B. McManus, a businessman and a prominent member of Fianna Fáil who was appointed to the first RTÉ Authority, made no secret of his suspicions of some broadcasters at a number of Authority meetings, asking pointedly at one stage whether there had been any representations to the Authority 'regarding Mr Justin Keating's political affiliations.'[83] Keating, a former member of the Communist party and a veterinarian by profession, was now finding a new political home in the Labour Party and a career as an exceptionally knowledgeable broadcaster on agricultural topics. MacManus was subsequently immortalised by the left-wing TD Jack McQuillan, in the couplet: 'When Eddie says no, it's curtains for the show.'[84]

Where the Catholic Church was concerned, the new openness created by the Second Vatican Council had encouraged more widespread criticism of that Church generally. In its Irish manifestation, it was being seen as crusty, backward, unwilling to change and restrictive of personal liberty – all characteristics which could conveniently be assigned to its most visible representative, now nearing retirement, Archbishop John Charles McQuaid.

In this broad general context, it is hardly surprising that the political establishment saw the newer breed of broadcast journalist as a threat – a threat which

---

82 Wesley Boyd, *40 Years of News*, RTÉ 1 Television, 20 December 2002. Mr Boyd, a former RTÉ Head of News, made no bones of his opinion that the Knights had exercised more influence within RTÉ than had the 'Stickies', i.e. the Workers Party. **83** RTÉ Authority, Minutes, 17 June 1965. **84** Quoted by Tom O'Dea, *Irish Press*, 25 September 1982.

was all the more dangerous, and difficult to deal with because it did not involve simply disadvantaging one of the mainstream political parties in order to advantage one of its rivals, but advanced a new framework of analysis completely. The fact that the core value of this new frame of analysis was partly Marxist, or at any rate left-wing, did not escape the political professionals for long. As this realisation deepened, the puzzlement and exasperation which had characterised the early reaction of Fianna Fáil in particular to the station's forays into Irish political current affairs began inexorably to yield to a loosely, but widely held conspiracy theory in which the Labour Party, in particular, was thought to be the sinister hidden influence within the station.

In the summer of 1967, Lelia Doolan moved to another programme area, on promotion. Muiris Mac Conghail, who had been editor of *Division*, was invited to replace Doolan at *Seven Days*, but opted, instead, for an amalgamation of both *Seven Days* and *Division* under a single programme, now entitled *7 Days*. The rationale for the change, which was not accepted everywhere with equanimity, was 'that politics and current affairs are so often intimately associated that to separate them sometimes means that less than justice could be done to pressing and immediate problems.'[85] The anonymous commentator added that while 'objectivity' and 'impartiality' were two words which were much heard about the station, there was a third one which was at least as important: 'That word is "responsibility."'[86] Mac Conghail, in his twenties, was to have a powerful influence on the early development of current affairs broadcasting. A vocational teacher by training, he had a tough political intelligence, a sharp appreciation of the foibles of politicians, and a mastery of the Irish language that provided him with a degree of political fire-proofing. He had a range of skills which spanned studio discussion and film, and is the person who – in spite of the briefer and meteoric career of Lelia Doolan – is probably most associated, not only in the public mind but in the minds of programme-makers generally, with the early *7 Days*.

Some four years later, he explained his view of the programme when he took it over. He indicated that he did not by any means eschew structural analysis – the need to 'explain the major developments of the day in terms of people'. He also saw the need to help audiences identify with what they saw on the screen by 'having people like themselves talking about their problems instead of having remote experts talking at them'. Above all, however, he identified himself with the mainstream of classic journalism, as he declared, 'Television is a case of habeas corpus. If you do not have the body that has made the news, will make the news or should have, you are just not in business.'[87] *7 Days* now had six directors, five reporters, the associated production facilities and budget, and was coming out twice every week. For the first time current affairs was beginning to be

---

85 *RTÉ Guide*, 28 July 1967. Unsigned article.   **86** Ibid.   **87** *RTÉ Guide*, 31 December 1971.

viewed by audiences in numbers comparable to those watching light entertainment. Even a crowded pub would hush as the programme began.

If the iconoclasm of 7 *Days* was not sufficiently upsetting for the political, religious and social establishments, they also had another programme to contend with, and it was a programme with a weapon which no other current affairs programme could employ. This was *Féach*, and its secret weapon was the Irish language. This in itself pointed up a paradox. In Irish society generally, the proponents and speakers of Irish had tended to become associated, in the public mind's eye, with an older, more conservative Ireland. The influx of new personnel into the recently-established television service, however (and indeed some of those who had transferred from the old radio station) included both older people whose attitude to Irish was imbued with a social and political radicalism, such as Seán Mac Réamoinn and Aindrias Ó Gallchóir, andalso younger broadcasters like Harris, Seán Ó Mordha, Proinsias Mac Aonghusa and Breandán Ó hEithir, who were effectively modernisers and mould-breakers. They did not by any means share a set of political convictions, but they were united in their desire to push the envelope of the new medium, and protected in that enterprise by the fact that they were doing it in the first official language. The first broadcast of *Féach*, on 16 July 1967, gave little hint of what was to come. Its anchor man was Andy O'Mahony, it was directed by John Williams, and its reporters included Seán Duignan and Micheál Ó Briain. It promised viewers, among other things, 'a weekly calypso in Irish.'[88] If this sounded like harmless fun, the reality was to prove considerably grittier.

The new 7 *Days* under Mac Conghail hit the ground running. It was initially a split programme. Its Tuesday programme would cover politics, its Friday programme a more general current affairs topic. Quite early in its run, however, there were shivers of apprehension about the interviewing style of some of the staff. A programme on 3 October 1967 generated a view at the station's Programme Policy Committee that John O'Donoghue, Brian Cleeve and Patrick Gallagher had carried aggressive interviewing too far. This concern was leavened by a certain amount of approbation: while there had been 'hectoring' at times, it was important not to give staff the impression that they were being reprimanded, because 'in "*65*" [a programme] of two years ago we had flabby, diffused, unpointed commentary. Now we had a planned, detailed, analytical type of enquiry. It was important that this evolution would not find disfavour at official level'.[89] The station managers were, effectively, in a dilemma. On the one hand, criticism by government ministers would help to persuade the public that the Vietnam affair had been no more than a flash in the pan, and that the station had a genuine measure of independence. On the other, such attacks could have a

88 RTÉ Guide, 28 July 1967.   **89** PPC Minutes, 5 October 1967.

chilling effect on an organisation which had not yet, perhaps, established its independence to the necessary degree.

Early in December 1967, the 7 *Days* programme editor and staff produced a manifesto outlining their approach, which was warmly welcomed by at least one commentator:

> If a point of view is implicit in any one programme, the public has shown that they will accept it as a 7 *Days* point of view, even if it be controversial or hard hitting, but provided – and this is important – that every effort is made to present the case fairly and comprehensively.[90]

Over at the *Late Late Show* production offices, the *éclat* and controversy surrounding current affairs had not gone unnoticed. Nor had the audiences which 7 *Days* was attracting. In November 1967 Gay Byrne phoned the secretary of the Department of the Taoiseach to ask him of the Taoiseach would meet him to discuss ministerial participation on his programme. 'He said', the Taoiseach was informed, 'that he hopes to get away from the present light entertainment type of programme and to turn it instead into a programme in which matters of public interest would be discussed in a serious manner.'[91] Byrne had already made informal approaches to no fewer than three ministers – Charles Haughey, George Colley, and Donough O'Malley, and O'Malley, at least, had indicated his willingness to participate if the Taoiseach was in favour of this experiment.

Reaction was swift and unambiguous. After a government meeting the following day, Lynch told his departmental secretary that he did not approve of ministers going on the *Late Late Show*; that there was already provision for political programmes; and that therefore there was no need for a meeting with Byrne. The whips of all the political parties told Mac Conghail and Jack White, at a meeting in Leinster House, that they took grave exception to the introduction of politics as such on other RTÉ programmes, and 'deplored the fact that RTÉ should vilify and ridicule politics and politicians in shows like "Late Late", "Seven Days", etc.' Gay Byrne was censured by the Director-General, Kevin McCourt.[92] At an internal RTÉ meeting it was noted that 'recent events are now encouraging the opinion that RTÉ is being run from underneath', a view which the Director-General described 'with some bitterness' as 'not entirely unfounded.'[93] Two days later, two members of the Cabinet – the Minister for Posts and Telegraphs and the Minister for Finance – came out to Donnybrook for a meeting with the Director-General at which he was left in no doubt about the strength of feeling in government circles about public affairs programming.[94]

---

90 Tom O'Dea, *Irish Press*, 9 December 1967.   91 NA, 98/6/19, note to Taoiseach, 1 November 1967. 92 Ibid., Lynch to Secretary of department, 2 November 1967; Childers to Carty, 4 November 1967; note of meeting, 5 November 1967. McCourt's track record suggests that the reprimand would have been a mild one.   93 PPC, Minutes, 9 November 1967.   94 UCD, Andrews papers, 091/71.

For the time being, at least, anyone tempted by the siren song of the *Late Late Show* would have to remain roped to the flagpole on government buildings.

It is worth noting, in passing, that political hostility towards RTÉ was not confined to the Government benches. The redoubtable and eccentric Fine Gael TD Oliver Flanagan (himself to be the subject of a special *7 Days* filmed report by Ted Nealon in June 1968) leaped on the bandwagon, asking the Minister for Posts and Telegraphs provocatively:

> Is it not a fact that very recently, on the instructions of Telefís Éireann, there has been a round up of certain well-known Communists for the purpose, first, of having them put on television for interview and, secondly, to ascertain their views?[95]

A few years later, the same deputy was to form part of a pincer movement with the Fianna Fáil Minister for Posts and Telegraphs, Gerry Collins, as the problems of Northern Ireland escalated uncontrollably from drama into crisis.

Although the broadcasters did not know it, they were now beginning to live on borrowed time. The government was proposing a referendum on changing the electoral system from proportional representation to the British, 'first-past-the-post' system. An analysis by David Thornley and Professor Basil Chubb of TCD in a December edition of *7 Days* suggested that, under the British system, Fianna Fáil would win a huge majority of Dáil seats: Fianna Fáil ministers were enraged, believing that RTÉ was setting out to undermine their policy. Then Brian Cleeve and Eoghan Harris suggested that a programme should be done about the Garda Special Branch in relation to the events surrounding the arrest of two members of the Communist Party, Michael and Georgia Murray. At the same time, research was going on into a controversial planning dispute at Mountpleasant in Dublin, which had political overtones.[96]

The Programme Policy Committee, headed by the Director-General and including all divisional heads, now began to address this series of problems (as it perceived them) in earnest. In January 1968, arising out of a discussion about the possibility of allocating a half-hour additional news programme to the news division at 10 p.m., the Head of News, Jim McGuinness, observed that the germ of the problem lay in relationships between news and current affairs, and argued that there had been a failure in news over the past few years in that it had not been covering Irish affairs effectively. He was, he said, 'quite aware of the explosive possibility of combining the two fields' but was prepared to accept the implications of this 'even if it might not be in the best interests of what is presently regarded as the News Division.'[97]

95 Dáil Debates, 7 November 1967. **96** Doolan et al., *Sit Down*, p. 116. **97** PPC Minutes, 15 January 1968.

Simultaneously, Mac Conghail had been planning to take a team to film a report on the breakaway of Nigeria's Eastern Region (now known as Biafra) and the ensuing civil war. On 24 January he went to Lisbon, where a charter plane had been arranged. The Controller of Programmes, Michael Garvey, who had replaced Gunnar Rugheimer in 1966, had been informed in advance and had agreed.[98]

The following day McCourt, who had also been informed, phoned the Department of External Affairs to say that RTÉ personnel were planning a visit to Biafra, and to enquire 'whether there was anything about Biafra he should know about.'[99] His interlocutor, the Secretary of the Department, Hugh McCann, warned him that any action taken by RTÉ which could be represented as partisan might endanger the safety of people in Nigeria, and would certainly be used for propaganda purposes. McCourt spoke to Andrews, then issued an instruction cancelling the project, and then rang McCann again to tell him what he had done. McCann had, in the meantime, phoned Aiken, who agreed fully with his view. McCourt was at pains to explain to McCann that he had not consulted the government and had not received any direction or advice from them. He hoped, he added, that 'any publicity which seemed inevitable would not give rise to embarrassment as the Vietnam affair had.'[100] In a Dáil debate much later, Aiken maintained that he had not heard that RTÉ were proposing to send a team to Biafra until he read in the papers that they had been called back from Lisbon, which puts quite a different gloss on McCann's memorandum in the archives and its implication that McCann had kept him fully informed. In the same debate, Aiken maintained stoutly that oil interests were at the bottom of it all – as indeed in some sense they were – and that RTÉ had been taken in by 'certain gentlemen' who had given $1 million to Col. Ojukwu [the Biafran leader] and that this money 'was used to buy a plane and they came to Britain and hooked up as many television teams as they could and also nobbled our television team to go to Biafra'.[101]

McCourt's hope that the Vietnam episode might not be replicated in the publicity surrounding the Biafra episode was, no doubt, a forlorn one, but the incident brought to a head the mood which had been developing in the upper echelons of the station. At a meeting of the Authority on 2 February 1968, McCourt (who had actually given in his notice in December 1967 and was due to retire on 1 April 1968) recorded his dissatisfaction with the editorial control of 7 *Days* – in particular the Biafra trip, about which he claimed he had not been advised, and about the proposed film on the Special Branch. He now proposed that 7 *Days*

98 Doolan et al., *Sit Down*, p. 116.   **99** NA 98/2/28, unsigned memorandum dated 25 January 1968, from which subsequent information relating to the Department of External Affairs is also drawn. A reference in the Andrews papers in UCD (P91/70) makes it clear that the author of the memorandum was the Secretary of the Department, Hugh McCann.   **100** Ibid.   **101** Dáil Debates, 28 October 1969.

should be transferred to the News Division, where it would come under McGuinness's direct control. Michael Garvey, who had agreed to the Biafra trip, was now caught in the middle: he first of all agreed to the proposed transfer, but then changed his mind and threatened to resign. Jack White, suggesting that censorship was involved, argued that the Biafra story should go ahead, and added, somewhat bitterly, that current affairs in RTÉ had been put in a 'very humiliating position'.[102]

The notice from McCourt announcing the change was posted on staff notice-boards on 12 February 1968, and there was an immediate uproar. Equity and the Workers Union of Ireland both threatened industrial action. As the contracts of Ted Nealon, Brian Cleeve and John O'Donoghue with 7 *Days* were cancelled, the National Union of Journalists added its voice to those calling for a strike. McCourt, explaining his decision, expressed the view that 7 *Days* was beginning to lack impartiality – required of the station under Section 18 of the Act – and that the decision to move it to the News Division would rectify the situation.[103] The Special Branch film was first of all shown to a special meeting of the Authority, who came to the conclusion that it did not meet the requirements of Section 18. It was then withdrawn, although bits of it were shown later in a different programme; the Mountpleasant film was shelved; and a report which Seán Egan had been preparing on the Dublin Housing Action Committee also bit the dust. There is little doubt, at this remove in time, that the transfer was essentially disciplinary, and influenced at least partly by the political pressure which had been building up externally. Almost simultaneously a 7 *Days* programme on the property developer Matt Gallagher, evidently an attempt to show that 7 *Days* had not lost its teeth or its analytical edge, was in the words of Tom O'Dea in the *Irish Press* a crudely-done 'disembowelment' which demonstrated that the programme-makers were 'less endowed with prudence than with honesty and courage.'[104]

Gossip ebbed and flowed intensely around these issues, especially in Leinster House where most opposition deputies were pre-disposed, in the wake of November 1966, to assume that the government had intervened yet again. A series of exchanges in February 1968, laced with innuendo, gives a useful flavour of the atmosphere of the times.

> Mr Cosgrave: The Minister is aware that, while the Minister may not have directly intervened, this Board is an entirely Fianna Fáil Board, and so acted, and the Minister can add that to his reply.

102 PPC Minutes, 25 January 1968.   **103** McCaffrey, 'Political communication and broadcasting', p. 232. Paradoxically, it could be argued that as much of news broadcasting is in the form of political controversy in serial form, it is impossible (certainly within the scope of any one news broadcast) to ensure 'impartiality', while current affairs programmes and documentaries, produced under more relaxed time constraints, could embody this concept to a greater extent.   **104** *Irish Press*, 17 February 1968.

Mr MacEntee: I should like to ask the Minister if he is aware that following a recent convention of the Fine Gael Party to select a candidate for Clare, a former Chief Whip of that Party presented himself in Montrose, forced his way into the editor's office complaining that the news bulletin was not to their liking and asking for a bulletin to the Fine Gael specification?

(Interruptions.)

Mr Boland: And not for the first time.

Mr P. Belton: Where did the Deputy get his information from?

Mr Cosgrave: He got it in Greece.

A Deputy: From his close touch with the members of the Board.

Mr Cosgrave: They are a Fianna Fáil Board and act as such.

Mr B. Lenihan: Do you put the Director-General in that category?

(Interruptions.)

Mr Davern: Whose furniture is moved with RTÉ vans?

Mr Cluskey: The Minister is stating categorically that there was no written or verbal communication with RTÉ in connection with any of the three programmes?

Mr Childers: There was no instruction of any sort given.[105]

The big battalions prevailed, as big battalions generally do. *7 Days* personnel who were unhappy with the transfer were eventually given the option of moving to other programmes. Eoghan Harris went to direct a programme called *Work*, safely removed from the control of the News Division: trouble followed him, like a tin can tied to a dog's tail. By May 1969 one of its programmes, on housing costs, had been castigated privately by the Minister for Posts and Telegraphs, Erskine Childers, as not being impartial within the terms of Section 18 (1) of the Act, and his criticisms had been echoed by the Authority.[106] He was joined there by Brian Cleeve and – a little later – Patrick Gallagher. There were turf wars between *Work* and *7 Days* – notably over a programme on the new oil storage facility at Whiddy island in Co. Cork. Harris subsequently migrated to *Féach*, where he joined Breandán Ó hEithir and Proinsías Mac Aonghusa: it was a troika which would – despite their frequently differing political views – provide management with a fair share of controversy in the period that lay directly ahead.

Of the *7 Days* team, others – notably Muiris Mac Conghail and Brian Farrell – stayed, but the new relationship, while workmanlike, was never an entirely happy one. McGuinness and Mac Conghail had always got on well in personal terms: unusually in the station, all their conversations about programming would

---

105 Dáil Debates, 20 February 1968.   **106** RTÉ Authority Minutes, 16 May 1969.

be carried on in Irish. There were rows from time to time: McGuinness, for example, explained at one meeting that the cultural difference remained: he, as Head of News, preferred to have stories done at speed, and he felt that the News Division was not psychologically geared to do this: *7 Days* was unhappy in the new arrangement inasmuch as it disliked having to do topics at five or six hours' notice, and preferred planned analysis.[107] It was evident that *7 Days* was determined to show that it had not been neutered by the transfer: a documentary by Ted Nealon on mental illness in the same month showed what the programme could do, given a bit of space and time. In March 1969 it tackled the problem of political corruption – a topic aired by the Catholic bishop of Killaloe, Dr Michael Harty: both programme and bishop were more perspicacious than either of them were aware at the time.[108]

As the black clouds rolled in from the horizon, however, there were still a few chinks of light. One of them, unexpectedly, was radio. If news had been the poor relation to current affairs in television, news had, especially since 1961, been the poor relation in respect of broadcasting generally. There were even indications that some of those in radio did not find this especially uncongenial. Roibéard Ó Faracháin, the Controller of Radio and an old Henry Street veteran, observed in the middle of one meeting on the *7 Days* issue that, in his opinion, current affairs was the lifeblood of television, and had less place on radio, which was more suited to drama and music.[109] His gentle, poetic voice came from another era.

In fact radio had already been nibbling at the edges of current affairs, and its news coverage was increasing. John Bowman, who had made his first broadcast as a schoolboy aged 16 in 1959, had inaugurated the current affairs programme, *Topic*, in 1962. Since then he had covered the John F. Kennedy visit, Pope Paul VI's trip to the Holy Land, and commentated on the occasional rugby international, as well as acting as a correspondent for a number of radio stations in the United States. Breandán Ó hEithir had started his broadcasting career by submitting weekly radio letters from Germany, where he was living in the early 1960s: when he returned to Ireland, he initiated a new fortnightly radio magazine programme, *An Ciocasán*. In 1965 *Topic* was joined by *This Is Your Business* and *Who's News*.

These were generally programmes produced under the rubric of Features – radio did not as yet have a specific current affairs division. But news was also improving. Towards the end of 1966 the government accepted proposals to increase the broadcasting hours in radio, which up to then had closed between 10.00 a.m. and 1.00 p.m., and between 11.20 a.m. and 12.20 p.m. on Sundays. In the same year the lunch-time news bulletin was extended from 10 to 15 minutes,

107 PPC Minutes, 18 April 1968.　**108** The present author discussed this with Dr Harty some time after the speech was made: Dr Harty observed that there had been such a hostile response to his speech that he would be slow to enter the same territory again. This illustrates the point that programme-makers were not the only ones taking risks at this time.　**109** PPC Minutes, 18 April 1968.

and the 'Topical Talk' was dropped and replaced by live and recorded broadcasts from locations at home and abroad. Day-long radio broadcasting, from 7.30 a.m. to 11.45 p.m., was to begin on 2 November 1968.

Other things were changing, too. There was a new Director-General: a selection committee comprised of Todd Andrews, Professor T.W. Moody, Dónall Ó Móráin and Fintan Kennedy (all members of the Authority), together with Maurice Gorham and the distinguished civil servant John Garvin, had chosen T.P. Hardiman to be the station's new Director-General.[110] The field had initially included Dr Conor Cruise O'Brien, who was not even given an interview: his application was summarily rejected by Andrews.[111] Hardiman's appointment was greeted with reserve by broadcasters: although he had been with the station as an engineer for a number of years, and had latterly been assistant Director-General, his attitude towards programme-makers was unknown.

For the seven years of his tenure, news and current affairs were going to be the battle-ground over which the protagonists in an entirely new – and to most people unexpected – conflict would rage: the politicians, para-militarists and programme-makers involved as actors in, or observers of, in the conflict that was just about to erupt in Northern Ireland.

110 UCD, Andrews papers, P91/67 (3)   **111** Private source.

CHAPTER 3

The North erupts

As T.P. Hardiman moved into the Director-General's seat on 1 April 1968, Irish society was beginning to change at a faster rate than it had, perhaps, for many decades. In politics, Jack Lynch's Fianna Fáil government was about to take another bite at proportional representation, which it increasingly saw as an electoral system designed to frustrate the party's ambitions. It was an area in which it generally found RTÉ's attempts at analysis distasteful: in the Dáil, the Minister for Local Government, Kevin Boland, referred scornfully to the verdicts of television commentators such as Professor Basil Chubb and David Thornley (who had predicted that the abandonment of PR would result in 100 Dáil seats for Fianna Fáil) as the 'fanciful forecasts of otherwise eminent gentlemen.'[1] In the capital, the collapse of a number of tenements in Fenian Street, Dublin, in which some people died, gave social protest a new edge. The Dublin Housing Action Committee, in which Sinn Féin activists – among others – found a place and a voice, was increasingly taking to the streets.

Early in May, the religious programme *Outlook*, which had up to then been a soft-centred, devotional end-of-the-day mini-homily, branched out into social issues. Its presenter, Fr Austin Flannery OP, enraged Boland by choosing to discuss housing policy on one of his programmes which included, as one of his guests, the leader of the Irish Communist Party, Michael O'Riordan. Within the station, the producer, Seán Ó Mordha, was asked to re-jig the programmes so as to supply more 'balance'. He duly prepared a list of the persons, interests and agencies whose views would 'balance' the programme. The problem was that there were fourteen of them, and the programme duration was only four and a half minutes.

> The thing spluttered out in a kind of a sour joke. Fr Flannery went on showing the audiences, in an unbalanced and, presumably, totally distorted way, that the state of housing in Dublin was scandalous, *but debatably scandalous*. The Government was very angry.[2]

---

1 Dáil Debates, 3 July 1968. **2** Jack Dowling, 'Broadcasting: an exercise in deception?' (1973), p. 126. Emphasis in original.

The North – although few people in government or in the media were as yet aware of it – was beginning to bubble. In June, Austin Currie, the young Nationalist Stormont MP, illegally occupied a local authority house in Caledon in Tyrone to protest against discriminatory local authority housing policies. A 7 *Days* programme by Patrick Gallagher on Northern Ireland in July of that year exposed at least some of the complexities of that region to an audience in the Republic which had long ignored or derided them. Abroad, and even to some extent at home, student protests fanned the flames of social and political movements. It was a good time to be young and energetic and wanting to change the world; it was a difficult time to be in mainstream politics; and it was a deeply problematic period for broadcasting.

Relationships between government and broadcasters during the Lemass era had been occasionally fractious, but under Lynch the pressure on RTÉ became intensified as some ministers, in particular, pushed the boundaries of the relationship in an attempt to see whether the Lemass interpretation of the Broadcasting Act, as enunciated at the height of the NFA controversy in October 1966, could be stitched into a new praxis. This was not always done formally. On one occasion, there was a confrontation between a senior Government minister and a senior RTÉ executive on the fringes of a social gathering: the RTÉ executive concerned later wrote to the minister to apologise for his discourtesy, but did not resile from his firmly stated view that, if government wanted to intervene in broadcasting, they had an appropriate mechanism at their disposal – Section 31 of the Broadcasting Act.[3]

The problem about Section 31 and any directive that might be issued under it, from the Government's point of view, was that it was a blunderbuss rather than a rifle. It had never been used. Nobody was clear about what would happen if it were used – apart from the evident fact that any government which used it would immediately come in for substantial public and media opprobrium. It would evidently be preferable for ministers to achieve their objectives by indirect, less public means. In this context, and paradoxically, Section 31 – which had widely been seen at the time it was passed as a threat to broadcasting freedom – was at this particular time actually a form of protection for the station. It allowed broadcasters to reject inappropriate pressure by pointing out to government that there was a statutory method of getting their way – should they choose to exercise it. The broadcasters knew that if a directive was issued under the Act they would have no option but to obey it – but they also knew that the government was unwilling, for obvious political reasons, to take this particular course of action in any but the most serious circumstances.

This led to a situation in which Government and RTÉ circled each other warily, like fencers looking for an opening. Occasionally, Government ministers

3 Private source.

looked for time for ministerial broadcasts: RTÉ politely acceded, but in a context in which it made clear that it interpreted these requests – which it always insisted should be made in writing – as directives under Section 31. Three times in 1969, for example, ministers made such requests: the first, from C.J. Haughey, was for time for a broadcast in relation to financial and economic issues; later, the Minister for Defence asked for time to appeal for recruitment to the Army. In December, the Minister for Lands looked for time for a broadcast in connection with International Conservation year. The Minister, Erskine Childers, wrote to RTÉ to object that in his department's view, Section 31 applied only where a serious altercation had arisen, and where the serving of a directive would be the only way to ensure a required broadcast.[4] In effect, RTÉ had two objectives. One, a long-term one, was to ensure that RTÉ build up a number of precedents so that no ministerial broadcast could be made on a controversial matter without a formal written request. The other was to ensure that only significant material was contained in such broadcasts. As Hardiman noted: 'We are aware that the Minister's civil servants dislike our practice in this regard, but they are looking after their Minister's interests rather than the interests of RTÉ.'[5]

It was religion, however, rather than politics, which provided Hardiman with his first test. It is hardly an understatement to say that the events of Vatican II had struck many chords in Ireland. Equally, however, many of the implications of that epoch-making event had been subsumed, in the public imagination, into the narrower question of whether or not the Catholic Church would modify in any way its traditional teaching on birth control. This question had been removed from the competence of the Council by Pope Paul VI, who had subsequently entrusted it to a Commission. The Commission, meeting in secret, had come to the majority conclusion that a modification of the traditional teaching would be possible, and its conclusions were promptly leaked to the media. The Pope, however, in the encyclical *Humanae Vitae*, published in July 1968, reaffirmed the Church's traditional teaching, although he placed it in a more broadly-based, less mechanistic framework than had previously been the case. His decision provoked a major crisis within the Church generally, and *a fortiori* in Ireland. The newspapers were full of it: how would RTÉ deal with it?

As it happened, the new Director-General, T.P. Hardiman, had already met the man who was to become a central figure in this controversy. Hardiman was a member of the Hierarchy's Communications Council, and when Canon Cathal McCarthy, one of McQuaid's important sources of information on broadcasting matters, wrote to the archbishop on 6 May suggesting that a meeting with the new Director-General would be useful, McQuaid noted: 'Met him on 1st and will see him again. We shall need him, in view of the strange things priests are

4 PPC Minutes, 18 March 1969. Childers to RTÉ, 18 March 1969. 5 PPC Minutes, 19 December 1969.

doing on T.V.' [6] A few days later Hardiman had a meeting with the archbishop which lasted for two hours, and in the course of which he raised with the archbishop the possibility that he might be interviewed for the station. McQuaid, however, was 'most unhappy at the prospect'.

> He [McQuaid] had quoted the appropriate section from *The Imitation of Christ* on anonymity in the doing of the Almighty's work: it was obvious that although a public figure for almost 30 years, his personal distaste for the public arena had not abated.[7]

As it happened, within days of meeting Hardiman, McQuaid had received an anonymous letter from 'a group of priests' in Dundalk, which provided ample evidence of a strong anti-RTÉ undercurrent in clerical circles generally – although McQuaid's approach would undoubtedly have been more subtle and sophisticated. The priests asked, rhetorically:

> Have our esteemed leaders any idea at all of the harm that is being done to the Catholics of Ireland by the anti-Catholic, anti-Irish propaganda of the Late-Late Show? Surely the time is lamentably overdue for responsible leaders to see to it that the suave Mr. Byrne be prevented from providing a platform for the vermin of England, France, USA or anywhere such vermin can be picked up.[8]

On 27 July McQuaid arranged a press conference at All Hallows at which Monsignor P.F. Cremin, who had been McQuaid's personal theologian at the last session of Vatican II, explained the encyclical and its implications. It was an extraordinary performance, in that it was less a press conference than a formal lecture, where Monsignor Cremin spoke without interruption for some 40 minutes before a single question could be asked.[9] His satisfaction with the outcome of the papal deliberations was manifest, as was that of his patron. A 7 *Days* camera crew took copious film of the proceedings for a programme which was the subject of critical comment at a Programme Policy Committee meeting immediately afterwards. Coincidentally, the presenter – Brian Farrell – was coming under notice, partly for his style of interviewing, which was thought to be too aggressive, and partly in relation to investigations which the programme was carrying out into the Potez Aerospace factory, an industrial white elephant which happened to be a pet project of the former Taoiseach, Seán Lemass. One 7 *Days* programme on Potez was criticised by the Deputy Director-General for its 'unconcealed hostility' to the enterprise[10] and, when the project finally collapsed,

6 DDA, AB8 XXVI (c). **7** PPC Minutes, 18 May 1968. **8** 13 May 1968, DDA AB8/B/ XXVI (c). **9** The present writer reported this press conference for the *Irish Times*, 28 July 1968. **10** PPC Minutes, 28 June 1968.

executives expressed the hope that its television obituary would be dispassionate, rather than take the form of a 'gloating inquest'.[11]

The 7 *Days* programme on birth control brought both problems into focus. The Head of News was concerned that the film had been used to 'send up' the press conference, and that there had been a risk of distortion by way of paraphrase. Farrell in particular was criticised for his 'predilection for a rather dramatic or high point ending' in both programmes.[12]

This was not, however, to be the end of the affair. Eoghan Harris now proposed to Jack White that a special programme – taking the birth control issue as its starting point – should be broadcast on the crisis of authority in the Catholic Church. The idea was that this would be a one-off, public affairs programme under the stewardship of Jack White, rather than a current affairs programme under the aegis of the News Division. A number of preparations were made, involving among other things a meeting in Portlaoise at which the bishop of Kildare and Leighlin, Dr. Lennon, agreed in principle to participate: this would have been a major *coup* for the programme-makers. According to the version of events subsequently published in *Sit Down and Be Counted*, this proposal was aborted after the Director-General had expressed the opinion that it should be transferred to the News Division because it was essentially a current affairs programme, i.e. one requiring continuing editorial supervision, rather than a once-off study of problems in the community.[13]

The criticisms rumbled on. The Minister for Posts and Telegraphs contacted RTÉ in relation to the Potez affair to complain that there had been a breach of the duty of impartiality.[14] In August, David Thornley wrote to the *Irish Times* criticising the teaching of *Humanae Vitae* in scarifying terms, leading the Director-General to query the propriety of using Thornley as a commentator on this particular topic (although no decision was taken to bar him from doing so).[15]

Thornley's letter, as it happened, formed part of a wider discussion which was to be carried on intermittently at senior management level, and which reached particular intensity as domestic politics, and the involvement of broadcasters in events outside the station, converged. Proinsías Mac Aonghusa, the free-lance radio broadcaster, had already occasioned comment for writing a letter to the *Evening Herald* which had cast Cardinal Stepinac, an Iron Curtain country prelate who had been ill-treated by the Communists, in a 'dubious light'.[16] As

11 PPC Minutes, 26 July 1968.   12 PPC Minutes, 30 July 1978.   13 Doolan et al., *Sit down*, pp. 154-8. This account describes the proposal as originating jointly from Harris and the present author. In my recollection, Harris was the sole originator of the proposal, although I was present at some of the planning meetings described, including the meeting with Dr Lennon. Dr Harty, the bishop of Killaloe, was not present at the Portlaoise meeting, although the book says that he was.   14 PPC Minutes, 2 August 1968.   15 PPC Minutes, 16 August 1968.   16 NA, 25 May 1962, copy of memo from Pearse Kelly, Head of News, to John Irvine, 10 April 1962. Irvine, then a civil servant, subsequently transferred to RTÉ, where he had a long and distinguished career, his experience on both sides of the fence helping to defuse many potentially explosive situations. He has also been, in the mode of León Ó Broin, a doughty defender of the con-

broadcasters were more and more encouraged to lend their considerable, screen-based authority to non-broadcasting causes in which they personally believed, the problems of management accumulated. Seen from the broadcasters' point of view, this was no more than their rightful freedom of expression: and they cannot have been insensible to the weight the public expression of their opinions might carry. Irish television, after all, was less than a decade old: its presenters and commentators had rapidly become household names, more admired than the politicians – masters of the universe, almost. The station managers, on the other hand, whatever their own political views or inclinations, were understandably apprehensive about the degree to which the station's much-vaunted, but still fragile, independence of government might be compromised by broadcasters who were too free with their – usually critical – opinions of government and its policies in other fora.

In 1968, Farrell was writing a column in the *Irish Independent* which was 'causing a problem'. Two years earlier he had been the author of a regular column in the *Irish Press*, which had ended with that paper's change of editor. It was now thought necessary to let Farrell know that his column should be confined to foreign affairs, and perhaps be suspended five or six weeks before a general election. The young journalist Cian Ó hÉigeartaigh was written to twice about this time; others to receive raps on the knuckles included Nollaig Ó Gadhra and the producer Jim FitzGerald whose association with the left-wing Catholic group 'Grille' came under notice. In general, in Hardiman's view, persuasion of staff was a better instrument than coercion, but this was a problem that was to assume more substantial proportions in the months and years ahead.[17]

There was another area, however, in which controversy was simmering behind the scenes, and in a context which would – if it had not been dealt with firmly – have had very serious affairs for news and current affairs programming generally. This was the degree to which tapes and other material made by RTÉ, whether broadcast or not, could legitimately become the subject of police investigations. Even before Hardiman's time as Director-General, there had been rumours within the station that members of the Garda Special Branch had been attempting to bribe members of staff to release information on the content of the film (which at the end of the day was never shown).[18] That could legitimately have been regarded as unofficial or irregular Garda pressure; but semi-official and regular pressure now became more marked. At one point, the Secretary of the Department of Justice, Peter Berry, sent a list of people whom he wanted kept off the air to the Chairman of the Authority, Todd Andrews. Andrews had the

cept and practices of public service broadcasting. He is the author of (so far unpublished) Thomas Davis radio lecture on 'Broadcasting and the public trust' (mimeo, 19 January 1976).   **17** PPC Minutes 20 August 1968, 27 August 1968, 5 September 1968, 11 October 1968.   **18** PPC Minutes, 22 October 1968, where reference is made to the allegation as having been made in 1967.

good sense not to show the list to anyone else in RTÉ, and was similarly unco-operative when charged by his party colleague, Erskine Childers, with making things difficult for the government by giving airtime to undesirables (presumably members of Sinn Féin). On one occasion, when Childers rang Andrews to express these views, Andrews told Childers sharply that if his [i.e. Childers'] government locked them up, they wouldn't be in a position to trouble anybody.[19]

Gardaí had for years operated within a culture within which all the resources of the State, and particularly information under State control, could readily be made available to them. They assumed that the State broadcasting system would be similarly co-operative, and were surprised when their initial overtures were rebuffed.[20] There was in fact a major issue of principle here, which emerged first in relation to the case involving Seán Bourke, the Limerick man who had arranged for the escape of the spy George Blake from Wormwood Scrubs Prison in Britain, and whom the British authorities wished to extradite. Almost simultaneously, it arose in connection with film which Gay O'Brien had taken of the civil rights march in Derry in October 1968. Later, it became an issue in relation to the Scarman Tribunal. Finally, it overshadowed the major controversy over the radio broadcast by Kevin O'Kelly in 1972 which led to the dismissal of the Authority.

The Bourke case first arose in November 1968 when the State Solicitor's office wrote to RTÉ looking for a wide range of material – not only film, but access to journalists and producers who had been involved in its production – and threatened to issue subpoenas if the required cooperation was not forthcoming. The State Solicitor was tersely told that

> As to the request that members of the Authority's staffs (and presumably contract broadcasters) should be at the disposal of the Gardaí for investigation into a matter arising out of their broadcasting duties, Radio Telefís Éireann does not consider this to be a reasonable request or one that it could enforce.[21]

Before this issue had been resolved, the question of the Derry film arose, when it appeared that the RTÉ film might be needed as evidence in court cases that were being brought in the wake of the disturbances at the civil rights march. The RTÉ position was clear: they would not hand over any of their material without a court order. This presented a certain problem, in as much as an order made by a court in Northern Ireland was obviously not enforceable in Dublin. Hardiman met this by requiring that a note of counsel's opinion, accompanied

---

19 Author's interview with Dónall Ó Móráin, 3 February 1994. Ó Móráin, A member of the Authority under Andrews and later its chairman, was discussing Authority business with Andrews in the latter's office when the telephone call was made. 20 Private source. 21 PPC Minutes, 20 November 1968.

by a statement from the Derry magistrate or justice of the peace that it would be in the interests of justice and in the general public interest that the RTÉ film should be made available to the court. Both these statements were prepared in Derry and on foot of this RTÉ released the film.[22]

Meanwhile, the wrangling continued about the Bourke case. Hardiman refused a further Garda request in December to make RTÉ material relating to Bourke available, despite coming under substantial pressure from the State Solicitor's office, from the Attorney General, and from an official in the Department of Posts and Telegraphs. When the official reported Hardiman's attitude to his Minister, Gerry Collins, Collins suggested that RTÉ were being less cooperative than the BBC would be in similar circumstances. Hardiman was contacted again, but said that he had gone as far as possible, and would not entertain requests for names and addresses of staff, the production of their notes, and so on. At this point Hardiman contacted the BBC for information on their policies, and was able to inform the department that the BBC cooperated with the authorities 'to a limited extent' in preliminary enquiries, but that they would regard as 'unthinkable' any request to be allowed access to BBC staff for purposes of interrogation.[23] As Hardiman made clear at the time to the Attorney General, 'RTÉ did not attempt to set itself above the law, but the particular considerations involved in broadcasting were such that cooperation should be seen to be achieved in public'. This could best be done by producing material only on the basis of a court order.[24] A similar stance was taken in relation to a request from the Scarman tribunal a year later,[25] but the overall effect can in retrospect be seen as contributing substantially to the growing sense of annoyance, which was to modulate into impatience and open hostility, on the part of government and senior officials towards what was seen as RTÉ's high-handed attitude in the sensitive area of State security. Although some Bourke material was provided on the basis of a subsequent court order, this did little to assuage government feelings, and the nature and importance of the principle on which RTÉ had taken its stand was unappreciated or even regarded as mischievous by a government which was coming under increasing pressure at home and abroad as the Northern Ireland crisis escalated out of control.

A related but less significant issue, but one which surfaced from time to time, was whether government ministers or departments should be given, at their request, tapes of radio or television programmes. This issue had first emerged in the 1940s and the Minister responsible, P.J. Little, had always resolutely refused to provide Opposition TDs with tapes of programmes with which they had found fault, or to put transcripts of news broadcasts in the Oireachtas library.[26]

22 PPC Minutes, 10 December 1968. In the event, the film was not used as evidence. 23 NA 2001/78/44. Memoranda to Minister from 'S. O'D', 6 December 1968 and 12 December 1968. 24 PPC Minutes, 10 December 1968. 25 PPC Minutes, 23 September 1969. 26 Dáil Debates, 6 February

Now, of course, RTÉ had been moved out of direct Government control, and Government ministers were unable to change the policy even if it suited them – as undoubtedly, on occasion, it would have. Successive Authority chairmen and directors-general, whatever their own political views, found this a convenient policy to adopt, often in the face of considerable pressure from ministers and civil servants. Indeed, had they weakened, it is difficult to see where the process would stop. Ultimately, however, the exigencies of the Northern situation, and the political implications of RTÉ coverage of the North, was to weaken the Authority's resolve in this area.

RTÉ was encouraged in this policy initially by the very high cost of video-tape: occasionally, tape required for a programme would cost more than any of the other ancillary items. It was primarily this factor which led to the erasing of much invaluable material, such as recordings of performances by Seán Ó Riada, which later generations came to regard as a dreadful loss. Gardaí and ministers were, however, from time to time offered facilities for private viewings of controversial television programmes, and the policy adopted in relation to radio programmes was more liberal: at one point the then Chairman, Dónall Ó Móráin, invited the Minister for Posts and Telegraphs to ask the Director-General for a tape of a programme on Ian Paisley if he had missed it.[27] Later, Bishop Michael Browne of Galway was sent a tape copy of a radio programme on Protestants in the Republic: he had asked for a transcript, which was not provided.[28]

Largely unaware of the external pressures to which the station was being subjected (or assuming on the basis of somewhat limited evidence, that the station capitulated too readily to such pressures), a number of producers and directors were becoming increasingly frustrated. They had already voiced their concerns in a letter signed by eighteen of them and sent to the RTÉ Trade Union Group on 18 October 1965: their views were embodied in a memorandum which the Group sent to the Authority on the same day.[29] This was – and was seen as – an indirect attack on the Controller of Programmes, Gunnar Rugheimer, who had been the object of some xenophobic, and unfair, public criticism by the Gaelic League and in some newspapers.

The anti-Rugheimer protest had fizzled out, and indeed some of the signatories to the letter later admitted that insofar as they had aimed it at him they had been unfair and inaccurate. The controversy which erupted now, however, was far more serious, and had its origins in continuing resentment at the transfer of 7 *Days* into the News Division. It was triggered by Bob Quinn, a creative producer who was a friend of Jack Dowling, Lelia Doolan and Eoghan Harris,

1941: reply to Risteárd Ua Maolcatha. **27** PPC Minutes, 1 May 1970. **28** PPC Minutes, 25 April 1972. **29** Doolan et al., *Sit down*, pp. 62-76. The signatories included James Plunkett Kelly, Maeve Conway, Aindrias Ó Gallchóir, Jim Fitzgerald and Padraig Ó Raghaillaigh.

who was, in May 1969, working on a social history project for the station's schools division, Telefís Scoile. Now, writing unexpectedly from Clare Island in Co. Mayo, where he was 'snagging turnips and conceiving my first son' with a camera crew he had 'hi-jacked' from RTÉ,[30] he addressed a general letter to his friends and colleagues. He felt, he said, that the time had come to challenge what he described as 'the Factory' [i.e. RTÉ] which had become 'a bloated and swelling corpse, feeding the increasing number of parasites but incapable of directing itself because there is no life, no human spirit to quicken it.'[31] He added:

> What do I propose to do about it? Mine is a personal responsibility of responsible irresponsibility. It attempts to counter the organisation's pseudo-philosophy of irresponsible responsibility. If you follow me, I propose to get in a boat and sail off, Charlie Bubbles-like, into the setting sun. All contributions will be tolerated, and appreciated if they're in the form of moral support.[32]

Despite the imprecise nature of this call to arms, Quinn's letter created a ferment within the station. It is fully, if sometimes confusingly, described in *Sit Down and Be Counted: The Cultural Evolution of a Television Station*, the book he wrote in conjunction with Lelia Doolan and Jack Dowling and which was published later in that year. An informal meeting of his friends took place on 19 May. On 20 May, Programme Heads met to discuss it, and it was also discussed at the Programme Policy Committee meeting on 22 May. The latter meeting did not seem disposed to take his criticisms too seriously: one of those present said that the letter had 'stirred up a number of those who were probably ready to be stirred up in any case'.[33] The situation, however, escalated rapidly with the resignations of Jack Dowling and Lelia Doolan on 26 May, and a mass meeting in the RTÉ canteen was attended by both Dowling and Lelia Doolan: together with other speakers, they upbraided the station's senior management. The Programme Policy Committee took strong exception to programme heads criticising management in public like this, and opinion was hardening.

Jack Dowling's resignation was accepted. Hardiman wrote to Lelia Doolan to tell her that she could be retained in her executive post (she was at this stage Head of Light Entertainment) 'if you cease to carry out what amounts to a public campaign of dissent from the form of organisation that exists and from the structure within which responsibility in RTÉ is exercised'.[34] Doolan's contract

---

30 Bob Quinn, *Maverick: a dissident view of broadcasting today*, pp. 11, 64. **31** Doolan et al., *Sit down*, Appendix III, pp. xxiv-xxxv. **32** Doolan et al., p. xxxv. Letter dated 14 May 1969. The author is referred to at one point in this book as 'Bill' Quinn. Following his resignation from RTÉ he embarked on a career as an independent producer, and was finally appointed to serve a term on the RTÉ Authority itself in 1995. He resigned before the expiry of his term of office, on the basis of a policy disagreement related to advertising and programming for children. **33** PPC Minutes, 22 May 1969. **34** Doolan et al., *Sit down*, Appendix III, p. xl. Hardiman to Doolan, 29 May 1969.

was due to run out in August 1969, but she replied immediately with her resignation, endorsing Quinn's and Dowling's view that the station's programmes were 'dangerously and increasingly trivial, emasculated, and contrary to the national cultural spirit'.[35] Eoghan Harris, who had planned to address another meeting in the canteen, was advised 'forcefully and emotionally' by his superior Jim Plunkett Kelly, a senior figure within the Workers' Union of Ireland, of the implications of doing so: Harris interpreted this as a threat of suspension, but the PPC minutes suggest that this advice was related to 'students on the site and the avoidance of unnecessary problems with them [a small number of students from the Students for Democratic Action organisation were involved].'[36]

The documentation from the period suggests that, despite the hard line being taken by management, the producers were not entirely without support at that level. At one meeting, the view was expressed that some of the concerns of the producers were genuine; at another, the Deputy Director-General, John Irvine, expressed his own view that the station's decision to back down on the Vietnam issue had been a mistake.[37] The speed with which the controversy escalated, however, backed both protagonists into their respective corners. Threatened in public, management moved into a defensive, uncompromising mode. Their critics, however, also miscalculated: Doolan's and Dowling's resignations, in particular, failed in one of their primary purposes, which was to radicalise the heads of the various departments within RTÉ. Resignation is a gun that can be fired only once, and on this occasion it missed.

Hardiman's lengthy justification for management's response, running to seventeen foolscap pages, was the object of a further rejoinder by Dowling and Doolan in June 1969, but the controversy – although it left much bad feeling in its wake – subsided until the publication of *Sit Down and Be Counted* later in the year. Bruised by the public nature of the controversy – and in the long term more seriously by the departure of Doolan in particular – managers and programme-makers alike settled back into an uneasy truce. The publication of the book occasioned much debate within the Programme Policy Committee, where the general view was that management could only lose by getting into a public debate with the Dowling/Doolan group.[38] However, a radio discussion about the book was chaired by Michael Littleton in October, and in November it was the subject of a discussion on the *Late Late Show*, which evoked an 'unfavourable' audience reaction.[39] Most of this reaction referred to the problem which had arisen about the *7 Days* projected programme on the Special Branch, which had never been transmitted, and the Deputy Head of News, Desmond Fisher, felt that the station was being further damaged by the controversy, and argued

35 Loc. cit. 36 PPC Minutes, 30 May 1969. 37 PPC Minutes, 27 May 1969, 30 May 1969. 38 PPC Minutes, 30 September 1969, 9 October 1969. 39 PPC Minutes, 11 November 1969.

against 'putting out programmes for non-programme reasons – i.e. using them to solve our internal difficulties.'[40]

Overall, the episode represented a nett setback to RTÉ's claims to be independent of outside pressure. The arguments about politics and culture which found expression in *Sit Down and Be Counted* were elaborated in language which on occasion fought communication to a standstill. Although the evidence presented for the censorship thesis remained flimsy enough, and depended in part on a Byzantine analysis of the relationships between named individuals within RTÉ, there would have been a greater degree of sympathy for Doolan's Brechtian view that culture was not the plaything of an elite, or the table-talk of the over-educated, but communication between people in the broadest sense:

> We have the language, religious and ethnic differences, we have the divisions between rural and urban life. All these make people individuals, and my idea of television, or indeed any communications medium, is to more or less set them at each other, rather than beaming some two-dimensional interpretation of culture at them and expecting everyone to be entertained and informed in exactly the same way.[41]

The controversy generated in the newspapers nonetheless left its mark on the public consciousness. The image of RTÉ producers as tireless seekers after truth and justice who were being continually frustrated by an obsequious or cowardly station management was stereotypical and over-simplified, and for that reason easily mediated to a large and non-specialist audience. In the longer term it can best be explained less as a defining moment in the history of the organisation than as yet another skirmish – though a substantial one – in the perennial struggle for control of audio-visual content, a struggle which was as often waged between producers themselves as between producers and management, or between management and government. The contemporary response to these events, however, was probably best summed up by the actor and *raconteur* Niall Toibín, describing a visitor to RTÉ expressing her admiration for a newly-constructed building.

> – What a magnificent studio, she said.
> – No, ma'am, said the porter. This here behind you is the studios. That is the admin block. You see – he added helpfully – in here there's about three hundred people making programmes. Over there, there's two thousand people trying to stop them.[42]

40 Ibid.   **41** Maeve Binchy, 'The TV rebel', *Irish Times*, 14 June 1969.   **42** Niall Toibín, *Smile and be a villain* (1995), p. 160.

Within days of the particular PPC discussion mentioned above, however, another event occurred which could not have been more opportune for a station management anxious to portray itself as a defender of journalistic freedom, although it was certainly not designed as such. This was the broadcast on 13 November of a *7 Days* programme on illegal money-lending in Dublin, on which the reporter was Bill O'Herlihy.

The programme was notable in a number of respects. It used hidden cameras. It reconstructed money-lending transactions on film. And it said, without doing much to soften its message, not only that illegal money-lending was a major social problem in Dublin, but also – and more significantly as it turned out – that the Gardaí were not doing enough to stamp it out. Two days later, the Director-General noted that the programme – which he considered excellent – had raised a number of questions about broadcasting practice, on which he was preparing a paper for the Authority: it was already evident that controversy was in the air.[43] Jim McGuinness, the Head of News, had discussed the problems involved in making the programme with the team some weeks earlier, and they had satisfied him that there was no other way of doing it. Now, although he was glad that he had agreed to *7 Days* doing it, he felt that it would be inappropriate for public service broadcasting to engage in a series of '*exposé* type' programmes.

Within days, the temperature had increased considerably. The Director-General, together with the Head of News and RTÉ's senior legal officer, met two senior Gardaí, one of whom implied that if RTÉ failed to cooperate it could be threatened with 'misprision of felony'.[44] The Gardaí had been politely told that they could view the film privately if necessary, but that a court order would be required if any tapes or transcripts were to be handed over. On 19 November the station issued a statement – partly drafted by the programme editor, Muiris Mac Conghail – standing over what had been transmitted. The Minister for Justice, Micheál Ó Móráin, also viewed the film, and – surprisingly in view of what happened later – expressed himself as being satisfied with the integrity of the programme but not with the degree of cooperation being afforded to the Gardaí.[45]

The two key issues, as they seemed to be emerging, were the use of hidden cameras, and the question of whether participants had been suborned by having had drink purchased for them. In point of fact, RTÉ had spent only fifty shillings on drink for participants during the three weeks that the programme took to make; K Security, a private firm employed by RTÉ as consultants on the project, had spent a further two pounds.

The RTÉ Authority supported the programmes, and went as far as to protest to the Minister for Justice about the approach by Gardaí to RTÉ staff. The Authority then met the Minister for Posts and Telegraphs, Gerry Collins, and told

43 PPC Minutes, 13 November 1969. **44** PPC Minutes, 18 November 1969. **45** PPC Minutes, 25 November 1969.

him, too, that they endorsed the programme. Collins, however, was unhappy: the Authority statement would not only contradict the Gardaí, but would put him in a difficult position in relation to the Minister for Justice, and would 'represent a re-escalation of a situation which in the general public interest required de-escalation'.[46]

Unknown to the Authority and the Director-General, the situation was now one in which the Minister for Posts and Telegraphs was not in a position to defend the station, in the unlikely event that this would be his preferred course of action. The Garda pressure on Ó Móráin had become intense, to the point where he effectively manoeuvred the Taoiseach, Jack Lynch, and by extension the Government, into agreeing to institute a sworn public inquiry into the matter.

The Government announced the composition of the Tribunal, and its terms of reference, in December. It was immediately evident that the inquiry would not be into either illegal money-lending or the Garda response to this problem, but into the programme itself. As Fisher remarked, the intention was plainly to 'put RTÉ in the dock'.[47] In spite of this, management remained optimistic: as late as the end of February, when the Tribunal had been sitting for thirty-two days, the Programme Policy Committee felt that the judges were persuadable of the merits of RTÉ's case.[48] By the time the Tribunal ended at the beginning of April, such optimism was noticeably on the wane. When its report was published in August, the Tribunal came down heavily against the broadcasters, accusing the programme of inauthenticity and, by extension, of failing to observe proper journalistic standards.

The prediction that RTÉ was to be put in the dock had essentially been proven to be correct. RTÉ's weakest point, in retrospect, had been its failure to indicate, when broadcasting filmed reconstructions of money and children's allowance books changing hands, that this had not been film of actual events, and the absence of any procedures to cover the use of hidden cameras. The latter difficulty had been met by the adoption of a set of guidelines in May 1970 (earlier, in January, there had also been new guidelines on payments to programme participants) but these inevitably had no effect on the Tribunal's findings. Janet Moody, one of the researchers on the programme, was particularly – and unfairly – singled out by the Tribunal for criticism. One RTÉ employee, Níall Andrews – a son of the former Chairman of the Authority, Todd Andrews – later expressed the opinion after he had been elected a Fianna Fáil TD that the inquiry should never have taken place and that broadcasting had 'never been the same since,'[49] but this was very much a minority opinion within the party.

Although the Authority subsequently issued a statement expressing its support for the programme-makers, there was a discernible chilling effect. In an

46 PPC Minutes, 2 December 1969.   47 PPC Minutes, 16 December 1969.   48 PPC Minutes, 24 February 1970.   49 Dáil Debates, 1 March 1983.

unpublished memorandum to the Minister for Posts and Telegraphs outlining its response to the Tribunal's report, the Authority defended itself stoutly, not least because, in its view, 'the official summary issued with the Report was not an adequate synopsis of the findings.'[50] By far the most difficult aspect of the tribunal report, from a programme-maker's point of view, was the implication that programmes like these would have to be able to furnish judicial standards of proof of wrong-doing in the future. In organisational terms, the only change made was a decision that the editor, Muiris Mac Conghail, would devote himself more completely to continuous editorial supervision, and would divorce himself from the details of programmes and the direction of individual programmes. He would agree to the initiation of all work, and would check on progress at intermediate stages. The Director-General, T.P. Hardiman, indicated that the team had had a complex history: 'there had in the past been problems relating to authority within the group itself; multiple decision-making with little clear decision taking resulting in a tug of war among individuals, leaving in question the detailed decision on the appropriate treatment of a programme idea'.[51] The age of those involved is also worth noting. At the time of the publication of the tribunal report, Mac Conghail was only 28, O'Herlihy 30, Janet Moody 24, and the editor, Rory O'Farrell, only 28. Few facts could have illustrated more dramatically the inter-generational tension which contributed both to the sense of outrage expressed in the programme, and to the thunderous response of the Gardaí and senior government ministers. Mac Conghail resigned as editor of *7 Days* in July 1971 after a total of 300 programmes, noting that he was 'tired'.[52] He had planned to take a year's sabbatical, but ended up, as noted earlier, working in radio in Henry Street.

In a sense, this was no more than a re-statement of the old dilemma: too loose a system of supervision encouraged risk-taking and got the station into trouble, especially with an already edgy political establishment; too tight a system limited creativity and encouraged self-censorship. Symbolically, the inquiry 'came to be regarded as the re-establishment of the control of broadcasting by politicians'.[53] The dilemma itself was now to be brought more sharply into focus than ever before, not primarily by the money-lending programme and its aftermath, which would rapidly disappear into the shadows, but by the emerging political crisis in relation to Northern Ireland, which was to shape news and current affairs in RTÉ as no other set of events had done since the station had been established almost a decade earlier.

Northern Ireland had, by this stage, been pushing itself to the forefront of the public affairs agenda for more than a year. The emergence of the civil rights

50 Memorandum, 15 Mean Fomhair 1970. Text in NA, Department of the Taoiseach, 2001/6/440. **51** PPC Minutes, 11 September 1970. **52** *Irish Times*, 7 July 1971. **53** Peter Feeney, 'Censorship and RTÉ', p. 63.

movement in the autumn of 1968 marked changes both in policy and tactics. The policy change, on the part of those agitating for political developments in the North, was that the new movement eschewed constitutional objectives: it was campaigning for change within Northern Ireland, rather than as part of an all-Ireland settlement. It was therefore an even greater threat to the Unionist political and social establishment, because it could not be simply dismissed as a recrudescence of old-fashioned Republicanism. This did not prevent Unionism from reacting as if it were. But that reaction – indeed, over-reaction – was powerfully countered by a new tactic, which had been urged on the early leaders of the civil rights movement by their supporters in the British Labour Party at Westminster: use of the media, and in particular television. To this already combustible mixture two further ingredients could be added: the conscious endorsement of a civil rights rhetoric that had been pioneered in the Southern states of the USA; and the fact that, nearly a decade after Britain had started a process of peaceful disengagement from her colonies in Africa, she now had what could be regarded as a colonial problem on her own doorstep. All these factors combined to heighten the media visibility of the situation; but its international dimension was as nothing compared to the convulsions it would generate both north and south of the border dividing the two parts of the island.

RTÉ cameraman Gay O'Brien's film of the Derry civil rights march in October 1968 had already been used in many stations across the globe, and Northern Ireland would now become a staging point for television crews from many countries. As far as RTÉ itself was concerned, however, there were personnel and technical problems to be overcome, even though the source of the news pictures was little more than 100 miles up the road from Dublin. There were also, paradoxically, audience problems. These arose primarily from the impartiality requirements placed on the station by the 1960 Act: how was the station to observe impartiality in a context which included the constitutional claim to the island's six north-eastern counties? Evidently, no self-respecting news operation could simply espouse the Nationalist – or even the civil rights – arguments. Equally evidently, any attempt by RTÉ to broadcast interviews or reports which in any way gave airtime to the Unionist political viewpoint (or, *a fortiori*, to the RUC viewpoint on security issues) would raise communal and political hackles in the Republic.

The situation, however, was not as simple as that. A substantial proportion of the national audience for RTÉ would have instinctively sided with the civil rights marchers, and would have seen Northern nationalists as 'our' people: this segment of the audience would have had a gut reaction against the presentation of Unionist or RUC viewpoints. This feeling would have been even stronger among members of Fianna Fáil, who would have been surprised – in some cases even outraged – by the national television station giving any prominence at all to what they would have perceived as anti-national views. These feelings would have been fed upwards through the party and the Parliamentary Party to the Cabinet, and transmitted from there, in various ways, to RTÉ. As early as January 1969, a resolution was put down for the Fianna Fáil Ard-Fheis alleging that RTÉ had 'failed to project a proper national image'.[54] The discussion – although not recorded by the newspapers – ranged far and wide, including specific accusations directed at James Plunkett Kelly, Head of Television Features, at 7 *Days*, and at 'subversive elements in the community.[55] And yet RTÉ was caught in a double bind: as well as a sizeable proportion of its audience which had difficulties with impartiality, there was another sizeable segment which – conditioned by half a century of partition and anxious about the possible overspill of Northern violence into the Republic – wanted to have little to do with Northern Ireland, regardless of its problems. One audience research survey early in 1970 recorded 58% of the audience expressing the opinion that there was 'too much' news from Northern Ireland, especially on television.[56]

The personnel aspects of the problem were also fascinating. The two key executives involved in making editorial decisions about Northern Ireland were both Northern Ireland-born: Jim McGuinness, the Head of News, was also a former member of the IRA. His deputy, Desmond Fisher, who had effectively become Head of Current Affairs (although without divisional status and authority) since the integration of 7 *Days* with the News Division, was Derry-born. Northern Unionists might have been forgiven for thinking that they could not expect much in the way of impartiality from such a hierarchy, and nationalists might have been led to expect an easy ride. Both were to be disappointed.

A straw in the wind was the appointment of the station's first Northern Ireland correspondent. The first person to be sent up there, however, was not the first Northern Ireland correspondent, but a young UCD graduate named Patrick Cosgrave. Cosgrave, who came from a Dublin working-class background, was energetic and intellectually adventurous, and doing post-graduate work in history at Cambridge: McGuinness, who was intrigued by the disagreements between France and the UK about Common Market entry, first noticed Cosgrave's name attached to an article about de Gaulle in *The Spectator*. Muiris Mac Conghail, who knew him personally, effected an introduction, and Cosgrave was taken on board and sent briefly to Northern Ireland as part of his training before being formally appointed as the station's first 'London Representative' in July 1968.[57]

The station as yet, however, had no Belfast correspondent.[58] The Belfast office was formally established in February and Martin Wallace, a Belfast news-

---

54 *Irish Times*, 23 January 1969.   **55** PPC Minutes, 31 January 1969.   **56** PPC Minutes, 3 March 1970.
57 PPC Minutes, 11 July 1968. He later left RTÉ, and became a full-time journalist for print, radio and television in London. Most notably, he wrote a biography of Margaret Thatcher, whom he had come to admire. He died on 16 September 1991.   **58** PPC Minutes, 6 May 1969.

paperman (and a Protestant to boot) was appointed as full-time Belfast corre-spondent in early May 1969. Wallace, who was to be a key figure in the station's coverage of Northern news for the next two years, was later joined by John McAleese, and by March 1970 requests were being made for a third reporter: in what was to become a familiar refrain, McGuinness was told that this could not be envisaged until the licence fee had been increased.[59]

Staffing, however, was only part of the problem. The technical difficulties, in these early days of television, amounted to a major constraint on what could and could not be broadcast. These constraints principally affected the use of film. In order to be in time for the 6 p.m. television news bulletin, film had to be put onto the 2.30 p.m. train from Belfast to Dublin. Film for the 9 p.m. news bul-letin had to make the 5.30 train from Belfast. Because of customs requirements, each can of film travelling to Dublin had to be accompanied by substantial amounts of documentation: the paperwork involved was so time-consuming that the new Belfast studio, with its live link to Dublin, was more frequently used. This meant that news film of the early part of the Northern conflict was sparse – even though, as will be seen, documentary coverage in time helped in part to make good this deficiency. These difficulties were compounded by the fact that few of the station's staff, either in news or in the programme-making divisions, had much personal experience of working in Northern Ireland, and some were reluctant even to travel there. This put a considerable burden, in the early days of the conflict, on senior executives. On the news side, McGuinness and Fisher, and on the programmes side, Muiris Mac Conghail, were to spend considerable amount of time in the North.

In these circumstances, the radio service – which had been re-vitalised in stages since early in 1968 – was beginning to come into its own. The tape recorder, the microphone, and the telephone were infinitely more flexible than the television camera with its retinue of technicians. At the same time McGuin-ness, who had always been keen to allow his journalists opportunities for a type of work that would echo some of the output of the Programmes Division, set up in 1968 the News Features operation, as a self-contained element within the newsroom. The first editor of News Features was Seán Duignan: he was to be succeeded in September 1971 by Kevin O'Kelly, who had been involved with News Features from the beginning. The other key members of the operation were Mike Burns and Gerry Barry.[60]

In some respects, the format of the programmes presented by news features were derivative: the influence of the BBC, and in particular of William Hard-castle's programme *The World At One*, could readily be discerned. But the fact that the formula had been devised elsewhere did not make it irrelevant, or inca-

59 PPC Minutes, 24 March 1970.   **60** Burns remained in broadcasting; Gerry Barry, after a period as political correspondent of the *Sunday Tribune*, returned to RTÉ, where he continues to present *This Week*.

pable of adaptation within RTÉ. Such was its success, in fact, that within the station News Features actually became the part of the newsroom which most attracted reporters: television was becoming the poor relation, bedevilled not only by its cumbersome technology but by inadequate production values.[61]A failed attempt to launch a similar early-morning news programme – later successful as *Morning Ireland* – did not dissuade the pioneers, and radio went from strength to strength.

Nor was this only in the News Division. Over in Henry Street, where the remaining elements of the radio service were still isolated pending the construction of the new Radio Centre at Donnybrook, new developments were also taking place. Muiris Mac Conghail became head of the newly-formed Current Affairs and Features grouping in radio after taking a break from television in 1971, and remained in that position until he transferred into Government service as head of the Government Information Bureau for the 1973-77 Coalition Government. Under him, Michael Littleton, assistant head of features and current affairs and general editor of the Thomas Davis lecture series, and Pádraig Ó Néill, editor of the morning discussion programme *Here and Now*, overhauled and redesigned the complete features, current affairs and documentary output in 1972/3. *Here and Now* was an amalgam of two programmes – the *Liam Nolan Hour*, which had run from 11 a.m. to midday, and *Day to Day*, which had run from noon until 1 p.m. Initially it dealt with current affairs up to noon, and arts material thereafter. By July 1972 there were complaints that it was 'straying' into news and changing from a magazine features programme into a current affairs one.[62] By the end of the 1973, extraordinarily, news, features, current affairs, talks and documentaries on the station's single radio channel accounted for 37.3% of the total radio output, compared to 31.4% for music.[63] As ever, the borders were increasingly permeable. By 1974 – the first year in which radio output in current affairs was categorised as such, that category accounted for 9% of all radio outpout, compared with 10% for news (which had fallen from a high of 17% in 1962).[64]

The increasing virility of current affairs broadcasting on both radio and television was not going unnoticed. Ironically, the Minister who decided to make a major issue of this was none other than Erskine Childers, who in an earlier incarnation in the same post in 1954, had been largely instrumental in developing the process which was to set RTÉ free of direct government supervision. There was in all probability an administrative sub-text to this development. León Ó Broin had been succeeded as Secretary of the Department in September 1967 by Proinsías Ó Colmáin, a man of a different stamp entirely. Much more interventionist than his predecessor, and lacking the same degree of philo-

61 Seán Duignan interview.   **62** PPC Minutes, 11 July 1972.   **63** Mac Conghail, 'Wireless', p. 77. Michael Littleton died in 2002, after a lifetime of vital, but often unsung, service to radio.   **64** Kealy, *Data*, p. 62.

sophical commitment to the concept of independent public service broadcasting, Ó Colmáin was not slow to make senior RTÉ administrators aware of his views on programming issues. In Childers, moreover, he had a minister who – despite his background as a Minister committed to the concept of at least qualified independence for broadcasters – was personally fascinated by media (his father, after all, had been a gifted publicist during the War of Independence), and seemed on occasion even to imagine himself in the role of editor-in-chief.

These factors help to explain the extraordinary series of developments in early 1969 when Childers decided to intervene directly, not just in overall policy at RTÉ, but in programme style. What he was exercised about was over-aggressive interviewing. This had intermittently surfaced within the station as long ago as 1967, and had been commented on in the media. In his regular column in the *Irish Press*, for instance, Tom O'Dea noted after a programme on the proposed merger of University College Dublin and Trinity College, that 'Mr Farrell is a fine interviewer, but one of these days he is going to bite somebody's nose off. Physically bite it off, I mean – and close to the face withal.'[65] Childers first intervened in private, meeting the Authority on 17 January 1969 to express his concerns. The following month, he took advantage of the fact that he was introducing a supplementary estimate for his Department in the Dáil to spell out his concerns, and to acknowledge the action he had taken. The grounds for his criticism were explicit. Ireland was a Christian country, and he therefore rejected the idea that 'the most easy path to sensational shock-creating broadcasting is to cast doubt on every form of philosophy which embraces fundamental truths based on revealed religion.' He had been receiving many criticisms.

> A national broadcasting service should not follow the prevailing trend of stirring up protest in such a way as to emphasise all the weaknesses of human nature and defects in the social and economic structure leaving not an impression of constructive policies to be pursued but a cynical and destructive impact on the viewer and listener [...]. There are countries where there is among young people a pervasive unrest whose principal cause is the absence of any philosophy to replace religious doctrine. Having regard to the majority view in this country on such matters, I will not have RTÉ used to create a murky cynical atmosphere in regard to what, ultimately, are problems due to inadequacies in character in people as a whole.[66]

He was also concerned that RTÉ programmes on moral and religious issues should always include commentators who could 'present the views of the great

---

65 *Irish Press*, 22 April 1967.   66 Dáil Debates, 27 February 1969. Other quotations from this debate are from the same source unless otherwise stated.

majority of our people', but his prime emphasis was on interviewing. He was now satisfied, he said, that the Authority 'has taken steps to modify the recent trend in interviewing persons of all political and social opinions in a manner which has aroused the strongest criticism.'

Support for – and opposition to – his views came from the most unlikely quarters. Oliver J. Flanagan, the Fine Gael TD who had been vociferously criticising RTÉ for allegedly giving airtime to Communists only two years earlier, now weighed in to support the station, alleging that the Government was simply frightened of being confronted by interviewers who knew their business. In the circumstances, he was an ally RTÉ could probably have done without. More surprisingly, he was supported by Patrick Norton TD, son of the former leader of the Labour Party, William Norton, who accused RTÉ interviewers of 'cheap, blatant career-building at the expense of the public and the person whom they are interviewing.'[67] Concluding the debate, Childers announced with satisfaction:

> It was perfectly obvious from what people on both sides of the House had said to me that a habit had been instituted in RTÉ of rude interviewing, and I mean rude interviewing. This has now stopped. I wanted to get consent from everyone. I do not want to have the Frost type of interviewing in this country. It is totally unsuited to our needs.[68]

Another recurring problem was related to the political activities of staff – both contract and full-time – outside the station. The appearance of Eoghan Harris on a special edition of the *Late Late Show*, where he spoke passionately against the Common Market, evoked the criticism internally that it was 'undesirable' that members of staff should appear to have easy *entrée* to programmes to give their views on social, political and economic matters.[69] The role of Howard Kinlay, a former student activist who had been employed as a producer and continued to edit *Nusight*, the current affairs magazine with which Vincent Browne was also associated, came under notice from time to time during 1970, and he was eventually asked to terminate his association with it. This, and similar problems, generated guidelines on the political involvement of broadcasters in 'Restricted' categories (i.e. reporters, comperes or commentators) who had to obtain advance agreement from the station even for involvement in minor political activities, and who were required to take whatever steps were necessary to ensure that they were not identified publicly as employees of RTÉ whenever they were expressing their personal views on political matters in pub-

---

67 Dáil Debates, 6 March 1969. Norton, who had initially been elected as a Labour TD before becoming an Independent, eventually joined Fianna Fáil.   68 Dáil Debates, 12 March 1969.   69 PPC Minutes, 20 October 1970.

lic.[70] Coming up to the 1969 election, the political correspondent of the *Irish Independent*, Arthur Noonan, observed that RTÉ appeared to be 'a hotbed of politics, from the Board to the technical level', and asked pointedly:

> One may legitimately wonder to what extent its attraction for people of political leanings of one kind or another is associated with its protests and troubles. The latest wave of these has come, interestingly, in the heat of an election campaign. One might also ask to what extent such political commitment and consequent loss of objectivity bedevils RTÉ in broadcasting politics and public affairs?[71]

Noonan, who had been a participant on the *Hurler on the Ditch* political discussion programme which had been axed in 1966, was appointed the station's political correspondent in October 1973, and became a member of the RTÉ Authority in 1979. In both capacities he would have had the opportunity to give practical effect to his concerns.

The disciplining of Kinlay – no doubt not entirely coincidentally – happened at around the same time that *Wednesday Report*, a weekly television current affairs programme on which he had been working, fell foul of the station's management for a programme on Spain which had been scripted by Patrick Gallagher, one of the refugees from 7 *Days* after its transfer into the News Division. The criticisms were general and particular. The particular criticism was that the programme had employed the 'empty chair' device to signal that an individual or spokesman for an organisation had been unwilling to come into studio to give an account of themselves. This device had been employed at various stages since the station's current affairs programming had become more adventurous. It had been stopped by Gunnar Rugheimer, and was later re-introduced only on condition that senior management would validate the producer's decision in any given set of circumstances.[72] On this particular occasion, the empty chair was used to highlight the absence from the programme of an invited representative of the Opus Dei organisation.

In more general terms, the programme attracted the ire, not only of the Programme Policy Committee,[73] but of the Spanish Ambassador, who wrote to the Minister for External Affairs to complain, demonstrating as he did so that he possessed a fine diplomatic sense of humour. Pointing out that Mr. Seán MacBride – at the time general secretary of Amnesty International – had only very recently sent a telegram to the Spanish head of state congratulating him on the introduction of a new law in Spain to take account of the wishes of conscientious objectors, he enquired mildly: 'Can it be that Mr MacBride is more

---

70 RTÉ, *Personnel Information Bulletin*, 46 issued on 7 February 1973, which repeats the guidelines originally established in 1970.   **71** Arthur Noonan, 'Candidates from RTÉ set a poser', *Irish Independent*, 5 June 1969.   **72** See, e.g., PPC Minutes, 20 October 1970.   **73** PPC Minutes, 24 April 1970.

kindly disposed to the government of Generalissimo Franco than Radio Telefís Éireann?'[74]

Wednesday Report's neck was now on the block, and when it was terminated in the summer of 1970 Gallagher migrated to the similarly titled *Report* programme, introduced as part of a general shake-up of current affairs. This shake-up, in the view of Michael Garvey, the Controller of Television Programmes, was organised primarily to move away from the 'emotional' aspects of 7 *Days* and *Wednesday Report*. Their elimination, he suggested, would 'allow current affairs programming to be considered more rationally and dispassionately'. Although 7 *Days* was not, as Garvey had intended, taken off the screen, it did not survive in precisely the same form.

These episodes reflected ongoing tensions within the station which were never entirely resolved. They had, however, already been pushed into the background by current events themselves, which were now taking a number of dramatic turns. The problems relating to the behaviour of particular individuals within the news and current affairs area now took second place to the over-riding problem of how to report the evolving, and frequently chaotic, situation in Northern Ireland.

The government was now expressing increasing concern in this area. At an off-the record briefing with journalists from the print and broadcast media early in August 1969, the Taoiseach, Jack Lynch, had expressed his concern at the level of activity on the part of the re-emergent Irish Republican Army. Desmond Fisher, who attended the meeting on behalf of RTÉ, reported that Lynch had been particularly anxious that terminology should not be used which tended to glamourise the organisation and its activities – he instanced the phrase 'an expert job'. Lynch also reminded the journalists that it was technically a criminal offence under the Offences Against the State Acts (which dated from 1939) to refer to the IRA by name: he accepted that this was now anachronistic, but expressed the hope that RTÉ in particular would still refer to it from time to time as 'an illegal organisation' in order to stress its outlawed position.[75] Hardiman concurred: any publicity for the IRA should be avoided, especially when dealing with its issued statements, except when it was felt essential in the interests of accuracy in the news.[76]

One programme which unexpectedly fell foul of this climate of vigilance was a series of *Outlook* broadcasts in which Fr Jerome O'Herlihy OP had advised viewers to look at news programmes about the Northern crisis with a critical eye: umbrage was taken at the implication that RTÉ news was being 'slanted', and management cancelled the programme at short notice.[77] The News Division, plainly, was not going to accept criticism from within the station meekly.

74 NA 2001/78/79, Juan José Pradera, Ambassador of Spain, to Dr Patrick Hillery, 31 March 1970. **75** PPC Minutes, 8 August 1969. **76** Ibid. **77** PPC Minutes, 22 August 1969.

This, however, was only part of the problem. The other element of it was the difficulty of carrying news from, and interviews with, Unionist and Northern Ireland security sources. As early as April 1969 concern was being expressed at the apparent failure of a 7 *Days* programme on Derry to provide an airing of the RUC case.[78] This criticism was aired again the following year, but in a different context, when McGuinness told the Programme Policy Committee that there had been criticisms of RTÉ's news bulletins for having been one-sided in favour of republican elements in the North. He told the Committee:

> It is RTÉ policy, and all reporters on assignment to the North are briefed accordingly, that on every occasion where a Republican viewpoint is given, an opportunity must be given also to the Unionist side to express their version of events. It would appear that in regard to the raiding of the houses on the Falls Road where British soldiers were portrayed as performing that search of the houses in a brutal fashion that British Army commanders are embarrassed: in any event when asked to make a statement for RTÉ news bulletins they declined.[79]

McGuinness further instanced two other programmes – the 7 *Days* programmes on Derry and another on Belfast – that could have been regarded as unbalanced. However, the explanation given by the reporter on those programmes, Rodney Rice, was that when he had sought a Unionist or protestant viewpoint he had been received in a 'violently hostile manner'. On the other hand, a series of interviews on radio by Mike Burns on the *This Week* programme on 28 June 1970, had evoked criticisms of the station from civil rights people as being pro-Unionist. And, whatever the station did in relation to Northern Ireland, it was too much for some viewers and listeners: there was also criticism of the station because of its coverage of social ills in Northern Ireland 'to the exclusion of those obtaining in the Republic'. To objections like these, the RTÉ managers presented a firm and united line: if audiences did not want to hear about the North – well, it was 'just too bad'.[80]

Well before this, of course, the situation had become extraordinarily tense, more particularly in the wake of the disturbances in Belfast and in Derry on 12 and 13 August 1969 – the former disturbances engineered at least in part by Republican elements to draw British forces away from Derry. The nett effect of much of this was to generate a somewhat visceral response among the generally apathetic, or only mildly interested population in the Republic, and more particularly in the ranks of Fianna Fáil itself. On 12 August Lynch made his 'we shall not stand by' speech on RTÉ: he arrived at the station with a typescript which was so covered with alterations and amendments that it had be typed out

78 PPC Minutes, 25 April 1969. **79** PPC Minutes, 9 July 1970. **80** PPC Minutes, 5 September 1969.

for him again by RTÉ staff. Within weeks, he had another off-the-record meeting with senior print and broadcast journalists at Government Buildings at which he volunteered the observation that the mobilisation of the front line reserves, which he had announced in his 12 August speech, had prevented 'maverick action down here.'[81] The mavericks, as subsequent events were to prove, had not gone away, and some of them were ensconced at the heart of his own government.

If the problem of providing adequate airtime for the Unionist point of view was a legitimate concern of the programme-makers and administrators at this time, it was rapidly overshadowed by another: the reporting of the resurgent IRA and its activities and, more particularly, the interviewing of its spokesmen. A *7 Days* programme at the end of August 1969 captioned Cathal Goulding in his role as Chief of Staff of the IRA, which cannot have contributed much to the Cabinet's collective peace of mind: tensions were already escalating within that body about the most appropriate response to the Northern crisis. In October, the Minister for Justice, Micheál Ó Móráin, wrote formally to the Minister for Posts and Telegraphs, Erskine Childers, to complain about a number of people with para-military connections appearing on the station, and instancing in particular Seamus Costello.[82]

The temperature increased noticeably in April 1970, when *Hibernia* published an article on a bank robbery which had allegedly been carried out on behalf of Saor Éire, a left-wing splinter Republican group, and in the course of which a member of the Gardaí, Garda Fallon, had been murdered. *7 Days* invited Ó Móráin to discuss the situation on air. *Hibernia* had asked for a public enquiry into the matter.[83] *7 Days* sent six advance questions in to Ó Móráin: the flavour of their planned line of enquiry can best be judged from the fact that it invited the Minister specifically to comment on three men who were on the Gardai's wanted list, and asked him to comment on an article in another publication, *This Week*,[84] to the effect that a proposed raid on Saor Éire had been halted 'on instructions from some higher authority'.[85] Even without the benefit of hindsight, it is plain that questions along these lines would have seriously prejudiced any future criminal proceedings.

Peter Berry, on Ó Móráin's behalf, responded testily that 'to discuss such matters at all on television at this time would ... constitute an utter disregard for the principles governing the administration of justice in this country.' Hardiman, after receiving this reply, spoke privately to Ó Móráin. The programme,

81 PPC Minutes, 4 September 1969.   **82** Dáil Debates, 3 March 1973. The existence of this letter was revealed in the course of the debate by the then Minister for Posts and Telegraphs, Dr. Conor Cruise O'Brien: the text has not yet been released to the National Archives under the 30-year rule.   **83** *Hibernia*, 17 April 1970.   **84** A short-lived but valuable current affairs magazine, with the same title as the radio programme, edited by Joseph O'Malley.   **85** NA, 2003/16/17 contains the full set of files in relation to this incident, from which related quotations are also drawn.

which was due to have been transmitted on 17 April, was cancelled, and RTÉ issued a statement partly agreeing that the proposed treatment 'could later have been prejudicial to the interests of justice' but suggesting also that the reason for the programme's cancellation was to allow further close examination and detailed treatment of the issues raised.

In the circumstances, Ó Móráin was immediately blamed for having engineered the cancellation of the programme, and the Fine Gael TD Gerry L'Estrange immediately put down a Dáil question to Lynch suggesting that this had been the case. The behind-the-scenes discussions between Lynch, his departmental secretary Nicholas Nolan, and Berry on this issue were very revealing, not least because of the way in which Nolan watered down Berry's draft response to L'Estrange. This was particularly the case in respect of Berry's aggressive stance on the issue of communications between ministers and RTÉ. In Berry's draft for Lynch,

> the right to communicate in this way is a right available to every member of this House, and indeed to every citizen, and I am not prepared to accept that a member of the Government has any lesser right or that he must disclose the content of any such communication either in reply to a Parliamentary Question or otherwise.

Nolan, in a note to Lynch, counselled caution.[86]

> To stress such ministerial right ... is more than likely to give rise to acrimony, the raising of the matter on the adjournment, etc. If Opposition deputies enquire why Section 31 of the 1960 Act was not invoked, they could be informed that it was not necessary to invoke it, that RTÉ are a responsible public body who, as indicated in their own statement, did not wish to prejudice the cause of justice.

Nolan's advice was taken, but the official view as to RTÉ's ability to regulate itself responsibly was to undergo a dramatic change within a very short time. Unknown to at least some of the players in this mini-drama, political matters were moving rapidly to a head. On 5 May 1970 Micheál Ó Móráin resigned, ostensibly on health grounds. It has been generally accepted since then that his resignation was a forced one (although he plainly had an alcohol-related health problem), and that the real reason was because he had failed to keep Lynch fully informed of the activities of some of his Cabinet colleagues. Ó Móráin's resignation prompted a wave of speculation, confirmed dramatically two days later, on 7 May, when Lynch dismissed his Minister for Finance, Charles Haughey,

---

86 Ibid. Nolan to Lynch, 29 April 1970. Not for nothing was this most conscientious of public servants known by his contemporaries as 'meticulous Nicholas'.

and his Minister for Agriculture, Neil Blaney, on the grounds that they did not fully subscribe to government policy on Northern Ireland. Kevin Boland, the Minister for Local Government, resigned on the same day. Haughey and Blaney were subsequently arraigned, with Captain James Kelly and Albert Luykx, on charges of having conspired to illegally import arms into the State. Similar charges against Blaney were dismissed in the District Court, and the other defendants were later found not guilty after two jury trials, the first of which was aborted for technical reasons. It was an astonishing sequence of political events, second only to the Civil War in its long-term effects on the body politic.

Outside the Dáil as well as inside, greater risks were being taken. The IRA announced that they would be holding a press conference in Wynn's Hotel in Dublin on the evening of 12 May. The Head of News, Jim McGuinness, noting that the proposed press conference was a direct challenge to the government, expressed his concern at the thought that coverage would be limited to straight reporting. What the Irish public needed at present, he said, was more information, and informed comment: for this, feature type treatment and even speculation as to the likely course of events would seem desirable.[87] Events were to cast this admirable objective in a somewhat different light.

Ó Móráin's replacement as Minister for Justice was Desmond O'Malley, a solicitor by profession (as indeed Ó Móráin had been) but of a younger generation, who had won his spurs as parliamentary secretary to the Taoiseach and Minister for Defence since the 1969 election. His replacement as parliamentary secretary was David Andrews, a son of the Chairman of the RTÉ Authority, Todd Andrews. Andrews senior wrote immediately to Lynch to resign his position, on the grounds that, given the possibility that there could be differences of opinion between RTÉ and the Government or the political parties on matters of current controversy, he would not want to find himself in the position of having a conflict of interest.[88]

He was succeeded by an existing member of the Authority (but no relation to the former Minister), Dónall Ó Móráin, the head of the Irish language organisation, Gael Linn. This organisation, as it happened, had unsuccessfully sought in 1957 the award of a franchise to run the national television service before the Government decided to establish it as a semi-State organisation.[89]

The new ministerial team set to work with a vengeance, not only to strengthen Lynch's hand in the political situation in which he had dismissed and was now prosecuting for criminal offences two of his most powerful cabinet colleagues, but to ensure as best they could that the 'maverick elements' as Lynch had earlier described them, could not, through RTÉ, act further to de-stabilise an

---

87 PPC Minutes, 12 May 1970. In the event, a decision was taken to send a reporter to the press conference, with a camera crew standing by. **88** NA 2002/8/264. Andrews to Lynch, 11 May 1970. **89** Robert Savage, *Irish television: the political and social origins* (1996), pp. 185-7.

already perilous situation for the Fianna Fáil Party.[90] Two months after his appointment to Justice, O'Malley wrote to the Minister for Posts and Telegraphs, Gerry Collins, who had succeeded Childers in the government re-shuffle following the crisis. He wanted, he said, to 'protest very strongly against the irresponsible behaviour of RTÉ in glamourising persons who are known to have engaged in subversive or criminal activities.'[91] O'Malley instanced coverage given to a wide range of individuals such as Máirín de Burca ('Miss Maureen Burke, secretary of Sinn Féin ... and a member of a number of pseudo-protest bodies'); Tomás Mac Giolla, Cathal Goulding, Jim Sullivan (Belfast), Seán Keenan (Derry), and others. He asked Collins:

> When is this going to stop? Is the RTÉ Authority going to sit back and allow the television and radio stations to be used by this minority to brainwash the public? If the answer to that is 'Yes' then I am faced with the unfortunate necessity to raise the question of the enforcement of the law ... and, if nothing else can be done, I propose to raise immediately the question of prosecuting them the next time that they publish seditious matter.[92]

Interestingly – in the light of subsequent events – neither Minister mentioned the powers available to Collins under Section 31. Even more interestingly, O'Malley's jibe at Collins about effective law enforcement evoked a distinctly flinty response. Instancing widespread newspaper coverage of the IRA, Collins quoted from an *Irish Times* description of Cathal Goulding, published only two weeks earlier, as 'Chief of Staff of the IRA' and commented: 'Any foreigner reading this article would assume that the IRA was a legitimate recognised army in the State and many of our fellow-citizens must be feeling that it has Government blessing as well as toleration.' Pouring salt onto the wound, he continued:

> I don't know what the Department of Justice has done about all these matters, but until the situation which has been allowed to develop is changed, RTÉ cannot reasonably be forbidden to publish news items about the IRA which the newspapers – their competitors – freely publish. These matters are news and it would be absurd of RTÉ to draw a veil over them while the newspapers flaunt them.[93]

---

90 As both the opposition parties were resolutely on Lynch's side – although doubt was later cast on his absence of foreknowledge of the events for which he dismissed his ministers – the institutions of the State, and more particularly the pre-eminence of the Dáil, were in no way threatened. Fianna Fáil unity – and therefore power – on the other hand, undoubtedly were. **91** Dáil Debates, 3 March 1973. This letter from 1970, and the reply to it by the Minister for Posts and Telegraphs, were read into the record of the Dáil by the Coalition Minister for Posts and Telegraphs, Dr Conor Cruise O'Brien, shortly after he had assumed office. **92** Dáil Debates, 3 March 1973; O'Malley to Collins, 13 July 1970. **93** Dáil Debates, 3 March 1973; Collins to O'Malley, 17 July 1970.

Plainly, Ó Colmáin in Posts and Telegraphs was not going to allow his new Minister to be wrong-footed by a Minister who had only two days' seniority over him. But there was common concern, at least, on the issue of left-wing tendencies among RTÉ staff, which Collins now underlined in a more eirenic vein.

> I have no doubt that the left wing and some pretty extreme elements of it have a good footing in RTÉ, but it would be very easy in attempting to deal with that situation to do a great deal more harm than good. It is perfectly natural that a new exciting service such as RTÉ would attract very many young people to its staff and without considering the possibility of deliberate infiltration by hard-line Communists. The probability in present-day circumstances is that a great number of these young people will be of left-wing sympathies. There can be no question of eliminating these influences in RTÉ, but what we can and will do is to ensure to the utmost possible that they will not use their influence to bring about the presentation of programmes biased in favour of their views.

This avuncular advice was accompanied by a promise to take further action if any further programmes came to O'Malley's attention 'which you feel are condoning illegality.'

Haughey's acquittal, in October 1970, was the occasion for a special 7 *Days* programme, which included a film insert prepared in advance, giving a somewhat soft-focus image of Haughey as a country squire and vote-catcher. This would, if anything, have added to the convulsions within Fianna Fáil.

Apart from 7 *Days*, however, one of largest flies in the government's ointment was *Féach*, which Eoghan Harris was now producing. His reporters were politically diverse: Breandán Ó hEithir, from the Aran islands, was a writer who combined sensitivity, a superb command of his native language, and a gift for mockery. He was also a nephew of Liam O'Flaherty (who had fought with British forces on the Somme). Mac Aonghusa, a free-lance journalist and independent radio producer, had earlier been expelled as vice-chairman of the Labour Party. He now believed that his former party was controlled by 'small sinister groups' and had told a meeting of Tuairim in Limerick that Fine Gael policies, if fully implemented, could radically improve the State.[94] Harris himself had, he told an RTÉ interviewer many years later, been a member of Sinn Féin since his youth,[95] but – with the split in the organisation into 'Official' and 'Provisional' Sinn Féin – had sided decisively with the former organisation in the belief that its leader, Cathal Goulding, was bent on radicalising and ultimately de-militarising the movement. A *Féach* interview with the editor of the 'Official' news-

94 *Irish Times*, 30 January 1969.   **95** RTÉ, *Today-Tonight*, 26 April 1990, RTE ref BP20/008822.

paper, *The United Irishman*, carried by the programme in May 1970, was effectively a major scoop on the story about where the money had come from to buy guns for Northern Republicans.

Both wings of Sinn Féin, and RTÉ's coverage of them, were now attracting considerable government attention, and the archival evidence suggests that O'Malley was being successful in putting pressure on Collins, although Collins was still reluctant to interfere directly. Twice in the summer of 1970 Collins had meetings with station executives. At the first, at the end of June, Collins, while expressing the Government's concern, said that he saw his role as being concerned with broad questions of national policy on broadcasting matters and not having any involvement in day to day affairs of RTÉ.[96] Collins, however, had another meeting with RTÉ management less than a month later, in which his tone had noticeably hardened.

RTÉ was represented at this meeting, in the absence of the Director-General, by the Deputy Director-General, John Irvine, and the Chairman of the Authority, Dónall Ó Móráin. At this meeting, Collins complained vociferously about the prominence being given by RTÉ in its news and current affairs programmes to the activities of the IRA, Sinn Féin, and 'other left wing and protest organisations.' Ó Móráin counselled strongly against any attempt to ban elements of news reporting which would have the effect of undermining RTÉ's credibility as a news medium, especially in the light of the fact that neither the BBC nor the print media were in any way restricted. The RTÉ representatives at the meeting formed the impression – somewhat over-optimistically, as it turned out – that the Minister would judge RTÉ for himself in the light of its performance from then on.[97] As it happened, other forces were coming into play which would put fresh pressure on the government and, in turn, on RTÉ.

The political involvement of Harris and other individuals continued to cause ripples at senior management level in the station. The Director-General had gone on record with his concern about the degree to which not only *Féach*, but the *Late Late Show* had all dealt extensively with 'societies and groups advocating social revolution'.[98] Mac Aonghusa and Breandán Ó hEithir were criticised for their journalistic commentaries on current events in *Hibernia*, on the grounds that audiences would not be able readily to separate their roles as committed political commentators in print, and statutorily impartial interviewers on RTÉ.[99] Mac Aonghusa's role in a mock 'trial' of President Nixon during the latter's visit to Ireland in October 1970 occasioned fresh concern. Then there was a brouhaha in December, when Garvey had vetoed an invitation from Harris to

96 PPC Minutes, 2 June 1970.   **97** PPC Minutes, 24 July 1970.   **98** PPC Minutes, 16 October 1970.
99 PPC Minutes, 27 October 1970. At the same meeting, the future Director-General, Oliver Maloney complained that a 'small elitist group appeared to be involved in all communications media', instancing John Horgan, Seán Mac Réamoinn, Michael Viney and his wife Ethna.

the President of Provisional Sinn Féin, Ruairi Ó Brádaigh, to take part in a *Féach* programme, and Tomás Mac Giolla, anxious to debate with his erstwhile comrade, had walked off the set in protest.[100]

Within days of this episode, Garvey disclosed that he had written to Harris some time previously to warn him that if he continued to express his opinion on topical problems or questions in the press (Harris had told the print media that he disagreed with the decision to veto Ó Brádaigh), he would not be allocated to produce current affairs type programmes for RTÉ since his credibility in this function would be affected with the public. Hardiman, while he shared Garvey's concern to a degree, responded that, of its nature, broadcasting needed such people – but it should be able to manage them. Producers and programme makers should be judged primarily on the quality of their work and, on this basis, Harris was 'justly held in some regard'. He advocated common sense as the best way of dealing with the problem.[101] Harris did not make matters any easier for his dwindling band of protectors by refusing to accept a Jacobs Award for the programme. As a supportive commentator noted:

> The philosophy and political stance of the producer, Eoghan Harris, often obtrudes; but it is clearly visible, and you either like it or not, agree with it or disagree with it. Breandán Ó hEithir leaves his own views outside the studio more often than the others.[102]

This commentary, of course, begged the central question. Political views, especially those of the producer, were simply not supposed to obtrude. Whether the audience agreed with them or not, recognised them for what they were or not, was irrelevant. According to the station's ethos, and indeed its regulations, it was inadmissible. At one level, this again raises the whole question of impartiality – a difficult enough concept at the best of times, despite its seeming clarity, and especially problematic in relation to media. As Dr Samuel Johnson said when he was asked whether his report to Parliament had treated the different parties impartially he replied: 'yes, but I take care that the Whig dogs shall not have the best of it'.[103] This issue, and the management problems it created, sometimes resulted in outright confrontation, more frequently in guerilla exchanges, as broadcasters tested the limits of what was permissible, had shots fired across their bows, and tried another tack. Meanwhile, outside, the politicians were watching. One of the most colourful, the independent TD Joseph Leneghan, less anxious about the way in which he might be portrayed on the airwaves than some of his contemporaries, expressed the pungent view that most people in RTÉ were 'nothing other than woodlice'.[104]

100 PPC Minutes, 8 December 1970.   **101** PPC Minutes, 11 December 1970.   **102** Tom O'Dea, *Irish Press*, 31 October 1970.   **103** Quoted in Joseph Dunn, *TV and politics* (1971), p. 17.   **104** Dáil Debates,

There were two issues involved in relation to coverage of the escalating Northern crisis, although they were frequently conflated, both by broadcasters and their critics. The first was whether, in the interests of comprehensiveness (a less glamorous but perhaps better word in this context than 'impartiality') members of, or spokesmen for, illegal organisations should be not only visible but audible on a national State-owned television and radio service. The other related to the personal political views of those who controlled the gateways to the airwaves.

Both issues were now to be addressed in earnest. When Dessie O'Hagan was referred to on another *Féach* programme in February 1971 as an 'IRA officer,' there was reluctant agreement that a policy of not naming the IRA could not be adhered to in circumstances which were so different from those obtaining a year ago: at a PPC meeting, Desmond Fisher, the Deputy Head of News, pointed out that at no time had the Taoiseach been given an undertaking that IRA activities would not be covered. He had merely been assured that they would not be glamourised.[105] Unknown to the station managers and broadcasters, however, the invitation proffered by Collins to O'Malley was being enthusiastically taken up. From now on, not only the IRA, but RTÉ's coverage of its activities, were to come under increasing scrutiny.

11 March 1971. **105** PPC Minutes, 9 February 1971.

CHAPTER 4

Censors and sackings

RTÉ's policies and practice in relation to news and current affairs generally, and the government's reaction to these, cannot be analysed independently of the political context of the times.[1] Relationships between the Irish and British government were deteriorating as the situation in the North deteriorated: there, the resignation of James Chichester-Clark as Northern Ireland's prime minister in March 1971 was followed by the election of Brian Faulkner as his successor. This did not prevent Unionism from beginning to tear itself apart, not least under pressure from Rev. Dr Ian Paisley. The British government attitude towards the recrudescence of violence in Northern Ireland, especially after internment was introduced in August, was based on two premises, both of them to a degree questionable: that it was all fomented by the IRA; and that the IRA was largely operating from safe havens on the southern side of the Border. The corollary of this was the view, frequently expressed by security spokesmen in Northern Ireland and in Britain, that if the government of the Republic took firm action against the IRA within its own jurisdiction, the problem would rapidly become much more manageable.

Lynch had his own problems. They were only partly to do with the IRA, in a national security sense, because that organisation was still largely indigenous to Northern Ireland. It did, however, have a substantial measure of political and financial support in the Republic, and Lynch's own party harboured a number of back-benchers, not excluding former ministers, whose support for the political objectives of the IRA was only mildly qualified by their rejection of that organisation's methods. Some of these, in any case, saw militant nationalism – provided its activities were safely confined to Northern Ireland – as less of a political threat than the left-wing variant which had emerged after both Sinn Féin and the IRA split in January 1970, and which looked like taking root in the Republic. Political instability was therefore the endemic condition in both parts of the island. In this context, anything that RTÉ might do which could be interpreted as adding to that instability, or as weakening the position of the Irish government in its continuous exchanges with the British government on security matters, attracted instant, and hostile, government attention.

1 See Appendix 1.

Within RTÉ itself, a number of key personnel developments and changes were taking place, some of them involving individuals who would feature prominently in later controversies. In the North, Martin Wallace was succeeded as RTÉ correspondent in October 1970 by the gifted journalist Liam Hourican, who had originally been employed by RTÉ for its London office. Mike Burns was Features Editor in the News Division; Seán Duignan was News Features editor on radio. Hourican was succeeded in London by John O'Sullivan; and the increasing demands on staffing in Belfast led to the appointment – initially on a temporary basis – in that office of Kevin Myers. Myers was required to pay some attention to his fluency in Irish and, after attendance at courses in Belfast, he satisfied his employers on this account, and was appointed to a permanent position.[2] Myers's appointment was interesting for one other reason. Although he was an NUJ member, senior members of the Union in RTÉ were apprehensive at his appointment. They feared that it was indicative of a new staff policy in the making – one which would prefer bright young graduate reporters, and which would limit the promotional prospects of those who had come up the hard way through an apprenticeship in the provincial and national print media, and who did not necessarily have any third level qualifications. The official NUJ view at that time was that journalists should be able to become specialised broadcasters without any prior knowledge of the subject being required.[3]

The government, as it emerged, was not the only party concerned at RTÉ's practice in relation to reporting Northern Ireland. In March 1971 Cardinal Conway, the Archbishop of Armagh, had complained by telephone to the Head of News, Jim McGuinness, about the station's northern coverage. McGuinness immediately went North for a personal meeting with the cardinal, at which he responded to Conway's objection about the interviewing of Provisional and official spokesmen. There was a moral dilemma for RTÉ, McGuinness agreed – but RTÉ could not refuse to include interviews because the story might be less acceptable to its audience in the Republic.[4] Conway apparently accepted this argument, but was less accommodating in relation to RTÉ's tendency, as he put it, to 'put forward the advocacy of change or the progressive viewpoint to the detriment of the conservative, establishment, or status quo attitude'. He had been particularly upset by the way in which RTÉ had some time earlier intercut an interview by Liam Hourican with himself with another interview featuring Oliver J. Flanagan. Warming to this theme, he intimated to McGuinness that if RTÉ continued in this vein, 'the hierarchy might be forced to take what action it could to draw attention to this deficiency.' His views were echoed within RTÉ at a meeting where the organisation's Director of Personnel Oliver Maloney, wondered at the 'apparently disproportionate number of the audience [on the *Late Late Show*] who were members of civil rights organisations and communists'.[5] Similar concerns were expressed later, in relation to the station's coverage of the Women's Liberation Movement journey to Belfast to purchase contraceptives, when executives wondered whether RTÉ was being seen as 'over-concerned with the contraception issue.'[6]

The principal activity, however, was on the political rather than on the ecclesiastical or moral fronts. In April, Collins told the Dáil that the media should ignore statements released by illegal organisations. RTÉ's Programme Policy Committee, when it considered this request, concluded that every statement from the IRA simply had to be judged on its merits: the committee also reaffirmed its policy that no member of the IRA would be seen on television or interviewed on radio without prior consultation with, and the agreement of, the divisional head concerned. Coincidentally, the BBC reporter, Bernard Falk, was facing court action in London in relation to an interview he had carried out with an IRA spokesman in Northern Ireland, and was in fact briefly imprisoned for contempt of court when he refused to disclose details about his sources.[7]

On 1 June 1971 Dónall Ó Móráin was re-appointed as Chairman of the RTÉ Authority. Within three weeks, the station found itself in the throes of a major controversy in the course of which the government drew back only at the last minute from issuing its first ever directive under Section 31 of the 1960 Act.

Hourican, a journalist of prodigious energy and insight, planned a lengthy contribution to the Sunday lunch-time radio programme *This Week*, which had rapidly established itself as required listening throughout the country since its introduction on 3 November 1968. Hourican, who later became Government Press Secretary under Garret FitzGerald and then moved to a career in the EEC Commission, could scarcely have been accused of being an IRA sympathiser, much less a fellow-traveller. He told his Head of News, Jim McGuinness, that he had been the object of abuse both from Provisional and Official Sinn Féin. The programme was planned for 20 June 1971, and was to feature two interviews by Liam Hourican with Belfast members of the Provisionals. McGuinness went North to discuss the matter with Hourican and listen to the full tapes; the station managers maintained the position that if the interview contained important new information, RTÉ would have to take into account its real obligations to report the situation fully.[8] This created a 'major confrontation' with the government.[9]

The Minister for Justice, Desmond O'Malley, was informed on Friday 18 June about the planned programme, and invited by Mike Burns to participate by

4 PPC Minutes, 16 March 1971. **5** PPC Minutes, 4 May 1971. **6** PPC Minutes, 25 May 1971. The discussion was occasioned by largely hostile reaction from viewers as recorded in the station's telephone log. This reaction was echoed at an Authority meeting in June: PPC Minutes 8 June 1971. **7** Liz Curtis, *Ireland: the propaganda war* (1984), p. 250. **8** PPC Minutes, 15 June 1971. **9** NA 2003/17/278. Memorandum from Department of Posts and Telegraphs to Government, 24 November 1972.

way of live interview. There was a glitch: the staff member in the Government Information Bureau who normally dealt with RTÉ requests for Government ministers was on leave, and a less experienced official misunderstood some of the detail in the proposal and informed O'Malley that the programme 'would be concerned with the IRA' and that there would be wide representation from all wings of the Republican movement.[10] Considerably annoyed, O'Malley telephoned Ó Colmáin, Secretary of the Department of Posts and Telegraphs (Collins was back in his Limerick constituency) to tell him that he had declined to participate; that he strongly objected to the programme; and that he wanted to know if it could be cancelled.

Ó Colmáin rang Hardiman, who cleared up some misinformation about the programme, but confirmed that two Belfast members of the Provisional IRA would feature on it, in a pre-recorded interview by Liam Hourican in which they would be 'closely questioned'.[11] Ó Colmáin told Hardiman that the possibility of making a direction under Section 31 was under consideration, but Hardiman told him that they were going ahead, and was not asked to discontinue making arrangements for the programme. In Hardiman's words,

> The withdrawal of the interview with the Provisionals, or of the complete programme, on the basis of a direction, would, in my opinion, create much more difficulty in the assumptions that would be made and the wrongful conclusions that would be drawn from the inevitable ensuing publicity.[12]

The following morning – Saturday – Collins contacted Lynch, who asked that RTÉ be urged to drop the interview with the Provisionals and substitute something else. This was conveyed to RTÉ, again in the context of a possible direction under section 31. However, following telephone calls from Dónall Ó Móráin to O'Malley, and O'Malley to Lynch, Lynch decided that no action should be taken. Ó Móráin had in fact already agreed with Hardiman on the stance he (Hardiman) had taken. The programme, as eventually broadcast, was therefore highly anomalous in that included not only interviews with the Provisionals and with a dramatically wide range of political opinion, North and South, but was entirely without any representation from the Government or the Fianna Fáil party.[13] At a meeting of the Programme Policy Committee at the height of the crisis, Hardiman warned station executives that the issue had by no

---

10 PPC Minutes, 19 June 1971. **11** NA 2003/17/17, Memorandum to RTÉ Authority from Director-General, 22 June 1971. **12** Ibid. **13** Ibid. The programme lasted for some 77 minutes, of which the interview with the Provisionals accounted for some 18 minutes. The contributors included: General Tuzo, Rafton Pounder, Gerry Fitt, William Craig, Fr Desmond Wilson, John Taylor MP, John Hume MP, Eddie McAteer, Robert Cooper, William Deedes MP, Merlyn Rees MP, Robert Babington MP, Paddy Kennedy MP, Dr Conor Cruise O'Brien, Senator John Kelly, and Professor Patrick Lynch.

means been finally resolved, and that the widespread publicity given to the disagreement between RTÉ and ministers would make it difficult to convince ministers that the leakage had not been organised by RTÉ executives in an attempt to embarrass the government.[14]

This was a game for high stakes. If the government backed off, it would have lost a battle – if not the war – in the continuous attempt to restrict or even prevent IRA and Sinn Féin access to the airwaves. On the other hand Ó Móráin – and presumably, through him, the Government – would have been made aware, although probably not in so many words, that this was an issue on which Hardiman, as editor-in-chief, was putting his own reputation on the line. This interpretation is supported by the recollection of Mike Burns that, as the final preparations were being made for the transmission of the programme on the Sunday morning, Hardiman was present in studio to reassure staff, although the various telephone conversations which had taken place had indicated that the Government had decided not to take action. The knowledgeable political correspondent of the *Irish Press*, Michael Mills, reported subsequently that the directive had in fact been prepared and signed, but never issued.[15] It was that close.

The issuing of a directive, followed by the inevitably hostile newspaper publicity, would have been a far more serious blow to the Government, at least in the short term, and in the circumstances it was a wound it decided it did not have to take. It backed off, therefore, but there was a sense in which it was only biding its time. Lynch made no secret of his feelings in a telephone discussion with Ó Móráin on the Monday following the programme, and on the Tuesday Ó Móráin was summoned to a meeting with Collins, at which the same message was no doubt expressed.[16]

The matter, as might have been expected, was raised immediately in the Dáil. There, in reply to questions from Barry Desmond TD, Lynch told the House that the government had refused to participate because 'it was not in the public interest that members of illegal organisations should be permitted to use such a programme for publicising their activities' and that 'members of illegal organisations should not be invited to propound illegal activities on a service paid for by the taxpayer – activities that are against the public interest.'[17] In an adjournment debate on the same day, Collins reiterated Lynch's view, and said that so long as he had statutory powers in the matter he would exercise them. In retrospect, this can now be seen as an thinly veiled warning to RTÉ that any recurrence of such defiance would not be tolerated. It was not, however, interpreted by the station in such a definitive way. The showdown had merely been postponed.

In those Dáil discussions on 24 June, the Opposition was in fact attempting to put the Government into a double bind: if it had interfered in RTÉ's pro-

---

14 PPC Minutes, 19 June 1971. **15** *Irish Press*, 2 October 1971. **16** NA 2003/16/17, Memorandum to RTÉ Authority from Director-General, 22 June 1971. **17** Dáil Debates, 24 June 1971.

gramming, it was in the wrong – but it was also in the wrong for permitting militant Republicanism to have access to the airwaves. RTÉ executives were particularly perturbed at a suggestion in the course of the debate by Conor Cruise O'Brien, the academic and Labour TD, that RTÉ's radio programme had been the equivalent of the Provisionals being allowed to parade in uniform.[18] There was a delicious irony about this. Less than a fortnight earlier, Collins had written to Lynch about a planned series of nine educational programmes on RTÉ in the coming autumn, three of which were to be presented by O'Brien. Lynch was equally displeased, reminding Collins that RTÉ had been rapped over the knuckles about Dr O'Brien two years earlier, in August 1969, when it had employed him on a programme about Ireland's application to the UN for a peace-keeping force for Northern Ireland. Collins, believing that it was 'objectionable that an active politician, especially a member of a front bench in the Dáil, should be featured in this way', had taken up the matter with the Authority, who had told him that unfortunately O'Brien's contract had already been signed and could not be revoked. The Authority, he now told Lynch, had nonetheless reprimanded the Director-General: these things were not to happen again, and he was satisfied that 'internal disciplinary action of this sort is more effective than, and has many advantages over, overt action by me or the government.'[19] Collins's apparent belief in the efficacy of internal disciplinary action, as compared to government directives, was soon to be sorely tested.

On 6 July, as has been already noted, Muiris Mac Conghail resigned as editor of 7 *Days*, to be replaced by Seán Ó Mordha. The programme was coming under increasing criticism from politicians; that, and the gruelling tempo of the production schedule, must have suggested to him that, for a time at least, he should take a different course.

Just before doing so, he had written to one of the programme's presenters, John O'Donoghue, to remind him 'most forcefully' of RTÉ's policy that current affairs broadcasters should remain uncommitted on controversial matters in order to keep credibility with the public: O'Donoghue, who had chaired a 7 *Days* discussion on the then controversial community schools programme, had subsequently made a public comment on the issue. Proinsías Mac Aonghusa was again in trouble for public statements he had made.[20] This problem simply would not go away.

The station continued to feel its way forward with some caution in the new situation. The leaders of both wings of Sinn Féin, Ruairí Ó Brádaigh and Tomás Mac Giolla, were interviewed on 7 *Days* on 30 July, without any apparent objection from government sources. During the summer, RTÉ management spent some considerable time discussing Northern Ireland coverage generally, and Jim

18 PPC Minutes, 25 June 1971. **19** NA, 2002/16/17: Collins to Lynch, 11 June 1971; Lynch to Collins, 14 June 1971. **20** PPC Minutes, 6 August 1971.

McGuinness made frequent visits to the North to assess the response to RTÉ coverage. He found himself under pressure from some nationalists who found RTÉ's coverage too impartial; equally, the station found that balance was not always easy, partly because of the British Army's refusal to give interview to RTÉ reporters.[21] This was also the case with Ian Paisley, who initially agreed to an RTÉ interview, but subsequently changed his mind on the grounds that Lynch did not 'recognise' Brian Faulkner.[22] (He finally agreed to the first of his many subsequent interviews – on radio, with Liam Hourican – in November.) While there were warnings about the dangers of personal feelings influencing reporters, McGuinness maintained strongly that RTÉ coverage, overall, was balanced and impartial – compared to some BBC reports which he found 'emotional and unbalanced'.[23]

As the situation in the North continued to deteriorate, programme-makers were given a vivid reminder of the long institutional memory of the Department of Justice, when the *Report* programme was refused co-operation by the Department on the grounds that RTÉ had still to respond to allegations that it had been unfair to the Department on an earlier occasion. Investigations revealed that the Department was still exercised about a programme chaired by Bunny Carr five years earlier, in 1966, in the course of which a boy who was being interviewed alleged that he had been severely beaten while an inmate of a reformatory school. The investigation also revealed that the Department had, in fact, been given an opportunity to respond to the charge in the following week's programme in the same series. Almost four decades later, this issue was to re-surface to dramatic effect: but the 1966 episode demonstrates not only the cultural power of the official denial but also – and more hopefully – the slow widening of the media's social agenda.[24]

The beginning of August had seen, in the Falls and Ardoyne areas of Belfast, some of the worst disturbances in half a century. Nearly 4,500 nationalists fled into the Republic, where they were housed as refugees in military barracks – an experience which cannot have helped their growing sense of isolation. As well as the physical battle which had been joined on the streets of Northern Ireland, an ideological battle had broken out between rivals for the guardianship of the core values of Irish nationalism. On 6 September Lynch had his first meeting with Edward Heath at Chequers: the occasion was marked by an IRA raid on the RTÉ transmission mast at Kippure which did little to improve the government's temper. On 19 September Kevin Boland, who had lost the Fianna Fáil whip in the Dáil in June 1970, and who had resigned from the Dáil in November of the same year, launched a new political party, Aontacht Éireann, with the aim of regenerating traditional Republicanism. The measure of the gulf that was open-

21 PPC Minutes, 10 August 1971, 13 August 1971, 20 August 1971.   **22** PPC Minutes, 24 September 1971.   **23** PPC Minutes, 27 August 1971.   **24** PPC Minutes, 20 August 1971.

ing within Fianna Fáil can be gauged from the fact that Boland's invocations of the spirit of 1916 on this occasion were described by his former Cabinet colleague Seán MacEntee as 'squalid and furtive stunts [designed to] desecrate the memory of the dead.'[25] Lynch, in another attempt to engineer a de-escalation of the situation, returned to Chequers on 27 September, this time for a tripartite meeting involving Heath and Brian Faulkner.

This was the context in which RTÉ now planned a 7 *Days* programme to review political developments, to be broadcast on the evening of September 28th.[26] There followed a rapidly escalating series of confrontations, fuelled in part by RTÉ's institutional memory of having faced down Collins earlier in the summer, and in part by an unintended but dramatic combination of visual effects which added to the government's conviction that things had now gone too far.

Sheamus Smith was the editor of the 28 September programme and Colm Ó Briain its producer. Lynch was travelling back from London and unavailable. On Monday 27 September Ó Briain phoned Bart Cronin, the press officer for George Colley, who was then Tánaiste and Minister for Finance, to ask if the Minister would appear on the programme. More critically, a decision had also been taken to invite onto the programme both Cathal Goulding and Seán Mac Stíofáin, Chiefs of Staff of, respectively, the Official and Provisional IRA. Colley was informed, and expressed his objections in the strongest possible terms. The Secretary of the Department of Posts and Telegraphs then phoned Hardiman, also on the Monday, to express the Government's concern, and indicated that it expected the programme to be withdrawn. Hardiman stood his ground, explaining that the interviews with Goulding and Mac Stíofáin were to be recorded, but that all the politicians taking part would be involved in a live discussion. By midday on the Tuesday, Hardiman had also spoken to the Chairman, who had – after questioning him closely – endorsed his decision. Collins phoned Ó Móráin on the morning of 28 September to object to the intended IRA interviews, and on several other occasions during the day.[27]

At this point, the choreography of what appeared on screen assumed an unexpected significance. Lynch, travelling back from London, was interviewed briefly at the airport about his summit with Heath and Faulkner: the 7 *Days* programme followed. However, because the participants from the political parties (excluding Fianna Fáil, which had declined to send anyone) were totally opposed to taking part in any programme in which they could be portrayed as affording Goulding and Mac Stíofáin equal political status with themselves, the two para-military spokesmen were, as has already been noted, interviewed separately, and the interviews were pre-recorded. However, these pre-recorded interviews were trans-

---

25 *Irish Times*, 25 September 1971, letter to the editor. **26** The chronology from this episode has been derived from PPC Minutes, 28 and 30 September 1971; NA 2003/16/278, and the *Irish Times*, *Irish Press* and *Irish Independent*, 28 September–4 November 1971. **27** RTÉ Authority Minutes, 1 October 1971.

mitted first. As well as this, which certainly afforded them some prominence (although the intention was that subsequent speakers would be able to comment on and criticise what they had to say) the setting in which they were interviewed caused some comment. This involved a black 'limbo' background, with continuous captioning of their names, which dramatically enhanced the impact of the presentation. The Dáil politicians, in contrast, were seated together in a studio lit individually in the normal way, but without a black background.

Nobody on the production team thought that the different settings had any political significance; insofar as the matter was commented on at all, the feeling was that the visually different treatment of both sets of speakers served positively to underline the fact that there was a huge gulf between the para-military spokesmen and the democratic politicians. This, however, was not how the politicians interpreted it. Lynch's own view, in particular, was provided indirectly to the public via the *Irish Independent*, whose reporter explained that 'the Taoiseach had been at some pains at Chequers to explain all that his government was doing to curtail illegal activities, so [the programme] was a considerable embarrassment to him.'[28]

On Wednesday 29 September Collins rang the Chairman to express his concern. The following morning a tape of part of the programme – that section involving the pre-recorded interviews with the two Republican leaders – was shown to members of the cabinet at Government Buildings. On Friday 1 October the Government, after discussing the matter, issued the following directive:

> In the exercise of the powers conferred on me by Section 31 of the Broadcasting Authority Act, 1960, I, Gerard Collins TD, Minister for Posts and Telegraphs, hereby direct you to refrain from broadcasting any matter of the following class, i.e. any matter that could be calculated to promote the aims or activities of any organisation which engages in, promotes, encourages or advocates the attaining of any particular objective by violent means.

Simultaneously, the Authority was meeting in Donnybrook. After viewing a recording of the full programme, the Authority came to the conclusion that the decision to include the two IRA leaders had been justified, but was 'highly critical of some aspects of the programme.'[29] At this point, Collins phoned the Chairman to tell him that the letter was on its way, and what its contents were. Ó Móráin then – accompanied by Irvine and Hardiman – went immediately to Government Buildings in an attempt to get Collins to rescind the directive

---

28 *Irish Independent*, 2 October 1971, article by Michael Brophy. **29** RTÉ Authority Minutes, 1 October 1971. The minutes, as originally drafted and before amendment, read that the Authority 'endorsed the decision to include the two interviews but criticised aspects of the presentation of this part of the programme, in particular, the length of the interviews.'

before it could be published. In the course of this meeting he argued strongly – according to the Government's version of events – that if the directive were withdrawn, it would be possible for the Authority to find a formula enabling it to effectively carry out the policy implied by the directive. Collins, no doubt remembering the way he had been out-manoeuvred in the summer, replied tersely that if the Authority had adopted this attitude the previous June, there would have been no directive. He reminded Ó Móráin that he had asked him not to put on the programme, and had tried very hard to persuade him, 'knowing what would happen'.[30] The RTÉ side was left under no illusion but that Collins had little or no flexibility in the matter, and was simply acting in pursuance of a government decision. At the resumed Authority meeting, the members heard a warning – prophetic, as it turned out – from a senior counsel, Eoin Liston, that as the Act did not provide for any sanctions for breach of a directive, the sanction presumably would be the dismissal of the Authority.

The first casualty was *Féach*, which had planned also to interview two paramilitary spokesman on its programme the following Monday. There was a palpable sense of shock within RTÉ: the Authority issued a statement defending the programme, which was welcomed by the National Union of Journalists. At the programme policy committee, decisions were taken in principle that from now on, in radio and television news programmes, there would be an embargo on broadcasts which would amount to enabling members of illegal organisations to put their point of view across: that apart, the existing arrangements were to be maintained. Current affairs presented 'more difficulties'; there would be no direct participation by members of illegal organisations, and divisional heads had to scrutinise plans by programme-makers carefully and, where appropriate, refer the matter upwards to the Director-General for a decision.[31] And there was now a significant difference of opinion between the programme policy committee and the Authority on the most appropriate course of action. The committee felt that seeking a closer definition of the government's decision was inadvisable; the Authority – as it explained in considerable detail in a letter to Collins on 15 October – asked for clarification, presumably in the expectation that the self-same government which had appointed it would not leave it in the lurch. In the event, no clarification was forthcoming: Collins told them bluntly that his directive 'speaks for itself'. From now on, broadcasters were to be in the unenviable position of having to second-guess the Government's opinion of their interpretation of a noticeably imprecise directive. It was so imprecise, indeed, that it could have been interpreted to ban reporting of groups as disparate as the African National Congress in apartheid South Africa, and the Anti-Vivisection League in Britain. Hard cases make bad law; but it was law nonetheless.

30 NA 2003/16/278, Memorandum for Government on earlier events, 24 November 1972. **31** PPC Minutes, 4 October 1971. **32** *Irish Press*, 4 October 1971.

Lynch went public on the Government's decision at a meeting in Cork a few days later, when he said that the 7 *Days* programme had allowed itself to be used as 'a recruiting ground for illegal military activities', and that the programme had been 'one of the worst examples of propagandizing those activities'.[32] Reaction from the print media was in part what might have been anticipated, in part nuanced. Aidan Pender, editor of the *Irish Independent*, no doubt reflecting the commercial tensions between the different media, chose to highlight his belief that RTÉ had 'sold its soul to the Government by accepting financial aid'. His counterpart at the *Irish Times*, Douglas Gageby, no doubt mindful of Lemass's 1966 intervention, said more bluntly that 'RTÉ is an arm of the government and has just got a directive from its boss'.[33]

Although they were –with the evident exception of the *Irish Press* – critical of Government, the newspapers editorially were less resolute in their defence of RTÉ than might have been expected. This may have been partly related to the growing sense of rivalry between the media, the invasion of the advertising market by RTÉ, and the fact that most of the broadcasters now in the firing line were not journalists – in the sense that they were not members of the NUJ. The furthest the *Irish Independent* would go was to maintain that the directive was too sweeping and should be clarified as quickly as possible. On the substantive issue, it had little doubt:

> It is a corollary of the right of free speech that the public have the right to hear freely all sides of a question. If one side, or one of several sides, gets a lion's share of the time then all the other sides are corresponding-ly curtailed and the right of the public to hear all sides is thus impaired. A governmental directive which seeks to redress imbalanced presentation in vindication of this right is therefore acceptable in principle. It is worth stressing that this principle applies particularly where there is a monopoly of a medium of communication.[34]

This, of course, begged at least one question: the effect of the directive would not be to allow the public to hear 'all sides', but to exclude one 'side' from the debate completely. The *Irish Press*, although it described it as a 'troublesome' directive, and warned about the need to maintain a full and free flow of information, declared that 'for the Taoiseach, for Mr Collins, the Minister for Posts and Telegraphs, to state that Telefís Éireann must not in any way aid in the process of taking innocent lives is not only justifiable, but essential'.[35] *The Irish Times* praised the Authority's response to the money-lending tribunal, and to the Government's attempt to veto a programme earlier in the year, but then pro-

---

33 *Irish Independent*, 4 October 1971 (report of radio programme broadcast on RTÉ on 3 October). **34** *Irish Independent*, 4 October 1971, editorial. **35** *Irish Press*, 2 October 1971.

ceeded to distribute blame widely. RTÉ had been guilty of 'errors of judgement'; on the other hand, the way to clear the screen of the advocates of violence was 'in the hands of the government, not of the media'. Hinting at the possibility of staff changes, it concluded that a service which made some mistakes was nonetheless better than one which people in the North, for example (the context suggests that the observation was confined to nationalists) would now 'take to be merely Mr Lynch's mouthpiece.'[36] Not all journalists, however, were singing from the same hymn sheet: James McGuire of the *Western People* supported the government's decision to issue a directive. So did the *Irish Times* journalist (and erstwhile political commentator on RTÉ), John Healy.[37]

The Fine Gael TD Richie Ryan welcomed it; his Fine Gael colleague, the constitutional lawyer John Kelly, who appeared on a 7 *Days* programme on the directive on 6 October, managed simultaneously to support Erskine Childers (who had presented the government's point of view on air) and criticise the government. Donal Kelly of the NUJ in the RTÉ newsroom protested to Lynch on behalf of his organisation, and sought a meeting with the Taoiseach and the Minister for Posts and Telegraphs to discuss the directive and the Act itself. This was refused, and the difficulties of journalists were exacerbated by the Authority's refusal to issue any policy statement or written guidelines to its staff. At an inconclusive meeting between RTÉ NUJ officers and senior station personnel in March 1972, Mr Hardiman told the journalists that Sinn Féin statements and IRA activities, legal or illegal, would be reported without question, but without direct participation by IRA members. This decision, however, 'would not be published or written down ... because a written decision would be binding on RTÉ, and could be used against them if at some later stage it was desired to change the policy.' He was supported by the station's Head of News, Mr Jim McGuinness, on the grounds if the current interpretation of the directive were put on paper, 'many people would interpret the directive much more narrowly.'[38]

Eoghan Harris found himself featured in both the *Irish Times* and the *Irish Press* for his view that the directive would provide 'insuperable' problems for the Authority, would seriously damage the information flow to the general public, and that it was inevitable that Irish Republicans would appear more frequently on Irish language programmes since they tended, on balance, to have a good command of the Irish language.[39] Tony Heffernan, the press officer for Official Sinn Féin – the party of which Harris would later acknowledge he had for many years been a member – suggested that it was 'the first stage in the implementation of a secret deal between Lynch, Heath and Faulkner'.[40] Although the latter comment was undoubtedly wildly inaccurate, given the extremely tense rela-

---

36 *Irish Times*, 2 October 1971. **37** *Irish Times*, 8 October 1971. Maguire became a member of the Authority appointed by the 1973–7 coalition government. **38** NUJ 1972, minute, 5 March 1972. **39** *Irish Times*, 2 October 1971, *Irish Press*, 2 October 1971. **40** *Irish Press*, 2 October 1971.

tionships between the three leaders at this time, it served to underline the political difficulties being created for Lynch by the fact that Heath, in particular, was increasingly endorsing the Unionist position that the whole root of the problem lay South of the border, and with the Dublin government.

Despite the protests and the anxiety about future coverage, the initial reaction within RTÉ was that the directive was, in essence, manageable, although its application to a range of programmes inevitably raised problems. In its initial response to the Minister, the Authority indicated that it would from then on be governed by an interpretation of the directive which would prohibit the direct participation in broadcasting 'of persons who through that participation would succeed in promoting the aims or activities of those organisations described in the direction.'[41] Work began on the production of a set of guidelines, essentially drafted by John Irvine and Desmond Fisher. There were informal discussions with the heads of both Official and Provisional Sinn Féin, after which the Director-General formed the impression that both wings 'seemed moderately surprised at the way we handled the direction.'[42] There were, nonetheless, teething problems, in current affairs rather than in news. On 1 November, *Féach* had covered the Ard Fheis of official Sinn Féin, and the report had featured interviews with Malachy McGurran and Liam McMillan, both from Belfast and both known to be members of the Official IRA. Liam Ó Murchú, the producer now with overall responsibility for the programme, was rapped over the knuckles for this: he argued that he had not been aware that there was an outright ban on such individuals.[43] The *Féach* interviews, as might have been expected, raised eyebrows over in the *7 Days* office, where they were under no illusion about the extent and effect of the new policy – a policy which not only prevented such interviews, but precluded programme-makers from broadcasting the so-called 'health warnings' to alert viewers to the fact that the programme had been made under certain restrictions. McMillan featured again in a different context almost immediately, when Kevin Myers recorded an interview with him in Belfast on his own initiative, and objected forcefully when Mike Burns, the News Features Editor, rejected it as being inconsistent with the directive.[44] This did not prevent occasional slips: on 31 January, in the immediate aftermath of Bloody Sunday, an RTÉ reporter, Eddie Barrett, reporting from Derry, had included a tape of a member of the Official IRA saying that all members of that organisation had been put on alert with instructions to shoot British soldiers in retaliation for the events of the previous day. This was deemed inappropriate 'irrespective of any question of the direction' and it had been removed from later broadcasts of the report.[45]

---

41 2003/16/278, Ó Móráin to Collins, 15 October 1971. **42** PPC Minutes, 22 October 1971. **43** PPC Minutes, 2 November 1971. The programme was also coming under notice for the increased amount of English spoken: PPC Minutes 16 November 1971. **44** PPC Minutes, 11 November 1971. **45** PPC Minutes, 1 February 1972.

At management level generally, there was now considerable watchfulness and – as indeed was understandable – a degree of edginess, which extended not only to programmes about Northern Ireland but into other areas as well. What now came under notice was an article in an issue of *Feedback*, which in management's eyes was simply a bridge too far.

Feedback was a classic example of what has been described as the mosquito press: small, unofficial, and generally anonymous. Its first issue had appeared in August 1970, and its intermittent appearances thereafter provided its readers with a cornucopia of anti-establishment views, frequently as critical of the broadcasters as of the station management. There is no truth, it told readers of its first issue, that 7 *Days* was to be replaced in the autumn schedule by 'a weekly HOUR WITH HUME'.[46] Its second issue, a month later, accused RTÉ of having transmitted 'very few programmes containing an analysis of the basic relationships in our community' and argued that 'Programmes like the *Seven Days* story on money-lending are not a real threat to the imbalances in our society.' Plainly, the spirit of Jack Dowling, and of the original *Seven Days* team, was still alive and well within the station. In October, it reviewed developments in religious broadcasting – and in particular the involvement in RTÉ programming of Fr Joe Dunn and the *Radharc* team – as evidence for its assertion that 'RTÉ a semi-state organisation is now locked at multiple levels in breach of the Broadcasting Act with the agents of one religious denomination.' A riposte published in *Intercom*, the journal of the [Catholic] Communications Institute, evoked a cyclostyled *Feedback* in December which declared roundly that Eoghan Harris was not the producer of *Feedback*, was not a founder of the magazine, and had never been a member of its editorial panel. The same issue leaped to the defence of the Controller of Programmes, Television, Michael Garvey (who might not have welcomed such support), alleging that his role had been emasculated by Hardiman because he had no control over the commitment of studio, outside broadcast and film facilities. In the summer of 1971, it was to be found raising the issue of an interview which had taken place with Cardinal Heenan, and accused those responsible of 'cowardice'. Apparently at Archbishop McQuaid's insistence, and over the objections of some RTÉ staff members, the interview had been carried out by Nodlaig McCarthy, a freelance broadcaster who also lectured for the archbishop at the Mater Dei Institute in Drumcondra. In October 1971 it was alleging – in the context of a controversy involving a *Report* documentary on Michael O'Riordan, leader of the Communist Party of Ireland, that 'Section 31 that was brought in to keep the IRA off the screens is now being applied to everyone else'.

The offending *Feedback* article, which expressed opposition to Ireland's proposed entry to the EEC and alleged that RTÉ's coverage of the issue had been

---

46 RTÉ Reference Library, where a number of copies of this journal are on file.

unbalanced in favour of EEC entry, was unsigned.[47] In the *Irish Press*, Tom O'Dea described the allegations it contained as 'a bit wanton'.[48] O'Dea, who said that he carried no torch for Harris, nonetheless defended *Féach*, not on the grounds that it was unbiased, but on the grounds that while it had 'frequently left a positive afterglow of the lineaments of the producer's mind', he doubted that it had 'ever engaged in raw propaganda'.[49] Raw or not, *Feedback* was now too much for management to swallow. Michael Garvey noted that Harris had denied any involvement in this particular issue of the meeting, and had indicated his intention of withdrawing from *Feedback* 'in his own time'. These protestations notwithstanding, Harris was transferred out of *Féach* to other duties, and all other staff involved in the production of the magazine were also in the process of being identified and reprimanded.[50]

Not even this episode, which was centred on the EEC referendum rather than on Northern Ireland, pushed the larger issue off centre stage for long. Issues both of principle and of practice were involved. In relation to principle, the question arose of what attitude should be adopted where cameramen had been allowed to film certain events relating to the IRA only if they agreed to IRA-imposed conditions. In one case, permission had been given only after the cameramen had given an undertaking not to make the film available to the BBC; on another, the condition had been laid down that individuals' faces should not be shown. As these situations had generally arisen without prior warning, the undertakings required had been given. Back at Montrose, however, the view hardened rapidly: such undertakings should not be given and, if they were, the film should not be used.[51] In terms of practice, there were growing tensions between programmes division and news division, in the sense that news executives felt that programme division broadcasters were frequently over-stepping the mark, and getting away with it.[52] Paradoxically, staff in *7 Days* were beginning to feel that the shadow cast by the news division over their activities was becoming ever longer, and that 'the NUJ is taking over'.[53] Its internal dynamic had become faulty, and three of its staff requested transfers. In an episode which even at the time appeared ludicrous to some of those involved, a programme on a dispute involving a post office at Leitir Mór, in County Galway, generated a

---

47 This particular issue listed the following as members of its 'Work Panel': John Caden (Accounts), Bob Collins (Floor managing), Ian Corr (Sound Operations), Fergal Costello (Cameras), Oliver Donohoe (Research), Brian Eustace (Sound), Harry Houston (Electrical Services), Billy Keans (Technical development), Leonie Kelly (Audience Research), Howard Kinlay (Producer), Brian Mac Lochlainn (Producer), Patsy Murphy (Production Assistant), Liam O'Flanagan (Sound), and Breandán O hEithir (Broadcaster). A subscription to six issues cost 50p. In October/November 1972, five RTÉ staff members were at first threatened with dismissal for their activities in connection with *Feedback*, but this threat was lifted after they signed assurances for management that they would be of good behaviour: ten others were reprimanded. *Irish Times*, 9 November 1972.   **48** *Irish Press*, 26 February 1972.   **49** Ibid.   **50** PPC Minutes, 22 February 1972.   **51** See, e.g., PPC Minutes, 21 March 1972.   **52** PPC Minutes, 28 March 1972.   **53** PPC Minutes, 25 April 1972.

special meeting of the Authority at which this particular programme was the only item for discussion. There was a sense that the programme was losing its way.

The Government was continuing to keep a close eye on proceedings. The attitude of RTÉ's journalists was alluded to indirectly as the directive began to bite. A 7 *Days* programme on the Provisional Sinn Féin Ard Fheis was transmitted on 16 October 1971, which included mute film: a sound recording of part of the proceedings had been transmitted on the lunch-time radio programme. Subsequently the Department of Posts and Telegraphs rang the Chairman of the Authority with a request for a script: he sent it directly to Collins and, in later discussions with the Minister, discussed the operation of the directive generally. Ó Móráin then got the Authority's agreement for his view that it should keep in close contact with the Minister to ensure that a formal channel for discussion would be available in the event of any alleged breach of the direction. At the same meeting, it was recorded that the news staff had expressed 'satisfaction with the Authority's interpretation of the direction, and that RTÉ was 'continuing to produce news and current affairs programming which was authentic and meeting the needs of the community'.[54]

Commenting on these events later, the Head of News, Jim McGuinness, told the television critic Tom O'Dea:

> I said that an Irish government was perfectly entitled to give, in a lawful way, a directive to RTÉ, and that I myself was in the business of upholding the law. Therefore, notwithstanding my own feelings on the matter, which in many ways would be sympathetic to those who think the British are behaving in a questionable way on the North, I felt it was terribly important that nobody in RTÉ would seem to cunningly set himself above the law, and attempt to appear to acquiesce in the directive given by the government and at the same time to thumb his nose at it in a boyish way.[55]

The shooting of 13 civilians taking part in the civil rights march in Derry on 30 January 1972, however, inaugurated a period of dramatically increased tension.

Comparison of government documents covering this period and the minutes of the Programme Policy Committee, however, demonstrates a degree of divergence. While the committee's minutes note several instances of occasions on which the directive was – generally inadvertently – breached, government documentation tends to focus on one specific type of breach. These were the occasions on which statements or comments by the Taoiseach were juxtaposed with

54 RTÉ Authority, Minutes, 5 November 1971.   **55** *Irish Press*, 30 October 1971.

statements from Sinn Féin spokesmen. In February 1972 Lynch phoned the newsroom to get a correction of an erroneous statement (which had originated in a Press Association report) that field hospitals had been despatched to the Border at the time of the Newry Civil Rights March.[56] On 22 May 1972, exception was taken by the Department of Posts and Telegraphs to the fact that a statement by the Taoiseach in the late news summary attacking private armies was followed immediately by a report of a statement from Ruairi Ó Brádaigh of Provisional Sinn Féin to the effect that 'any extension of coercive legislation would not be accepted passively by Republicans.' Another broadcast in June, although it did not involve Lynch directly, interviewed Seán Ó Brádaigh on his release from jail after having been charged with being a member of the IRA (the charge was not proceeded with). Not infrequently, broadcasts like these were followed by Dáil controversy which had the further effect of annoying members of the government. Journalists working in the Dublin newsroom, as it happened, were more removed from the greatest pressure on this issue than their colleagues in Belfast. In April 1972 McGuinness, on a visit to Belfast, was given a letter signed by all the Belfast staff drawing attention to the problems created for them by the directive. Although Liam Hourican had not signed that letter, he had earlier made clear to McGuinness that he was experiencing an increasing sense of conflict between the demands of realistic broadcasting journalism and his responsibilities under the directive.[57]

If the government was aware of the other breaches, it chose not to follow them up in such detail. It is even arguable that it did not consider them to be breaches, or came to the view that the case was arguable and that it might lose credibility by getting involved in a wrangle about it. On 4 April 1972 Donal Kelly of RTÉ's political staff carried an interview with Ruairi Ó Brádaigh which was widely praised, offered to Eurovision, and taken for transmission by the BBC.[58] On three separate occasions, on 8 May 1972, 27 June 1972, and 10 July 1972, a number of people involved in the IRA were interviewed by Liam Hourican (and on one occasion by Liam Nolan), and the substance of the interview – rather than the interviewees' actual voices – reported for the benefit of the radio audience. On the second of these occasions, Mac Stiofáin had been interviewed by Hourican. Nonetheless, Collins had a special meeting with the Authority on 23 June to express his concern specifically with current affairs programming. By now, it was evident, any reservations he may have had about keeping a close watching brief on RTÉ were diminishing, no doubt under strong pressure from O'Malley. His departmental officials noted afterwards that 'improvement was observed, although there were certain items which might well have been omitted'.[59] In retrospect, it can be seen that the government's failure to notice – or

---

56 PPC Minutes, 25 April 1972.   57 PPC Minutes, 11 April 1972 and 18 April 1972.   58 PPC, Minutes, 6 April 1972.   59 NA, 2003/16/278, memorandum from Department of Posts and Telegraphs, 24

unwillingness to take further action about – the Mac Stiofáin interview on 10 July (after Collins's meeting with the Authority on 23 June) would have encouraged RTÉ management in the view that the policy it had enunciated in its letter to Collins on 15 October 1971 had in effect been accepted.

This form of words adopted by Collins's officials to describe the situation adds to the general impression that the government was prepared, even now, to exercise a degree of tolerance. Equally, the effectiveness of the directive could be gathered from a study carried out within the station in preparation for Collins's visit on 24 June. This showed that between 1 October 1971 and 9 June 1972, only four out of 132 7 *Days* programme items had featured Sinn Féin; three out of 62 *Féach* items; and seven out of 633 news items.[60]

As the summer wore on, the North generally remained at the top of the agenda. Coincidentally, Mike Burns left radio to take up a position as editor of television news, and in September 1972 Kevin O'Kelly replaced Seán Duignan as News Features Editor on radio. O'Kelly, whose gritty independence was being recognised by this promotion, was a journalist who combined a classic, hard news approach with a cerebral approach to his craft. He was to need all his human and intellectual resources for the ordeal that was about to follow.

The evolution of policy on the directive within his union, however, was by no means clear. The 1972 annual delegate meeting (ADM) of the NUJ heard the union's general secretary promise support to any branch planning industrial action to protest against the ban. Perhaps even more significantly, a proposal for a one-day token strike was discussed, but not even put to a vote, at a meeting of the RTÉ branch of the union in Dublin. This provides early evidence of serious divisions of opinion among those members of the union involved in broadcasting in Dublin.

In September 1972, as the first anniversary of the directive approached, NUJ members working for RTÉ in Belfast staged a token two-hour work stoppage in protest. Their spokesman, Kevin Myers, issued a statement in which he noted that the chapel's decision to move from private to public protest was because, due to the effects of Section 31, 'our credibility with a considerable section of the Northern Population had been steadily eroded'. Emphasising that the chapel's opposition to the section was 'in no way an endorsement of any political group', he added:

> Many people are now more critical of RTÉ's coverage, often unjustly, than they have ever been. Hostility arising from this lack of acceptance of our effort to be impartial has on occasion made our job more difficult. We feel we have been journalistically compromised, although we freely

November 1972. **60** PPC Minutes, 22 June 1972.

acknowledge that RTÉ management is ultimately not responsible for instigating those acts of censorship which necessarily followed the invocation of Section 31.[61]

This underlined the fact that there were divided opinions among RTÉ journalists, some at least of whom saw no conflict whatsoever between journalistic ethics and support for the government's policy. The NUJ Irish Council discussed the whole matter, and in particular the government's continuing refusal to meet an NUJ deputation, at the beginning of October 1972, as the security situation worsened. There had been lengthy gun battles between the IRA and British forces in July, and special courts were being set up in Northern Ireland in September to try those suspected of terrorist activities. The Union's Irish organiser, Jim Eadie, told the NUJ General Secretary in London, Ken Morgan, that the officers of the Dublin broadcasting branch of the Union had tried unsuccessfully to prevent Myers from going ahead with his protest. The fact that the Dublin broadcasters had subsequently decided to take no action, he told Morgan, was 'interpreted by the Chairman of the [Radio and Television] Branch as indicative of a rather mild feeling on this whole matter.'[62] The Irish Council's secretary, Maurice Hickey, provided further evidence of the Union's difficulties in a frank letter to Morgan a few days later:

> It is a dicey matter for the Union – leaving aside the basic principle of freedom from censorship – and in the final analysis it boils down to how much freedom should be given to the IRA on radio and television. I do not think 'militant' action is required and any 'extremism' would cause a rift among our RTÉ members.[63]

Three days earlier, police had closed down the headquarters of 'Provisional' Sinn Féin in Dublin under a section of the Offences Against the State Act.

Morgan agreed with Hickey's suggestion that the best way forward lay in an approach to the RTÉ Authority, perhaps supplemented by an attempt to 'whip up some public campaign'.[64] The problem about whipping up a public campaign in support of freedom of broadcasting, however, was that it would have to take place in an atmosphere in which not only political, but also public opinion in the Republic was hardening against the IRA, whose campaign in Northern Ireland was responsible for an increasing number of civilian casualties, and which generated fears among mainstream nationalists that the violence would inevitably spill southwards over the Border. In relation to possible industrial action, there was the additional problem that some RTÉ journalists, independently of their

61 NUJ, 1972, copy of Myers's statement. **62** NUJ, 1972, Eadie to Morgan, 3 October 1972. **63** NUJ, 1972, Hickey to Morgan, 9 October 1972. **64** NUJ, 1972, Morgan to Hickey, 11 October 1972.

feelings about the directive and its consequences, were unwilling to take industrial action at the behest of their colleagues in the print media who would, presumably, have remained in work and on full pay. Only a minority of those questioned on the RTÉ Audience Research Panel in October expressed disquiet at the issue of the directive by the government twelve months previously; although two thirds of the respondents regarded RTÉ's coverage of Northern Ireland as balanced, of those who thought it biased, almost all thought it biased in favour of the anti-Unionist point of view.

The final element of the context in which the events of November 1972 were to be played out was the relationship between London and Dublin. Even before assuming office, and while he was still in Opposition, Edward Heath had warned the then Tánaiste, Erskine Childers, at a social function in the Irish Embassy in London in 1969, that he 'took grave exception to the Lynch government's presumption that they had a right to intervene in Northern Irish politics'.[65] The British ambassador in Dublin, Sir John Peck, described one of the 1971 meetings between the two leaders as 'a dialogue of the deaf', [66] and papers released at the National Archives in Dublin in 2002 also revealed that, in the wake of Bloody Sunday, Lynch and Heath had a bitter and unproductive exchange of views on the telephone.

A bad situation was made almost incalculably worse when the two men met on the margin of an EEC summit in Munich on 4 September 1972 (Ireland having ratified the EEC treaties at a referendum on 10 May, was now a member). It had apparently been agreed beforehand that no statement would be issued to the press after the meeting, but the British side reneged on this agreement and briefed journalists to the effect that Heath had given Lynch a dressing-down on the topic of the IRA. Among the accusations rumoured to have been levelled at Lynch by Heath were that there had been 28 cross-border raids in the preceding 28 days; and that 'well-known Provos like Seán Mac Stiofáin are operating openly in the Republic.'[67] Lynch was forced onto the back foot, as all the Irish newspapers ran stories depicting him in defensive and reactive mode. Added to the internal political difficulties he was continuing to experience within Fianna Fáil, this international loss of face would not have done anything to improve his humour, or that of his government.

Fences were mended, to a degree, at another side meeting accompanying an EEC summit on 21 October. Heath, perhaps conscious of the difficulties he had created for a fellow head of government who was now also a colleague on the EEC Council of Ministers, was now beginning to react more positively towards Lynch, and, in the context of his government's work on preparing its projected

65 John Bowman, 'How Jack Lynch helped lay the foundations for power-sharing in the North', *Irish Times*, 1 and 2 January 2003. **66** Ibid. **67** USNA, Pol IRE-UK, XR Pol 13 –10IRE, Department of State telegram, 9 September 1972.

White Paper on Northern Ireland, began to move cautiously towards a willingness to explore Lynch's suggestion that a solution to the North might be explored within the context of European regional policy.[68] Then, on 16 and 17 November, Heath visited Northern Ireland, where he made clear that his government would not support a unilateral declaration of independence by the province, and that its future would be determined by the British Government and parliament alone. Immediately, RTÉ embarked on a process of seeking programme comments from the widest possible range of sources, ranging from loyalists to parliamentarians, on both sides of the Irish Sea. This was the context in which a new summit between Heath and Lynch was arranged, to take place in Downing Street on 24 November 1972.

Almost as Heath flew back to London from Northern Ireland on 17 November, however, a sequence of events was set in train which was to have cataclysmic consequences for RTÉ in general, and for the Authority in particular. RTÉ had, as part of its information-gathering exercise, sent out feelers to the Republican movement looking for its view on events, and in particular on Heath's visit to Northern Ireland. Then, as always, communications between the Republican movement and the media generally took the form of one-way traffic. A request for a comment or an interview could be transmitted, but when – or whether – any statement came back was entirely at the whim of the Provisionals. As Kevin O'Kelly made clear in an interview not long before his death, he had rung Daithi O Conaill, the Vice-President of Sinn Féin, in an attempt to ascertain the IRA's attitude to these developments, on Saturday 18 November, but had not received any response before leaving for home that evening. Then 'the phone call came at midnight out of the blue, and next I found myself interviewing the two men on the couch in my living-room'. This was on the evening of the same day, Saturday 18 November.

The timing of the phone call suggests strongly that the Provisionals, aware of Lynch's forthcoming London summit with Heath, and highly media-conscious, timed their intervention for maximum effect. The more significant of the two men was Seán Mac Stiofáin, born in England of Irish parents, who was generally known to be the commander (or as he was sometimes known, 'Chief of Staff') of the IRA. The second was Joe Cahill, the Republican leader who was also probably at that time a member of the IRA, and whose status as a veteran was most recently exploited at the 2003 of Sinn Féin Ard Fheis, where he gave the party faithful the message that 'The war is over. Now is the time to win the peace.'[69] Unknown to both men, however, they were being shadowed by members of the Garda Siochána. After a lengthy session at O'Kelly's house, the two Republicans left, only to be picked up by the Gardaí almost immediately.[70]

---

68 John Bowman, 'Foundations'.   **69** *Irish Times*, 31 March 2003.   **70** Cahill, apparently Chief of Staff of the IRA in 1968, had been interviewed by Liam Hourican in that year, on a radio programme on which

Some versions of the story suggest that the person the Gardaí had been shadowing was in fact Cahill; that they did not know who the second person was; and - because he refused to answer questions or to speak - that they did not recognise whom they had in custody until lunch-time on Sunday when they heard O'Kelly's radio programme. It is certain that they did not know that the house they had been visiting was a journalist's house until, in the early hours of the morning, they went back to interview its equally surprised occupants, who were unaware that both their nocturnal visitors had just been arrested.

O'Kelly, meanwhile, had been working further into the small hours transcribing the tape and preparing his own script for the broadcast. Although the voices of Sinn Féin leaders who had been presumed also to have an IRA role had been broadcast since the directive, it was evidently thought to be too big a risk to do so on this occasion and, in the event, O'Kelly's broadcast did not feature any of the original taped material, either from O'Connell or Mac Stiofáin.

O'Kelly's broadcast on the *This Week* programme at lunch-time on Sunday 19 November was unusually lengthy, in part probably because of the lack of time for listening, writing and editing, and in part no doubt due to O'Kelly's perception of the importance of the material.[71] It was followed by a live studio discussion with the SDLP's Austin Currie, and the British Tory MP Edward Gardiner, both of whom rejected Mac Stiofáin's views as unrealistic and irrelevant. Within RTÉ itself, the interview had not gone unnoticed. Muiris Mac Conghail, in his capacity as head of current affairs on radio, wrote immediately to his Controller, Roibeárd Ó Faracháin, to express his concern both at its timing and its length. It would, he said, make it virtually impossible to give a clear answer to staff and others who asked him what - in the light of the interview - RTÉ policy now was. He added: 'Ó faid na tuairisce ní thuigim go macánta cad é an difir idir agallamh a chraoladh agus tuairisc fada air a chraoladh chomh fada agus a bhaineann sé le nádur an mheáin.'[72]

The government's view was less nuanced. The first cabinet meeting following the broadcast took place on the following Tuesday, 21 November. At that stage Collins put before the meeting a draft of a letter to the station that concluded: 'It is essential that I should have the Authority's views before 6 p.m. on Thursday next, 23rd November.' At Lynch's suggestion, however, this was strengthened to read: 'It is essential that I should have an indication, in writing, of the action that the Authority proposes to take.' The official note of the meeting added:

---

both Conor Cruise O'Brien and John Kelly TD had defended RTÉ's right to broadcast the tape: Leo Enright, 'Recalling all that doom gloom and boom', *Irish Times*, 10 November 1993. Plainly a lot of water had flowed under the political bridges in the intervening four years. **71** See full text, Appendix 1. **72** RTÉ, Print Archive, Mac Conghail to Ó Faracháin, 21 Samhain 1972.

Informally agreed that, if RTÉ does not take action on the matter to comply with Minister's direction, all members – or all such members as do not publicly disassociate themselves from such a stand by RTÉ – would immediately be removed from office. Certain names mentioned as possible replacements. Ministers to consider matter further before next meeting on 24.11.72.[73]

On Wednesday in the Dáil, Lynch addressed the issue with what one perceptive commentator, Michael Mills, described as 'more than usual fire'.[74] He told the Dáil: 'I am going to insist on taking on all fronts, political, economic and otherwise.'[75] The following day, 23 November, as originally arranged, he left for England, accompanied by the Minister for External Affairs, Dr Patrick Hillery: he had accepted an invitation to speak at the Oxford Union on the evening before his summit with Heath.

The Authority's reply was received by government at 4.30 p.m. on Thursday, 23 November. Running to more than four closely-typed pages, it set out the history of RTÉ policy since the issuing of the original directive, including notes of previous interviews with Mac Stiofáin and others which had not evoked formal government censure or displeasure. The Authority had decided, the letter concluded, that no critical material of the type featured in the O'Kelly interview would in future be broadcast without prior clearance from the Director-General or his deputy, acting in consultation with the Chairman and such other members of the Authority who might be available at short notice, and who would accept responsibility on behalf of the Authority for the decision taken in the particular case. It concluded that 'the editorial decisions taken showed defective judgement in the context of the direction, a conclusion which is being conveyed to all those concerned'. Additionally, in a splendidly oblique reference to the cops-and-robbers scenario early in the morning of 19 November, that 'there were extraneous affairs quite beyond the control of the staff which undoubtedly had an adverse effect on the actual presentation'. As the letter was agreed for despatch to the Minister, the Authority took counsel's opinion, but this – extraordinarily in the light of the advice proffered by Eoin Liston at the meeting after the issue of the directive a year earlier – focused only on the legal issues surrounding the release of the tape of the broadcast.

This had arisen because, as the government met on the morning of 24 November to consider its action in the light of RTÉ's response, Mac Stiofáin was being charged in the Central Criminal Court with membership of an illegal organisation (i.e., the IRA) under the Offences against the State Act, 1939. Kevin O'Kelly had been summoned to appear as a witness.

73 NA, 2003/16/278. 74 *Irish Press*, 23 November 1972 75 Dáil Debates, 22 November 1972.

There was an additional complication. RTÉ had initially declined – in line with its long-standing policy – to hand over the tapes to the Gardaí without a court order. Hardiman, however, had made it clear to the Gardaí that if a court order were forthcoming, the tapes would be handed over immediately. The Gardaí indicated in the Special Criminal Court on the Tuesday morning that the tape would be made available on foot of a court order. The court, however, misinterpreting the RTÉ attitude as one of resistance, ordered that the tape should be produced in the court on the Friday. This is what eventually happened, but the government, no doubt unaware of RTÉ's willingness to cooperate, or misunderstanding the reasons for the delay, was no doubt in an even more volatile frame of mind. And, as if these factors were not enough, Mac Stiofáin had now gone on hunger strike, adding to the urgency, and political intensity, of the situation. Simultaneously, the government was introducing in the Dáil new security legislation under which a person could in certain circumstances be convicted of membership of the IRA if a Garda officer of Chief Superintendent rank gave evidence that he believed this to be the case.

The legal advice given to RTÉ in these circumstances referred only to the question of whether the publication of the Authority's statement might prejudice the Court proceedings. An equally serious issue, however, was the implication, for the Authority itself, of the Minister's clear view that a breach of the directive had occurred.[76] For its part, the Authority may have been encouraged to discount the earlier legal advice because the previous Mac Stiofáin interview, reported by Liam Hourican, had occasioned no Government comment or action. What it undoubtedly failed to give sufficient weight to was the character of the O'Kelly interview, which was far longer and more prominent than Hourican's had been, and the political context in which it had been broadcast. It might also – although this is pure conjecture – have been influenced by its over-familiarity with political culture in Ireland, and by a history of political patronage in which no statutory body appointed by any government had ever been dismissed by a government of the same political colour.

The stakes were now higher than they had ever been. On the RTÉ side, there was a strong feeling that the station should not be pilloried for adopting a technique that had not given rise to objection in the past. Equally, there was a patent desire to tie the Authority more closely into high-risk decisions of this kind that might have to be made in the future. This was the reason for the undertaking that the Director-General would consult with the Chairman and other Authority members who would 'accept responsibility … for the decision.' What is interesting in this context is that the Authority members, a number of whom made no bones about their fundamental loyalty to Fianna Fáil, had to an extent

76 RTÉ Authority, Minutes, 22 November 1971.

gone native, at least insofar as they were prepared not to dissociate themselves from this reply to the government. It was a reply that admitted fault, but stopped short of retributive action (apart from an unspecified reprimand to unidentified individuals) and merely promised to be more careful in future. It was a compromise between a minority of Authority members who wanted more drastic action, and a majority who felt that the matter could be dealt with safely by way of a firm purpose of amendment.[77] It did not advance (although it might have done) a defence on the grounds of precedent, as was evident from its promise of the establishment of different procedures to cover such circumstances in future.

On the Government side, however, the situation had become dramatically clear: battle had been joined, and it was a struggle in which there could be only one victor. The time for fudge was over. If the Taoiseach could not take a scalp with him to London, he would be offered one before he came back. Effectively, there were only two scalps available, either of which might have satisfied the government: that of the Chairman of the Authority, Dónall Ó Móráin , or that of the Director-General, Tom Hardiman. Of the two, Hardiman was the more likely target: he was effectively editor-in-chief as well as Director-General, and could be expected to accept responsibility for individual programming decisions (even though they might not have received his *imprimatur* as such) in a way in which the Chairman might not.

Once the members of the Authority had finalised and despatched its reply, it had in fact – although it undoubtedly did not know it – signed its own death warrant. The Minister for Posts and Telegraphs, Gerry Collins, remained on standby at Government Buildings, but went home at midnight, as the Authority's deliberations had not yet been completed. Interviewed just after the Authority meeting at 3 a.m. the Chairman, Dónall Ó Móráin, said that 'the matter of dismissal does not, I think, arise at all'.[78] Although Lynch had left for London before the letter had been received, contemporary newspaper reports indicate that he was in intermittent telephone contact on this issue with the Tánaiste, George Colley. In the event, the government meeting to consider RTÉ's response on the following day, Friday 24 November, was an unusually long one, lasting from 11 a.m. to 1.40 p.m. and from 3.30 p.m. to 4.55 p.m. The decision taken during this meeting was to dismiss the Authority; it was then communicated to RTÉ and to Lynch in London.

The Heath-Lynch summit concluded with a dinner at 10 Downing Street on the evening of the same day, at which the new-found spirit of co-operation between London and Dublin was much in evidence. The Irish ambassador to London, Donal O'Sullivan, who was present at the meeting, reported later to Iveagh House that when Lynch informed Heath that his government had just dismissed its broadcasting Authority,

77 Private source. **78** *Irish Press*, 23 November 1972.

This led to a general discussion on the problems which governments face with television and radio services. The Prime Minister admitted that he has his problems too and would wish at times to be able to take the same forthright action against the BBC.[79]

Professional discretion no doubt persuaded him to omit Heath's gloss on the affair. In response to Lynch's explanation, which included the detail that the dismissed authority had included no less a person than Phyllis Bean Uí Ceallaigh, the widow of a former President of Ireland, Seán T. Ó Ceallaigh, Heath observed with evident admiration that this would be the equivalent, in Britain, of the Prime Minister dismissing a BBC Board of Governors that included in its membership Queen Elizabeth the Queen Mother. Lynch's return flight to Dublin was delayed by a technical fault, so that the party did not even leave Downing Street until midnight: when they finally arrived in Dublin in the early hours of the following morning, 25 November, they were greeted at an almost deserted Dublin Airport by Mr Collins. Someone who observed the meeting described the atmosphere as one of barely disguised exhilaration, informed by a feeling that – at last – the government's tormentors in RTÉ had been sent a message which was incapable of misinterpretation.[80]

Reaction was widespread but – to a degree – predictable. Again, the newspapers were less forthright than might have been expected. The *Irish Independent* noted that the issues were 'by no means cut and dried' and that the new Authority should be 'above suspicion of being merely a front for the government'.[81] *The Irish Times* initially suggested that RTÉ's professionalism might have been of a higher standard, that it might have been 'running against the government in a blundering fashion' and that, if this had been the case, it had only resulted in further cutting down the flow of information to the public.[82] This criticism was echoed by its columnist John Healy, who warned – in terms which did not conceal his own preferences – that a 'hush-hush Republican grouping in Montrose is determined to have a confrontation with the Government Republican doves of Leinster House.'[83] Two days later, however, the *Irish Times* returned to the issue with a stronger editorial line, and charged that the government was 'tampering with the public's right to know what is going on in its own country and outside', and that locking up Mac Stiofáin on RTÉ evidence was 'discreditable and two-faced.'[84] The most surprising commentary was to be found in the *Irish Press*, which was controlled by the de Valera family and which traditionally supported Fianna Fáil governments. On the one hand, it maintained stoutly that it was 'highly debatable' whether the sacking of the Authority was the right

79 Bowman, 'Foundations'. **80** Private source. **81** Editorial, 25 November 1972. **82** Editorial, 23 November 1972. **83** *Irish Times*, 24 November 1972. **84** *Irish Times*, 25 November 1972. The editorial evidently accepted that O'Kelly's evidence had been the key factor in securing the conviction.

response. On the other, it commented – in words which might have been culled directly from the Mac Stiofáin interview – that

> The RTÉ upheaval is only a symptom of the disease that is eating at this country, and we will not have a cure, an end to the physical force tradition until our two communities are living at peace, under the umbrella of a declaration to withdraw the IRA's recruiting agent, the British Army, from Ireland.[85]

The fall-out elsewhere was more predictable, including protests by the NUJ and others, but the exchange of letters between Lynch and some members of the Authority he had dismissed indicated differences of opinion within RTÉ, and between the Authority and some RTÉ staff, which were to become more evident later. In particular, Stephen Barrett, a political opponent (he had been a Fine Gael TD representing Cork) but personal friend of Jack Lynch, assured Lynch that

> while I was on the Authority I did everything possible to ensure that elements I considered dangerous would be made realise that the Authority was the Authority. I am quite certain that we had made an impact on the elements in question over recent years. The forces we were dealing with were characteristically elusive and it was often quite difficult to put your finger on the offending spot. This, in fact, was quite the case up to the very end.[86]

Lynch replied, with characteristic under-statement, that he appreciated 'the difficulties that hindered you'.[87] The file also contains a letter in Irish, signed 'Liam O Murchú (RTÉ)' which, although it does not specifically refer to the sacking of the Authority, assured Lynch of his support: 'Tuigeann tromfach mór na gnáth-dhaoine na deacrachtaí atá agat agus tuigeann siad freisin, is dóigh liom, nach bhfuil aon bealach eile gan iad a láimhseáil ach na bealaí atá á nglacadh agat.'

The hubbub grew as the Mac Stiofáin case in the Special Criminal Court drew to its conclusion. Effectively, one of the main pieces of evidence against Mac Stiofáin was the tape of his original interview with O'Kelly. Although Mac Stiofáin refused to recognise the court, he intervened from time to time, complaining on one occasion – understandably in the circumstances – that 'they arrest me first, then they look around for evidence'.[88]

---

85 Editorial, 25 November 1972. **86** NA, 2003/16/278, Barrett to Lynch, 11 December 1972. **87** Ibid., Lynch to Barrett, 14 December 1972. **88** *Irish Press*, 22 November 1972.

O'Kelly, in his broadcast the previous Sunday, had said: 'Earlier today I talked to Seán Mac Stiofáin'[89] He now gave evidence to the Court in which he agreed that 'this tape recording is an accurate and authentic document in so much as I am satisfied that what is made on it is an interview with Seán Mac Stiofáin.'[90] He was then asked if he had recorded the interview, and replied, 'Yes.' The following question, however, gave him difficulties, as he said that he could not answer it because of problems it raised in relation to journalistic ethics. The difficult part of the question appears to have been the parenthesis uttered by prosecuting counsel, Gerard Buchanan, who was attempting to generate additional evidence as to the authenticity of the tape, and asked O'Kelly what had happened to the tape *'from the time that you recorded the interview, in the presence, presumably, of the man you were interviewing'.*[91] After refusing to answer this question, and several variants of it, O'Kelly was sentenced to three months in jail for contempt of court. He appealed against the severity of the sentence, and was released on bail pending the appeal. Although O'Kelly's stance evoked a considerable amount of sympathy from his fellow-journalists, Mac Stiofáin's conviction was eventually obtained on Garda evidence. NUJ members in RTÉ promptly went on a 48–hour strike in protest against O'Kelly's conviction, and were supported on this occasion by their colleagues in the print media, who also staged a stoppage. Producers in RTÉ also met in protest – the first time, apparently, that this had happened. The NUJ stoppage evoked some public criticism, illustrating the difficulty facing that union in that its most effective form of protest also deprived the public of a service which those who supported media freedom believed should be maintained. It was one of only two industrial stoppages by Dublin NUJ members on this issue, although the directive was to remain in force in one form or another for a further two decades.[92]

The review of the evidence at O'Kelly's appeal some time later revealed what the Court of Appeal, in the person of Mr Justice Brian Walsh, described as 'a considerable amount of confusion in Mr O'Kelly's mind on this matter.'[93] O'Kelly had agreed that the tape concerned – the actual tape on which he had recorded the interview as the basis for his own, scripted broadcast on *This Week* - was 'an accurate, an authentic document in as much as I am satisfied that the remarks on it by Mr Seán Mac Stiofáin are authentic'. He had, however, refused to answer the following question from prosecuting counsel, Mr Buchanan: 'Now, who was that interview that was recorded on the tape with?' In spite of Buchanan's belated attempts to persuade the judge that O'Kelly had to all intents and purposes answered the question in essence, Mr Justice Griffin held that he had not, and was therefore in contempt. A somewhat puzzled Justice Brian

---

89 See Appendix 2.   90 *Irish Press*, 27 November.   91 *Irish Press*, 27 November 1972. Emphasis added.
92 Cf. John Horgan, 'Journalists and censorship: a case history of the NUJ in Ireland and the broadcasting ban 1971–94' (2002), pp. 377–92.   93 *Irish Law Times*, Reports, *In re O'Kelly* (1974) 108 ILTR 97.

Walsh reduced O'Kelly's penalty from imprisonment to a fine because his refusal to answer the question 'while perhaps adding some little extra difficulty to the case, did not effectively impede the presentation of the prosecution's case'. He nonetheless added, as part of a judgement which emphasised that journalists could not consider themselves to be above the law, that

> The interview in question was one made for public broadcast and one of the essential features of the publication was the fact that the identity of the person interviewed was Mr Seán Mac Stiofáin. In fact, the whole value of the publication of the interview from Mr O'Kelly's point of view depended upon the fact that the persons to whom the interview would be published would be made aware that the person interviewed was Mr Seán Mac Stiofáin. Mr O'Kelly's references to the difficulties which might be placed in the way of promoting the public good by fostering the free exchange of public opinion appears to add further confusion to the matter because the object of the interview was the publication of it.[94]

In the intervening years, it has been obvious from judicial actions in a number of cases that judges will require journalists to disclose confidential sources only as a last resort; there have also been a number of developments in British and European law which extend a measure of protection to journalistic sources in certain circumstances. In 1972, however, the letter of the law prevailed, and, as Mr Justice Walsh noted, the exact grounds on which Kevin O'Kelly had made his stand were, and remained, unclear. Ironically, the subsequent passage of the new security legislation created a situation in which quite a few Republicans were convicted of IRA membership on the evidence of a Chief Superintendent's opinion that they were members. This remained the case for as long as republicans refused to recognise the courts. It eventually led, however, to a change in Republican policy, and after that any defendant who challenged, on oath, a Chief Superintendent's uncorroborated evidence was generally, in the absence of other relevant evidence, given the benefit of the doubt by the Court and acquitted.

The political temperature increased with the explosion of two bombs in the centre of Dublin on 1 December 1972, killing two people and injuring 127 others. Although the perpetrators were undoubtedly not Republican sympathisers, the time was not – to put it mildly – propitious for a campaign in support of loosening restrictions on reporting about para-military organisations. A new RTÉ Authority had been appointed, and Collins told its first meeting that he was confident that it would ensure that his direction would be observed in the future. Almost immediately, the new Authority issued guidelines to its staff on the interpretation of the directive: sound recordings or sound on film were ruled

94 Ibid.   95 *RTÉ Guide*, 20 December 1972; *Irish Independent*, 22 December 1972.

out, even factual material could be excised from reports at the discretion of the Head of News, and a detailed reference upwards system was instituted. As it happened, the new system did not differ markedly – except perhaps in the possible excision of factual material, and in a number of other points of detail – from the policy which had been endorsed by its dismissed predecessor just before it left office.[95] The inescapable implication of this is that government had not been looking for new structures, but for executive action by the Authority.

In the world of *realpolitik*, this meant a sacking. If the Authority failed to recognise this at the time, it was being singularly unimaginative. If it did recognise the government letter for what it was, but decided to ignore the implied threat in the belief that it was probably a bluff, it miscalculated. The most favourable interpretation – as far as the Authority was concerned – came in a lecture by the former Deputy Director-General, John Irvine, in 1976, who believed that the Authority 'could conceivably have saved itself at the expense of senior staff, but refused to do so.'[96] This generously implies that the Authority was aware of, and accepted, the risk that it was taking, but at this remove in time such an analysis is difficult, if not impossible, to confirm. It seems to be more likely that the Authority simply did not envisage the prospect that it would be sacked by the very government which had appointed them, and of which some of them were passionate supporters. Such things did not happen in Irish politics.

As things turned out, the Authority got the worst of both worlds: it had apologised – after a fashion – and was still sacked. Open defiance might have been a more courageous response, and indeed could have been defended on the grounds that the government had tolerated similar treatment of Mac Stiofáin earlier in the year. This, however, was an option which was to all intents and purposes precluded by the political views of some prominent members of the Authority itself. And the whole episode served notice on RTÉ in particular that the rules of the game were now being interpreted by government in a significantly different way. The same reality was expressed more forcefully by Lynch in a private conversation he had at this time with the author and broadcaster, Ulick O'Connor, who had also spoken at the Oxford Union debate. When O'Connor suggested that the decision did not say much for Lynch's views on freedom of speech, and that the Taoiseach would rue his decision, Lynch looked at him with a grin:

'Fuck them,' he said.[97]

---

96 John A. Irvine, 'Broadcasting and the public trust', typescript made available by the author.   97 Ulick O'Connor, *The Ulick O'Connor diaries, 1970–81* (2001), p. 126. O'Connor, however, places the Oxford Union debate on 24 November (it took place on 23 November).

CHAPTER 5

New brooms, new laws

The dismissal of the Authority evoked the protests which the Government had foreseen: the protests, in turn, were met with the government hard line embodied in Lynch's riposte. In private, as it happened, Lynch had become less abrasive. He was conscious of the political fall-out from the government's decision, and also of the impending election – it would take place in February 1973, and the government's sacking of the Authority inevitably influenced some elements of public opinion during the campaign. This, at any rate, helps to explain an apparently casual aside he made to Hardiman on his first visit to RTÉ after the sacking of the Authority: 'Don't do anything rash'. This plainly expressed an underlying concern on his part that the argument about the dismissal of the Authority should be allowed to die down and not be given added momentum by any high profile protest resignations.

In the Dáil, a number of speakers took the opportunity afforded by a debate on an amendment to the Offences against the State Acts to voice their criticism of the government on the issue, amid widespread allegations of censorship. Dr Conor Cruise O'Brien, for example, argued that the dismissal of the Authority was a 'most brutal intrusion' by the state on the legitimate autonomy of broadcasting and television. His party believed, he said, that a real threat to the State existed, but that the existence of this threat was being used not to defend democratic institutions but to erode them. Broadcasting, parliament and the press were, he said, one of the three pillars of democracy.[1]

An exception to the tone of this general chorus of disapproval was the former Minister, Neil Blaney, whose view of RTÉ's activities in relation to Northern Ireland was dramatically different from that of the Government of which he had up to quite recently been a member. The station, he said, was 'banning everything that is republican while reporting everything that is Unionist'. He went on:

> The blame cannot be placed on the heads of the newscasters because this situation has arisen by reason of the orders of the Government that were submitted to the authority and passed on to the operators of the service.

---

1 Quoted in Donall Ó Moráin, 'The Irish experience', p. 19.   **2** Dáil Debates, 1 December 1972.

Yet, that same authority, who did their work as instructed by the Minister, have been given the sack, but, worse than that, we are told that they ignored the dictates of the Government on the suppression of republican views. Had I been in a position to do so, I would have fired them six months ago because of their suppression of republican views. Therefore, I agree with the Government in their sacking of the authority, but my reasons are the reverse of theirs.[2]

The National Union of Journalists began to organise a campaign against Section 31 which would last for twenty-two fruitless years, and was generally marked by a protest outside the Dáil when the directive was renewed in January of each year after 1975. Kevin Myers, of RTÉ's Belfast staff, went further, resigning completely from the station. Implying that the situation created by the directive would itself have been enough ultimately to lead to his resignation, he maintained that the activities and intentions of illegal organisations were 'proper areas of investigation for journalists in Ireland today'. He added: 'I feel I cannot be associated with a news service which has been deprived of that freedom which is fundamental to the profession of journalism.'[3] Another journalist, John Feeney, was to resign from 7 *Days* in March of the following year, charging that 'a mood of defeat and caution has spread in the station'.[4]

The NUJ campaign took on an extra dimension when the union organised a march to the Dáil, this time to campaign protest against the proposed amendments to the OAS Acts which would, they argued, have the effect of further interfering with freedom of expression. However, RTÉ's political correspondent, Joe Fahy, who was one of the Union's most senior members, had a strongly contrary view which he now expressed in private correspondence to the Union's general secretary and copied to the Union's senior officials in Ireland. In his view, the Union had simply been hi-jacked for a political campaign, leading to 'the direct involvement of the NUJ in what is a political issue of the most fundamental kind – namely, the right of a democratically-elected government to govern in the national interest'.

He was highly critical of the tactics of union activists, suggesting that they were trying to set themselves above the law, and maintained that many NUJ members had not even been informed of the meeting of Dublin print journalists which decided on a work stoppage:

---

3 *Irish Times*, 29 and 30 November, 1972. Twenty years later, Myers argued that the reason for his resignation had been because of the dismissal of the Authority, but also that 'the reasons for the enactment of Section 31 were good reasons, because something had to be done to control the freedom of access of terrorist organisations to RTÉ in particular. But it should have been done by the station and by the Authority, not by the government'. *RTÉ1: 40 years of news*, 20 December 2002. 4 *Irish Times*, 22 March 1973. Feeney became a print journalist, and was working for the *Evening Herald* when he died in an air crash in November 1984.

Last October, a cleverly manipulated press campaign suggested that the Dublin Radio branch was going to have a one-day strike on the anniversary of the Section 31 directive, and that all journalists in RTÉ were up in arms against this restriction. When the strike motion had to be withdrawn, because its sponsors quickly became aware that it would not receive a majority, that fact was not considered worthy to be reported in the same public press, while distorted reports appeared in one magazine and, I am sad to say, in *The Journalist.* I have already told my Branch colleagues that I will not have my political attitudes or action determined for me by any Union [...] I will not support any direct challenge to the Government of Ireland on this issue, and I believe if there is one, it is doomed to failure. It will have absolutely no public support, and in my view will result in a prolonged shutdown of RTÉ, before the whole station is returned to direct Government control.

The restrictions had been imposed in part, he argued, because 'the broadcasting media were abused in favour of illegal groups' and because 'the men of violence have been portrayed on RTÉ as if they were the elected leaders of the Irish people.' He asked: 'Can it be stated with certainty that all of this has not had some effect, particularly on younger people, in regard to recruitment for illegal organisations, or the gaining of sympathy?'[5]

His main point was echoed by the NUJ Irish organiser, Jim Eadie, a fortnight later. 'I think that the last thing in the world that is needed in Ireland at the present time is a campaign by the NUJ on this issue, even if we are satisfied that legitimate journalism is being restricted', he wrote to Morgan. 'The Union cannot afford the luxury of looking at this problem of censorship in isolation from the general political and indeed military situation in this country.'[6] When the union's National Executive Council met a few days later, he repeated these views in person,[7] and the NEC's considered view was that it would be unwise to second-guess the complicated Irish situation or ignore the advice of their colleagues who were closer to the issue on the ground. The political tensions involved can be gauged from the fact that, only three days earlier, the IRA Chief of Staff, who had been one of those interviewed by O'Kelly and who had subsequently been imprisoned, had just finished a 58-day hunger strike which had occasioned substantial controversy.

One of the unknown – at the time – casualties of these events was a document which had been in the course of preparation by the dismissed Authority. Entitled 'A View of Irish Broadcasting', it would have been published during that Authority's brief period of office, but for the fact that it was felt that the time was

5 Horgan, 'Journalists and censorship', pp. 382–3.   6 NUJ, 1973, Eadie to Morgan, 16 January 1973.   7 NUJ, 1973, National Executive Committee, Minutes, 19/20 January 1973.

not opportune because of the issuing of the directive in 1971. One of its crucial passages, noted by Dónall Ó Móráin many years later, observed:

> The preservation of the status quo is not necessarily always in the public interest: neither is the public interest necessarily always in complete harmony with every action or lack of action by government. A democratic society assumes that its broadcasting system should serve the public interest. It requires a great deal of freedom to discharge this responsibility. Responsibility must, however, always be exercised with a proper sense of public purpose, notwithstanding sectional views and pressures seeking preferential expression.[8]

Had this been published at the time, it would at least have provided that Authority with an epitaph. National political events, however, were now achieving a momentum of their own. The Dáil was dissolved, for reasons unconnected with the broadcasting controversy, on 5 February 1973, and a general election was held on 28 February. After sixteen years of uninterrupted single-party Fianna Fáil government, a coalition composed of Fine Gael and Labour took office: the new Minister for Posts and Telegraphs was Dr Conor Cruise O'Brien. Television played a greater role in this election than it had in any preceding contest, not least because of the introduction, for the first time (and in a bid at emulating the BBC) of a computer to the *7 Days* election studio. The computer programme, however, had been written by a British technician who had not been informed of the differences between proportional representation and the UK electoral system, and was totally unable to cope. In the studio on the evening of 1 March the main presenter, Brian Farrell, quoted its prediction to the programme's resident political reporter, Ted Nealon, and asked him what he thought of it. Nealon, who was hot-wired with details of knowledge of the Irish electoral system and personalities to a degree that no computer could possibly match, expressed his view of the machine briefly and pungently and – within half an hour – delivered a forecast which was so palpably better than anything the computer could offer that the studio all but turned it off.

At a March 1973 meeting with a deputation from the union, O'Brien undertook to urge the RTÉ authority to review its guidelines, and invited the NUJ to make written representations to him on possible alterations to Section 31 of the Act.[9] The importance of this invitation was underlined by Eadie in a letter to Morgan: 'clearly having missed the boat once before we must not miss it again'[10] but, unknown to the senior officials involved, the whole initiative was about to founder.

---

8 Quoted in Ó Móráin, 'Experience', p. 21.   **9** NUJ 1973, NEC Minutes, 29/30 March 1973.   **10** NUJ 1973, Eadie to Morgan, 27 March 1973.

By 10 April, the NEC and the negotiators on behalf of the NUJ's Irish Council had adopted proposals to replace the offending sections of the Act, but the following day, according to a note from Morgan for the information of the NEC, 'to the surprise of its chairman, vice-chairman and secretary, the branch decided to ask that the union had no further discussions with Dr O'Brien about the re-drafting of the Act and that he should not be supplied with a copy of our suggested amendments to the [RTÉ Authority] guidelines.'[11] Relations deteriorated further at the union's AGM, held in Co. Wexford, when an emergency resolution was passed criticising O'Brien, and delegates voted to refuse to allow the Minister permission to address the meeting and take part in a question and answer session. Seven years later O'Brien, no longer a Minister, was an invited guest at the annual dinner of the union's Irish broadcasting branch, and told his audience cheerfully: 'I thought at that time, and I still think, that to refuse a hearing to someone you have attacked is a funny way of defending freedom of speech.'[12]

O'Brien had inherited not only the Section 31 controversy, but an agenda of matters relating to broadcasting on which decisions would need to be taken, many of them directly impacting on news and current affairs. The previous government had established a Broadcasting Review Commission to re-evaluate the broadcasting service after RTÉ's first decade; pressure was growing in the single-channel areas (effectively all the areas outside the east coast and a strip along the Border) for choice in broadcasting; and the provision of a colour service was also being mooted. All this was happening in which the gap between revenue and expenditure in broadcasting was narrowing. Although television set ownership (and the related license fee income) grew at an average rate of 12% a year between 1961 and 1977, the latter part of this period showed the rate of increase tapering off sharply as demand for sets approached satiety: by late 1977 some 83% of all homes had television.[13] The oil price shocks to the global economy in the mid-1970s had an immense effect on Irish economic performance indicators, and the decline in advertising, which was of course one of these effects, was only partly compensated for by licence fee increases in 1970, 1971,1973, 1974, 1976 and 1977. From 1974–5, when a deficit of some £350,000 was recorded, the station's finances were becoming increasingly lop-sided, with dependence on a violently fluctuating advertising market the key variable. The 1976 annual accounts showed that long-term indebtedness was the equivalent of 80% of total assets.[14]

Driven in part by the successes of domestic programming, and by the need to respond to the demand from the single-channel area, staffing was also increasing, not least in programming areas. Staff numbers generally grew by 132%

---

11 NUJ 1973, Morgan to NEC, 16 April 1974. **12** *Irish Times*, 5 March 1981. **13** Desmond Fisher, *Broadcasting in Ireland*, p. 58. **14** Ibid., p. 97.

between 1962 and 1977; in the ten years to 1977, the largest percentage growth was in news (67%).[15] This, in turn, reflected the new-found confidence in news under McGuinness: an element of competition had already been introduced since 1968 to the 'one-station nation'[16] with the launch of the radio News Features area, and plans were being laid to similarly revitalise television.

That confidence, in turn, had led to a decision within the News Division to commission a special report on that division's performance. The report, by Mike Burns (at that time in charge of the 1.30 p.m. radio bulletin) and a sub-editor, Eddie Liston, was nothing if not critical. It cast aspersions on – among other things – the way in which reporters dressed and spoke: they dressed badly, wore shaggy jackets, kept their hands in their pockets, and had poor diction. Foreign news was covered in a slap-dash, meaningless way. The provinces were largely ignored. There was a lack of discipline, rehearsal and pride. The newsreader was used merely as a way of disguising television's failure to give visual treatment to all stories. None of this, however, created as much of a stir as the observation that news should also include analysis, background explanation, and studio should in future incorporate 'an element of news-creation.'[17]

This report evoked some criticism from the NUJ, which issued a statement critical of both McGuinness and Fisher,[18] but the criticisms it contained, and others, surfaced again in a more significant context in the discussions and report of the Broadcasting Review Committee.[19] That Committee devoted a considerable amount of its time and energy to examining RTÉ's news output, and it is difficult in retrospect to avoid the impression that this was broadly in line with the government's agenda, even though the Review Body had been appointed under a government of a different political hue. It concurred with the Burns/Liston report in that it expressed the view that RTÉ did not cater adequately for the provinces, and that news presentation should be more attractive.

More serious and fundamental, however, was its conclusion that, almost a decade after its establishment, RTÉ still needed to exercise more care in the 'recruitment, appointment, training and supervision of staff'. This was a generalised and implicit criticism of the professional standards of the majority of RTÉ staff, and by extension of management. The plain inference is that the criticism was directed at news and the other programme output areas. Even more seriously, it suggested that the station was falling short of required standards in relation to impartiality and objectivity. To buttress its claims in this regard, it effectively endorsed many of the criticisms of the Tribunal of Inquiry into the 1969 *7 Days* programme on money-lending, whose report it believed had had 'beneficial results'. It also expressed concern at complaints from the Department of

15 Ibid., p. 82.   **16** I owe this phrase to Mike Burns.   **17** *Irish Times*, 27 May 1971.   **18** PPC Minutes, 8 June 1971.   **19** Broadcasting Review Committee, *Report 1974*, pp. 92–7. The Report was published on 15 May 1974.

Labour, particularly about 7 *Days*, which was alleged to present its material in a 'highly dramatic form', and to stress negative matters The Department had also complained that there were 'too few, if any, features on the measures, involving large sums of money, taken by the government to ameliorate hardship.'

Its most tart criticism, however, was reserved for the reporting of Northern Ireland. Although accepting that much of the reporting and commentary in the previous two years [i.e. since the issuing of the directive, although this was not mentioned] had been well balanced, the Commission said that it could not regard RTÉ's treatment of this area since 1968 'as having conformed to an adequate standard of objectivity and impartiality'. Its coverage had, on the contrary, exemplified all the dangers of the medium: lack of detail, bias, distortion, sensationalism, the crowding out of moderate by extreme opinions and the temptation to select items for television news for their visual excitement, or because film of them was available, rather than because of their real news value.[20] Ironically, and unhappily in view of the Report's conclusions, a planned session at which members of the Committee would have heard evidence in private from Jim McGuinness had to be abandoned when the building in which the Committee was meeting had to be evacuated because of a bomb scare. As they stood together on the pavement outside, the Chairman, Mr Justice Murnaghan, asked McGuinness: 'Did I ever send you to jail?' McGuinness replied, with deceptive mildness: "No, not yet." [21]

The day the report was published, a lengthy internal memorandum from Jim McGuinness was circulated to newsroom staff and others. It rejected the Committee's assertions and findings, particularly the accusations of bias or partiality, in the vivid, muscular language that was the hallmark of its author.[22] It accused the committee of suggesting that RTÉ journalists had been, 'for a protracted and vital period, acting in a professionally reprehensible manner'; it noted that the Committee had changed its mind, but had not given any reasons for such a change; it pointed out that the Committee had never mentioned the problems associated with the outbreak of violence in Northern Ireland since 1968, and had never held any of its meetings there; and it observed that the Committee had failed to mention the 1971 directive from the government.

During the period under review, McGuinness maintained, the station had been criticised on numerous, and generally self-cancelling grounds. It had been criticised for being too pro-Catholic or for being a lackey of Dr Paisley; for being pro-IRA and anti-IRA; for giving too much about Northern Ireland, and too little about it; for being more pro-Provisional IRA than pro-Official IRA; and it had been accused of being pro-SDLP, pro-Dr Paisley, pro-Mr Harry West and pro-Mr Bill Craig. McGuinness observed that most of the criticism

20 Ibid., paras 15.4 and 15.9.   **21** Private source.   **22** Thanks to one of the unfailing mysteries of journalism, this memorandum found its way, in its entirety, into the *Irish Times* of 16 May 1976.

had come from people in the Republic – mostly from people who accused RTÉ of improperly favouring those of whom they disapproved. In the North, the criticism came from a different source – from the Catholic ghettoes, from Catholic rural areas, or from people sympathetic to Irish nationalism or Irish unity.

> This criticism caused us concern, not because we thought it justified, but because we understood why it was made. It sometimes came from people of fairness and perception who were trying to keep the peace in the Catholic ghettoes and sustain people who were the daily victims of violence. They wanted us to be their allies even if this meant, or so it seemed to us, tacitly suspending correct journalistic standards. For our part we believed that the greatest aid and comfort we could bring all the people was, as far as possible, to report accurately and truthfully all that happened.

This was in many ways an *apologia pro vita sua*. Although the two events were unconnected, McGuinness had asked to be relieved of his responsibilities as Head of News, and his transfer to a post with responsibility for organising and providing source material for broadcasting and archival purposes had been announced just before the Committee's report was published.[23] He was to be succeeded on 10 June 1974 by another Northerner, Wesley Boyd.[24]

Some years later Liam Hourican, who was still Northern Correspondent at the time of McGuinness's move, described his relationship with the Head of News as near to being the ideal relationship between a journalist and his editor. ' "Balance" would be an anaemic word for the qualities he sought; he wished for nothing less than to have the full complexity of Northern realities rendered truthfully in every broadcast we produced.'[25] The tenor of that relationship, as it happened, was evident in the extraordinary freedom given to Hourican to present, on 20 March 1973, an extended television essay entitled 'An Irish Dimension' which gave the journalist a rare freedom not only to present, but to interpret, that complex reality for RTÉ audiences. The loyalty felt by many of McGuinness's staff was also expressed by Hourican's predecessor, Martin Wallace, who told McGuinness that he had 'never worked with another journalist for whose editorial judgement, integrity and absolute impartiality I have a higher regard'.[26]

---

23 *Irish Times*, 6 April 1974. **24** Boyd was Diplomatic Correspondent of the *Irish Times*, and a former journalist with, and London Editor of, the now defunct Unionist paper, the *Northern Whig*. He had joined RTÉ in 1969 as Duty Editor in the newsroom. **25** McGuinness papers, Hourican to McGuinness, 5 January 1988. Hourican, who was promoted to the new position of Diplomatic Correspondent in September 1974, later served as press officer to Garret Fitzgerald and in the European Commission. He died in 1993. He was replaced in Belfast by John O'Callaghan in October 1974. In April of the same year another member of the station's Belfast staff, Frank Dunlop, gave in his notice prior to taking up a new appointment as press officer for Fianna Fáil. **26** Ibid., Wallace to McGuinness, 25 January 1988.

McGuinness had suffered intermittently from ill-health. In addition, the strain of eight years in one of the most senior management positions in the station undoubtedly suggested that it was time for a change of direction. Ironically, and quite inappropriately, his decision to opt for a transfer preceded, by a matter of only a few weeks, the most extraordinary incident to arise in the context of the 1971 directive, one that could not possibly have been foreseen, and one that directly involved the newsroom. On 25 June Dr Rose Dugdale was convicted on serious charges in connection with the IRA, and made a controversial statement from the dock. The editor of the day in the RTÉ newsroom came to the conclusion that if RTÉ were it to carry a report of some of Dr Dugdale's remarks, it would be in breach of the directive. This resulted in the RTÉ reporter present in the court, Eddie Barrett, refusing to broadcast the item into the bulletin. The NUJ, which was at this time at loggerheads with the Minister, Dr O'Brien, about a possible re-wording of Section 31, then issued a statement claiming that the incident was an extension of censorship to court reporting, and saying that they would refuse to report the courts until RTÉ reversed its decision.

What was at issue was whether the directive actually extended to court proceedings. A common-sense attitude would suggest that court proceedings, which were in any case privileged, would fall outside the scope of the directive – and indeed a case could be made that the failure to report statements by a defendant in a criminal trial might be a breach of the impartiality requirements imposed on RTÉ under the 1960 Broadcasting Act. Both McGuinness and the Deputy Director-General, John Irvine, however, maintained that while RTÉ should be reluctant to apply the directive to material arising from court cases, 'it had to reserve the right to apply [the directive] to material from any source.'[27] It was only eighteen months since the Authority had been sacked because it had failed to repudiate unequivocally a liberal interpretation by staff of the directive: the chilling effect was still very evident.

RTÉ got legal advice which tended to support the decision of the executives concerned, and the row with the NUJ was defused. Almost immediately, however, the same problem reappeared, but in quite a different guise. This was in relation to a 7 *Days* programme on 21 June which featured a three-day conference of certain Protestant organisations in Northern Ireland with para-military connections. Ruairi Brugha TD, the Fianna Fáil opposition spokesman on broadcasting, had put down a Dáil question asking whether this broadcast had contravened the directive. O'Brien, who had consulted with the Chairman of the Authority and the Deputy Director-General, had assured Brugha that in his opinion the directive had been observed, and that he was sure that the Author-

27 PPC Minutes, 27 June 1974.

ity exercised great care in dealing with matters relating to violence. In private, O'Brien was scathing, not about the Authority but about RTÉ newsroom staff who, he told the Authority chairman, had an 'extremely peculiar concept of balance', and were reporting Northern Ireland in ways which would 'help to fan the flames of sectarian civil war'. In a comment which would have left the RTÉ Chairman in no doubt as to his views about where reponsibility for this lay, he urged Ó Móráin to ensure that

> The control of RTÉ news ... be placed in the hands of someone with a genuinely responsible approach who will not allow a spurious concept of journalistic ethics to be used to inject propaganda in favour of violence into the coverage of the news.[28]

The problem, in effect, was that the guide-lines which had been adopted by the Authority to cover the implementation of the directive had – like the directive itself – been necessarily vague in certain respects, because the government had not specified any organisations. This had been a deliberate decision, in the light of the fact that conditions in the North changed rapidly, and in order to avoid making unnecessary difficulties for Northern staff. Liam Hourican, still Northern Ireland correspondent, argued strongly that spokesmen for many of these organisations should be interviewed: he was 'of the view that they were largely fascist and that this should be made evident as part of RTÉ's obligation to present information as fully and accurately as it could.'[29] A Hourican interview with Andy Tyrie of the UDA in the news at 1.30 on 21 July created another *frisson* at PPC level.

Current Affairs was at this stage under the editorship of Gerry Murray. As 7 *Days*, produced by Seán Ó Mórdha (who was also producing *Féach*) and Pat O'Connor, now went out on three days a week, he assured viewers that in spite of growing anxiety about television's power and influence, impartiality was the goal.

> As long as controversy is not contrived, it is, in my view, not only legitimate to have it broadcast, but it is also a prerequisite for worthy communication, provided there is a balance of opinions and that freedom of speech does not mean freedom to fool people.[30]

The main news bulletin had lengthened and gone to 6.01, and the newsroom, as well as giving factual information, was striving to 'interpret and explain the complexities of events.'[31]

---

28 O'Brien to Dónall Ó Móráin, Chairman, RTÉ Authority, 18 July 1973. NA 2004/21/69. Documents for the later years of Dr O'Brien's tenure of office are still restricted by the 30–year rule. 29 PPC Minutes, 4 July 1974. 30 Gerry Murray, 'A question of balance', *RTÉ Guide*, 13 September 1974. 31 Wesley Boyd, 'News about news', *RTÉ Guide*, 13 September 1974.

This dilemma was partly responsible for the development and promulgation of a new directive which was issued by Dr O'Brien in October 1976 to replace the one originally promulgated in 1971, and which went into considerable detail in identifying organisations whose members should not be interviewed on RTÉ.

As the business of teasing out the implications of the new directive continued, a number of structural changes were also in train, and were to involve a substantial re-organisation of the way in which news and current affairs had operated since their amalgamation in 1968. RTÉ management had, under pressure from the unions (notably the Workers' Union of Ireland, which represented the producer grades) agreed to move 7 *Days* out of News and back into the Programmes Division. In late summer of 1973 this decision was apparently reversed, leading to fresh opposition from the WUI and a period of uncertainty, while various compromise solutions were explored.

In the summer of the same year, the RTÉ Authority was replaced. The new Chairman, Dónall Ó Móráin, had been chairman of the Authority that suffered dismissal in 1972: his reinstatement was, among other things, a calculated rebuff to the preceding Fianna Fáil government. One of the tasks that the new Authority inherited was to oversee the reorganisation process in News and Current Affairs that had been instituted by its predecessor in the wake of the Authority's dismissal. This involved dealing with the still evident discontent among some current affairs programme makers at their extended exile in the News Division, and at the apparent reversal of the earlier decision to restore a degree of autonomy to them. The outcome of this fresh consideration of the problem was essentially a compromise, involving the creation of a new structure, to be known as the Current Affairs Grouping. Although not a Division (the traditional line-management model in RTÉ at the time) it would have quasi-divisional status, with its own budget, establishment, and promotional opportunities. Created to avoid the duplication and rivalry that had been to some extent generated by the previous amalgamation, it would be 'firmly rooted in the programme-making ethos which has been successfully developed in RTÉ in the Programmes Division and in the News Features area.'[32]

McGuinness's understanding of what was proposed, however, was different; and, believing that the new arrangement would involve a take-over of news division broadcasting opportunities by the Programmes Division, argued instead that the new 'grouping' should be constituted as a full Current Affairs Division. A subsidiary argument was also in progress, relating to the issue of whether current affairs on radio should be separate from current affairs on television, or whether both should emanate from the same control grouping. In the event, one

---

32 Desmond Fisher papers: memorandum of conversation between Fisher and Hardiman on 2 August 1973, dated 21 August 1973.

editor was appointed with overall responsibility for radio, another for television, and each became answerable to Fisher who was, in turn, reporting to Irvine.

McGuinness's objections were, in effect, overruled, or his apprehensions allayed, and the new grouping was created, with Desmond Fisher appointed as its head with effect from 6 October 1973. *7 Days*, together with *Féach*, *Tangents*, *Involvement*, *Opinion*, and the current affairs element in *Here and Now* and the *News at 1.30* were all to be transferred to the new grouping and the whole was put under the overall control of the Deputy Director-General, John Irvine.[33] Later additions included *This Week* (excluding the preliminary news bulletin), *World Report*, *Dáil Report*, *Gaeliris*, and *Enterprise*. As finally constituted, the new arrangement to some extent contained the seeds of its eventual dissolution. It did not have full divisional structure; its head, Desmond Fisher, although he had a budget of sorts, was not given dedicated producer/directors, and had to apply to the Controllers of Radio and TV Programming[34] for the assignment of staff at this level; it was unable to develop a meaningful corporate identity, partly because it had no specific physical location; and lines of communication – and therefore of control – were weak because of the difficulty of establishing, and monitoring, appropriate reporting arrangements across a wide variety of programmes in which previous practices had differed and to which varying degrees of freedom had in the past been accorded. It was, in effect, something of a hydra. Sooner or later, someone would get bitten.

The wide range of the programmes to be transferred into the new quasi-division underlines the difficulty of coming up with any definition of current affairs broadcasting which holds good for all periods of the station's existence. Indeed, at this time even some religious programmes were extending their briefs into the current affairs area – such as *Encounter*, which was being presented by Seán Egan, and which dealt with subjects as disparate as abortion and Western development. The latter programme was eventually taken off the air in early 1974, after – and, as some suggested, because – a group of priests in Limerick took space in a local newspaper to dissociate themselves from views on marriage expressed on the programme by the theologian Fr Seán O Riordáin.[35] A decade after the end of Vatican II, this decision was an unmistakably retrograde one, and unfair to an excellent journalist.

There were overlaps between *Enterprise* and *7 Days* (now being edited by Sheamus Smith), although *Enterprise* was more film-based and *7 Days* now more studio-based. *Tangents* was being broadcast occasionally from the studio which had been opened in the Dáil in 1971, and was therefore to an extent treading on

33 RTÉ Reference Library, *Personnel Information Bulletin*, 24 September 1974. 34 Seán Mac Réamoinn and Michael Garvey respectively. Like all Divisional Heads, they were naturally unwilling to allow their human resources to be depleted, even if the staff concerned were keen to work in current affairs. 35 Tom O'Dea, *Irish Press*, 15 June 1974.

7 Days territory also. The cultural differences between News and Programmes Divisions were far from resolution, and the new arrangement focused attention on them rather than helping to resolve them. Part of the problem was, and continued to be for years thereafter, that the news culture had to all intents and purposes one fewer input layer than the programmes side, in that it lacked producer/directors, or at least employed them in a relatively subsidiary role. This was because newsroom personnel resisted their involvement. The view in the newsroom, essentially, was that production was a journalistic function: it was summed up in the frequently-heard phrase – 'We are our own producers.'[36] In programmes, on the other hand, producer/directors were, in a sense, the fulcrum of the editorial decision-making process, with a larger measure of freedom than would have been customary in news. Any new structural arrangement which limited that freedom of editorial decision-making was inevitably seen by them as a diminution of their area of professional responsibility, and resented all the more if it was thought to be politically motivated.

In the summer of 1974 the arrangement looked as if it was already beginning to unravel. The producers of *7 Days*, *Tangents*, *Enterprise* and *Féach* mooted running a 30–minute current affairs programme which would run on five nights a week, but this provoked a degree of dissent among both producers and reporters. At a meeting of the Programme Policy Committee, the Controller of Programmes, Television, Michael Garvey, indicated that he would not put pressure on any producer to join the new current affairs grouping against his inclination. Tom O'Dea, the television critic of the *Irish Press*, commented acerbically: 'RTÉ is a very friendly organisation and it takes good care of its own. But that doesn't mean that it works on play-school lines, or that nobody ever gets kicked in the head.'[37]

A further, and more substantial crisis erupted in October 1974 when *7 Days* ran two programmes on internment, both of them conceived and planned by Eoghan Harris. The first of these, broadcast on 17 October, was largely based on film material bought in from an independent, British-based production company, Lusia Films, intercut with some actuality material from RTÉ sources. Although the Lusia producer had been in contact with RTÉ about a possible sale of the material in the early autumn, the topic had been given an added intensity by the burning of the Maze prison on 15 October, and the whole process was suddenly revisited and accelerated. The material on which the programme was to be based, however, arrived in RTÉ only at 2 p.m. on 17 October, was edited and spliced with some RTÉ material, and was finally finished only a couple of minutes before transmission time at 9.20 p.m. The second programme, transmitted the following (Friday) evening, consisted of a studio-based discussion on internment and associated issues.

36 Private source.   **37** *Irish Press*, 20 July 1974.

The Labour Party's annual conference was meeting in Galway on that weekend. Desmond Fisher, head of the Current Affairs Grouping, was at the conference. So was the Deputy Director-General, John Irvine. So was the Minister for Posts and Telegraphs, Dr O'Brien. What transpired was, at one level, an indication that the degree of sensitivity being experienced by government in relation to the IRA had not in any sense been lessened by the departure from office of Fianna Fáil.

Opinion in the North itself was hardening: the broad Republican candidate, Frank Maguire, defeated the Unionist Party leader, Harry West, in Fermanagh/South Tyrone in the British general election on 10 October. On 15 October, as noted, Republican and loyalist prisoners set their huts in the Maze prison ablaze. Magilligan prison in Co.Derry was set alight by its inmates the following night. Within the Labour Party, an intense political struggle was taking place between those – principally the party leader, Brendan Corish, O'Brien, and Frank Cluskey – who were resolutely opposed to any softening of the line on Republican violence, and a small but vocal group who regarded themselves as the inheritors of a socialist Republican tradition, and who therefore blamed the British government as being primarily responsible for the violence in the North. Debates in and around these issues had become a feature of Labour Party conferences since 1969, and they were occasions of high emotion: there was a sense that there was a battle going on for control of the heart of the party on this issue at least as intense as anything that was going on in Fianna Fáil. Nor should it be forgotten that Labour had gone into coalition the previous year, for the first time in sixteen years, in the face of the vociferous objections of a large minority of party members, among whom the socialist republican tendency would have been prominent. This, therefore, was the context in which the internment programme was broadcast: it was one in which O'Brien's battles within the Labour Party were at least as significant as the external and internal pressures being brought to bear on Lynch two years earlier. The timing of the internment programme, in that sense, could hardly have been worse.

Fisher was with senior party members in the lounge of the Salthill Hotel on the Friday evening when they were approached by O'Brien who, in Fisher's words, 'waved a finger under my nose and said: "Just one more programme like last night's: just one more."' Fisher suggested that the Friday evening programme, which had just been transmitted, had been excellent. O'Brien replied: 'I am not concerned about tonight's programme, just last night's. And it's the last of its kind you'll do.'[38] O'Brien, as it happened, had not seen the programme, but the intensity of his reaction left little doubt but that it was perceived by him as something which seriously reflected, not just on his standing as Minister, but

38 Desmond Fisher papers, memorandum, Fisher to Deputy Director-General, 12 November 1974.

on his own political position on the IRA, and exacerbated the difficult internal debates within the party.[39]

On the Monday following the conference, he viewed the internment film at RTÉ in the company of the Chairman of the Authority. Within the station, the Deputy Director-General, John Irvine, had already received reports from Harris and Eugene Murray, both of which he considered unsatisfactory.

The Programme Policy Committee viewed the programme on 25 October, and came virtually unanimously to the conclusion that the programme, and its preparation by those involved, had been deeply unsatisfactory. Particular offence was taken at the fact that some of the RTÉ footage employed – of British soldiers batoning a civilian in Belfast – in fact pre-dated the introduction of internment. But there were also other major criticisms from senior executives: the documentary was seen as impressionistic, and one that could reasonably be interpreted as propaganda for a violent organisation; it was 'incoherent, quite unbalanced, and highly emotional,' and 'contrived and highly theatrical.'[40]

Eoghan Harris defended the programme concept on the grounds that it had set out to explore the complex issue of whether violence had caused internment, or internment had caused violence. The programme, he said, had been a 'fair and adequate' treatment of the subject, and charged that RTÉ had made 'no comprehensive effort to deal with the fact that 600 men are held without trial'; that no member of an illegal organisation had taken part in the programme and that there had been no incitement to violence.[41] The latter philosophical point was as irrelevant to most of the station's executives as they had been to O'Brien. Harris also maintained that 'the only substantial matter at issue is that Dr O'Brien is grievously offended.'[42] Gerry Murray – to whom Fisher had spoken after seeing the programme on the Thursday night – rejected the view that the programme could be interpreted as designed to promote the aims and activities of any organisation. He maintained that none of the three main participants was, to the best of his knowledge, a member of any illegal organisation; and that therefore he had not felt any need to refer the matter upwards.[43]

The final outcome of this process, insofar as the executives were concerned, was a decision that the quality of judgement required in the making of such a

---

39 O'Brien's personal and political rejection of militant Republicanism has been consistent throughout his career, although his attitude towards the question of national unity has been more varied. In his earlier days as a civil servant in the Department of External Affairs in the late 1940s and early 1950s, he was managing director of the Irish News Agency, which had been set up by Seán MacBride to trumpet abroad Ireland's complaints against Britain in the matter of partition. 40 PPC Minutes, 25 October 1925. 41 Desmond Fisher papers, memorandum, Harris to Murray, 23 October 1974. The PPC Minutes of 18 October 1974 maintained that an 'Official' (i.e. member of Official Sinn Féin or Official IRA) had been included in the programme and had been identified as such, and that this would of itself have warranted the invocation of the reference upward mechanism. 42 PPC Minutes, 28 October 1974. At a subsequent meeting Harris withdrew his charge that O'Brien had been engaged in a vendetta against him. 43 Desmond Fisher papers, memorandum, Murray to Fisher, 21 October 1974.

programme was lacking, that the arrangements for supervising the making of the programme were unsatisfactory, and that the appropriate RTÉ guidelines were inadequately observed. These conclusions were conveyed to the staff concerned (Fisher, Murray and Harris).[44]

Harris, however, was in hotter water than the other two. In April 1971 he had been warned of dismissal for unacceptable behaviour. In February 1972 he was removed from handling current affairs programmes, as already noted. He had also been involved in a matter related to an anonymous article about Proinsías Mac Aonghusa, a fellow member of the *Féach* team, which had led to the latter's resignation from the programme.[45] He was now, as a result of this controversy, assigned to a different area of production in RTÉ – to the Radio Features Department. Both the NUJ and the WUI became involved; the NUJ noted that no journalists, in their definition of the term, had been involved in the making of the documentary, whereas the WUI threatened to black any producer seconded to do Harris's work on 7 *Days*. Harris appealed his transfer, amid ongoing controversy. The 7 *Days* programme scheduled for 12 November was not transmitted, although the 'blacking' of the programme by the WUI was lifted the following day. Harris's reassignment was postponed, but he remained barred from current affairs assignments. In December, Murray was told to double up as a director to make up for Harris's absence.[46] As the dispute had also been discussed by the Authority, it appeared that the relevant documentation was being circulated to Authority members. This caused considerable concern among programme heads, who were later assured that personal files had not been among the documentation circulated, and that in future any relevant documentation would be made available at Authority meetings rather than being circulated in advance, as had happened in this case.[47]

When the dust had settled – Harris was re-instated in current affairs on 1 April 1975 – Fisher wrote to the Director-General to encapsulate his view on the controversy. The failure to establish the Grouping on a definitive divisional basis from the beginning, he argued, was the 'original sin' which had retarded its development, and this had been accentuated by union pressures which meant that the Grouping could be established only on an experimental basis.

> The consequent uncertainty among staff about the future stability of the Grouping and therefore of their own career prospects inevitably tempted them to refrain from committing themselves completely to the Grouping. The result was a degree of divided loyalties which combined with a continuing element of doctrinaire commitment to bringing cur-

44 Desmond Fisher papers, circular from Director-General, 17 October 1974. **45** 'Mac Aonghusa quits "Feach"', *Irish Times*, 21 February 1972. **46** Tom O'Dea, *Irish Press*, 7 December 1974. **47** PPC Minutes, 22 November 1974.

rent affairs back to the Programmes Division, has helped to prevent the Grouping from developing an inner dynamic.'[48]

Outside the station, events were being re-shaped by other forces. Ireland assumed the presidency of the European Community for six months on 1 January 1975. An IRA Christmas cease-fire was declared on the previous 20 December, following a meeting between Republicans and church leaders in Feakle, Co. Clare, at the beginning of December and on 2 January was extended for a further two weeks. This created fresh difficulties in relation to the observation of the Section 31 directive. One of them was related to the amount of coverage of Sinn Féin; another was related to the type of coverage. The quantity issue arose when, on 12 December, the *News at 1.30* had carried an eight-and-a-half minute interview with Ruairi Ó Brádaigh after the conclusion of the Feakle talks. The decision not to allow other programmes to interview him on the same topic was inevitably interpreted by the broadcasters concerned, and to some degree by the general public, as inconsistent. In fact it was the outcome of a balancing act: no coverage was unacceptable; so was too much coverage. An inevitable outcome of this flexible decision-making approach was that some programme-makers felt discriminated against, and it was a policy which could not be expressed in any written or unambiguous form.

The quality issue arose later, when Liam Hourican talked to Daithi Ó Conaill of the IRA on the telephone: this delicate issue was dealt with by having Kevin Healy, in Dublin, interview Hourican about his conversation with Ó Conaill: the tape of this interview was broadcast on *This Week* on 22 December. This particular technique – allowing the transmission of information about the IRA by the expedient of having one RTÉ journalist interview another – was one of the commonest devices employed to attempt to maintain some sort of information flow to the public in the context of the directive. Other techniques included, for instance, interviewing experts unconnected with the censored organisations, and interviewing community activists who had a greater or lesser degree of sympathy with the organisations concerned, but who were not actually members of them. RTÉ reporters, in fact, frequently prefaced such interviews by asking the interviewee, off-air, to confirm that he was not a member of any proscribed organisation, particularly after the issuing of the new directive in 1976. The organisations concerned may, for their part, also have ensured a steady supply of such non-member sympathisers in order to ensure that their viewpoint and commentary on current events was not entirely occluded.[49]

There was, however, one side-effect of the various directives which was not to become apparent until much later. This was its effect on the archival holdings

48 Desmond Fisher papers, memorandum, Fisher to Director-General, 28 April 1975. **49** Linda Mac-Dermott, 'The political censorship of the Irish broadcast media, 1960–1994' (1996), pp. 70–80.

relating to this particular aspect of news and current affairs. Because the directive, as generally interpreted, precluded the broadcasting of sound material in many instances, such recordings as were made for television were frequently made on mute film. The station could, without in any way breaching the directive, have made as many sound and vision recordings as it liked for archival purposes. There was always the possibility, in addition, that the directive might be revoked at any time, which suggested that the station should maintain a bank of material which could be drawn on in any such eventuality. The haphazard and half-hearted approach adopted to this problem can now – admittedly with the benefit of hindsight – be seen as a serious *lacuna*.

Where the broadcasters were concerned, there were intermittent protests. John Kelleher, on behalf of the WUI producers/directors, protested about the 'too rigid' interpretation of the guidelines, and this led to a meeting between a number of senior executives and representatives of the producers on 22 January 1975.[50] The NUJ also made its disagreement with the guidelines officially clear.[51] These prompted the institution of a revision process for the guidelines, and revised guidelines were issued on 5 March 1975. Differing points of view were apparent among members of the new Authority.[52] There were also external pressure points from time to time, as when Mary Holland interviewed Daithi Ó Conaill on ITV on 17 November 1974. Despite such flashpoints, however – and there were to be future flash-points as well – broadcasters' desire to challenge the directive directly seemed to have diminished over time. As Rodney Rice, an NUJ member, put it:

> The NUJ's main strength in the station at the time then as now was in its newsroom numbers. Traditionally they are less 'political' than the producer grades in both radio and television and my memory would be that while members objected to censorship in principle, most felt that they could get on with the job unrestricted in the reporting of what was happening in the North, even without the spoken words of the IRA and Sinn Féin. It must be remembered that the significance of Sinn Féin within militant nationalism was much less than it now is. There were many claims of self-censorship, but these were again discussed at branch meetings in a theoretical way since no-one admitted to having engaged in self-censorship. I think much of the issue lessened for most journalists as time passed, atrocities got worse, and no government was interested in altering the application of the law.[53]

50 PPC Minutes, 31 January 1975. The producers'representatives were Paul Gleeson, John Kelleher, Joe Mulholland and Seán Ó Mordha. **51** PPC Minutes, 29 November 1974, 17 January 1975. **52** Ibid. **53** Horgan, 'Censorship', p. 381.

Many years later, Muiris Mac Conghail expressed his considered view on the matter.

> Of course there were good and excellent programmes since 1972. How-
> ever an edge had been dulled in the area of investigative reporting and
> the RTÉ authority and management became overcautious and appre-
> hensive about government attitudes in general and what they might her-
> ald. They were both right and wrong. Right for trying to protect what
> editorial independence RTÉ had secured. Wrong for failing to stand up
> and argue, respectfully of course, about the issues of editorial freedom.
> However, in the context of RTÉ, the limits to such a freedom however
> are set by the legislative framework within which RTÉ functions. At the
> core of that legislation is the Minister.[54]

Peter Feeney, whose work in RTÉ over many years was frequently concerned with current affairs, observed that RTÉ had been better at resisting covert than over censorship, but that its resistance to the former was generally achieved 'without significant input from the Authority'.[55] In the circumstances, it was a modest enough criticism.

Inside the station, too there was one critical change: T.P. Hardiman left the position of Director-General on the expiry of his seven-year term on 31 March 1975. He had, in his seven years at the helm, overseen the most formative peri-od in Irish public service broadcasting. The first person from within the organ-isation to act as Director-General, he had to nurture the station through its most difficult period in terms of its relationship with government and with politicians generally. He had to encourage the growth of innovative and independent broadcasting, while at the same time restraining – without crushing – the exu-berance (and from time to time the exaggerated sense of self-importance) of an entirely new generation of broadcasters, when these attracted a degree of intru-sive political attention that imperilled the independence in public service broad-casting that he was trying to create and protect. Although his background in engineering was often seen as a fatal flaw by programme-makers, he had a very hands-on management style. He made a point of familiarising himself with all aspects of the organisation's activities, often dropping into a wide range of offices to see how things were going. He was also renowned for the rapidity with which he returned phone calls from staff members. Some of these qualities became more apparent to his critics in the years after he had left the station.

His replacement from 1 April 1975 was Oliver Maloney, formerly Director of Personnel and more recently Assistant Director-General. Maloney was, in many

54 Mac Conghail, 'Wireless'. p 77.   **55** Peter Feeney, 'Censorship and RTÉ' (1984) , p. 64.

quarters, thought to be a DG who was sympathetic to broadcasters, and to producers in particular: in the event, his honeymoon with the broadcasters was to be comparatively brief. There were few changes initially, partly because the Authority which had been appointed in 1973 now had only a year left in office. Wesley Boyd, Head of News since 1974, was a conscientious professional with a broad knowledge of politics, particularly of the Northern situation, who was unlikely to be wrong-footed by any turn of events.[56] There was one possible difference of emphasis from McGuinness, in that he was primarily a news man: McGuinness, as has been noted, sought expansion for the News Division primarily in terms of providing new opportunities for his team to show what they were capable of by developing new programme formats. Boyd's firm hand was needed frequently, as in March 1975 when the *This Week* programme was seen as seeming to mediate between Official Sinn Féin and its rebel off-shoot, the Irish Republican Socialist party. His capacity to take initiatives, however, was severely hampered by the financial stringencies which were beginning to affect the station. He had continually to bring the Programme Policy Committee's attention to unfilled vacancies in the newsroom. An additional problem was that the national newspapers' pay scales were now in some cases rivalling those of RTÉ: it was no longer possible for broadcasting, no matter how glamorous, automatically to assume that it would have the pick of the journalistic crop.

The problem of the current affairs grouping, however – and in particular the problem of 7 *Days* – could not be avoided indefinitely. 7 *Days* was doing consistently well in TAM ratings, with programmes on natural resources in March 1975 and on the legal profession in May 1975 (on which the president of the Incorporated Law Society declared incautiously that 'there are no wealthy solicitors in the country'[57]). Harris returned from internal exile (he had been producing *Cross-Country Quiz*) and celebrated his reinstatement with a typically pungent programme on the closure of Gortdrum Mines, enlivened by snatches of a local mining ballad.

By June, 7 *Days* was back in the Programmes Division, underlining Maloney's image as someone who was sympathetic to producers. Its new editor was Seán Ó Mórdha, who came to it from *Féach*. A month later, the editor under whom it had arguably made its biggest impact, Mac Conghail, returned from his sojourn in Government Buildings: he had resigned from the station in 1973 to take up the position of head of the Government Information Bureau with the incoming coalition government. He had never intended it to be a permanent move, and when the position of Controller of Programmes, Television, was advertised in 1975, he decided to apply for it. He was unsuccessful – the post

56 A small but significant milestone of his tenure of office was the introduction of the first News for the Deaf on 6 January 1975, a development which pre-dated similar moves in other, better-funded European stations.   **57** Tom O'Dea, *Irish Press*, 24 May 1975.

went to Jack White – but the Authority recommended that a suitable post be found for him, and he returned to oversee, initially, Raidió na Gaeltachta. It would have been difficult for him, in any case, to return to current affairs directly from a period as a highly politicised figure close to government, and in fact he was never to return to direct editorial involvement in the current affairs field, although he subsequently spent a period as Controller of Television Programmes. He developed, in contrast, a highly successful and influential role in other programming, notably in drama, where he was responsible for *Strumpet City* and a wide range of other output.

At precisely this time, his former political superior and Minister for Posts and Telegraphs, Dr O'Brien, was steering his Broadcasting Bill through the Seanad and Dáil. The significance of this new piece of legislation for news and current affairs was in a number of areas. In the first place, it altered the statutory obligations in respect of current affairs. In the original act, the statutory definition of the material to which the requirements of objectivity and impartiality should apply referred to matters of public controversy or current public debate. The new wording formally extended the requirement to all current affairs broadcasting, no doubt to take in the very broad brief that many programmes in RTÉ had acquired, whether or not they were strictly speaking managed from within a current affairs structure. It also created a statutory requirement for all such current affairs broadcasts to be fair to all interests concerned. In practice the change might not have been substantial, but it reinforced the view that, as far as the Government was concerned, the original definition had been too narrow. Secondly, it instituted a new requirement that the authority should not, in making its programmes, 'unreasonably encroach on the privacy of an individual.' No less significantly, it permitted the station to achieve balance over a number of related programmes, thus removing the straitjacket which had led, among other things, to wrangles about the 'empty chair' approach by producers to identify individuals who had been unwilling to appear on particular programmes.

Section 31 in its original form was abolished. Under the new Act, directives could still be issued, but only for a maximum period of a year, and could be debated, and if necessary annulled, by a Dáil or Seanad resolution. This was only one of a number of significant changes. Another was the decision to specify, in the directive, the organisations, both in Northern Ireland and in the Republic, to which it was to apply. This could be interpreted in either of two ways. Positively, it could be understood as a welcome clarification for broadcasters, in that there was no room for doubt in relation to certain organisations, and new guidelines could be drafted within the station to take account of this new, hard-edged approach. Negatively, it could be regarded as a further and more direct intrusion by government into the editorial decision-making policy and management – in effect, a vote of no confidence in RTÉ's editorial direction and management and a step back from the degree of autonomy envisaged by the 1960 Broadcasting Act. It was, at the very least, a mixture of the two. It also had the as yet unforeseen, but later critically important effect of banning all members of Sinn Féin from the airwaves regardless of the issue on which they might be speaking or the role they might occupy in society generally. Yet another aspect of the directive which was unusual, and possibly unique, was that it extended the scope of the ban to cover, not only the named organisations, but any other organisations which might in the future be proscribed under British legislation in Northern Ireland. This was effectively transferring legislative power from the Dáil to another entity, a development which was perhaps envisaged to a degree in Ireland's accession to the European Community, but hardly in this sort of context.

Elsewhere in the Act, and equally significantly, the Government's power to sack the Authority was now limited: this action could only be taken after a resolution in appropriate terms had been agreed by a two-thirds majority in both houses of the Oireachtas. This, in contrast to the terms of the new directive, was undoubtedly an important new development designed to protect and enhance the independence of the Authority from government. It was also something which implicitly recognised that persons of standing in the community might, in the wake of the dismissal of the Authority in 1972, be unwilling to accept nomination as a member of a future Authority. In the new Act, therefore, Authority members would – extraordinarily – be given legislative protection similar to that accorded, in the Constitution, to members of the judiciary. However, the non-appearance in Dr O'Brien's first Authority, appointed by him on 1 June 1973, of many of the members of the Authority who had been dismissed less than a year earlier, suggests that even this was not a sufficient guarantee, for some potential appointees, of the Authority's independence or standing in the future. Although we do not have archival access at this point to government discussions concerning the appointment of the Authority later than 1972, it is at least open to conjecture that O'Brien's attempt to restore the Authority's prestige in this way failed, and that the Authority's original function as a buffer zone between the government and programme-makers was, after 1972, seriously impaired.

The new Authority did take one immediate initiative, possibly at the instigation of the trade unionist Sheila Conroy. This was to move towards the appointment of an Economics Correspondent. The post had been briefly filled by a journalist named John Feeney[58] before his resignation, and was advertised in the summer of 1973. The initial choice fell on Jim Canning, a 32–year-old economics graduate of TCD with a background in agriculture. The problem was that he was not a member of the NUJ, and this appointment would be in the

---

58 A different person from the John Feeney mentioned earlier in this chapter.

News Division. As a result of NUJ objections, this appointment was shelved, and Patrick Kinsella took up the appointment with effect from May of 1974. He eventually formed part of the Industrial and Economic Unit, whose other members included Brendan Keenan (1976–83), Feargus Ó Raghaillaigh (1980–91) and Liam Cahill (1983–89). In the early 1990s the unit, as such, began to lose members to programmes such as *Today Tonight*, and it was not until the appointment of George Lee in 1995 that economics reporting again assumed a central, newsroom-based role.

Despite the continuing campaign by the NUJ on Section 31, and despite Dr O'Brien's change in the law to allow any directive to be debated in the Oireachtas under certain circumstances, no directive was challenged for a very considerable period. This underlines the degree to which the policy behind the directive had some degree of popular support, at least as experienced by public representatives. The legislative innovation notwithstanding, no member of the Dáil or Seanad rushed to table a resolution to nullify the directive for many years. In 1977, an NUJ questionnaire to its own members evoked the comment that

> The ultra-cautious atmosphere which Section 31 and the guidelines have fostered in newsroom and programme sections has meant that enquiries into controversial areas have not been encouraged...there is now a general anxiety about tackling stories which might embarrass the government on the issue of security.[59]

The first parliamentary challenge was not mounted until 1986, when Sinn Féin The Workers Party[60] put down a Dáil motion rejecting the renewal of the directive. It did so, however, in terms which indicated that its feelings about RTÉ were decidedly mixed. The motion noted:

> In some respects Section 31 has worked to the advantage of the Provisional IRA in that members of their political wing have been able to avoid having to try to defend Provo atrocities. At the same time many current affairs programmes feature supposedly impartial commentators, who may deny support for the Provisionals, but are quite happy to articulate and defend the Provo viewpoint.[61]

59 Liz Curtis, *Ireland: the propaganda war,* p 194.   **60** SFWP was born of the 1971 split in Sinn Féin. Its first incarnation was as Official Sinn Féin; its post-SFWP form was as the Workers Party, which subsequently split again, part of it forming Democratic Left, which finally amalgamated with the Labour Party. The Workers' Party is still in existence. Each of these groups was characterised by an increasing reliance on socialist ideology and terminology, and by a rather swifter move into constitutional politics than was to be the case for the mainstream of Republican activists of the period.   **61** Order paper, Dáil Éireann, 22 January 1986.

The resolution was never debated, as the deputies who tabled it doubtless knew it could not be, because they did not have a sufficient Dáil representation under standing orders to have an appropriate allocation of parliamentary time. The failure to have a Dáil debate, therefore, was in all probability passed over with quiet relief by all parties, including the party that proposed it. A survey of Dubliners the following year elucidated the fact that a third of respondents were not even aware of the existence of the directive, much less of its effects.[62]

Meanwhile, as the new Section 31 directive began to be incorporated into the working practices and guidelines of the station, RTÉ producers moved to influence the debate about future programming, which they hoped would, under Maloney, be more pro-active and innovative. Maloney had spoken to the staff generally about his ambitions on his appointment in April. After this meeting, at which the frustration of some younger producers had been articulated by the veteran James Plunkett Kelly, he issued a discussion document in which he suggested that RTÉ had a responsibility to articulate the sentiments of ordinary viewers more than those of the privileged 'in-group' to which they belonged.[63]

This was the producers' response.[64] It argued that current affairs should, together with variety and features, become one of the three pillars on which RTÉ would stand. It endorsed the reorganised structure of current affairs programming, as well it might given the new status of current affairs under Ó Mórdha after its long exile in the News Division and the abortive experiment of the 'Current Affairs Grouping', and recommended the introduction of humour, satire, and a 'discursive conversational style'.

More daringly, it suggested a re-evaluation of the traditional concept of objectivity and balance (which had been formally enshrined in the legislation since 1961) and 'consensus', which had not. Any attempt to justify these principles on any grounds but the empirical, it commented somewhat ambiguously, revealed how uncertain they proved as guides.

> We would urge that such notions are tempered by some new principles which are honoured in other walks of life. A passion for truth, a search for justice, and an invitation to compassion will prove no less reliable guides to what the public needs. In this regard objectivity will mean detachment from institutional views; balance may require speaking out for the inarticulate; and consensus may have to settle for an argument [*sic* – what is possibly meant is agreement] to differ without recourse to violence.[65]

62 Jane Horgan and Niall Meehan, *Survey on attitudes of Dublin population to Section 31 of the Broadcasting Act* (1987).   63 Tom O'Dea, *Irish Press*, 16 and 17 April 1976.   64 Summary in *Irish Times*, 17 June 1975. 65 Ibid.

The 1975–6 period indicated that, without waiting for an endorsement by the station's management (which was in any case not forthcoming), some current affairs producers were beginning again to push the boundaries of what was possible. In this context, Northern Ireland affairs moved to a degree into the background. In late 1975, the Director-General expressed his concern that RTÉ 'appeared to have slipped into a pro-contraception stance', and others identified a tendency 'to take a softer line with one side in a controversy than with another', not necessarily on contraception alone.[66] There was a feeling that programmes other than current affairs programmes were straying beyond their brief (*The Gay Byrne Hour*, and *Get an Earful of This* were instanced), but a desire to set up an efficient monitoring system faltered as managers imagined how such a development would be interpreted publicly.

Then, in November 1975, *7 Days* went to town on one of the most controversial issues concerning the capital: the question of building an oil refinery.[67] The programme, produced by Eoghan Harris under the editorship of Seán Ó Mórdha, was presented by Brian Farrell, Michael Ryan and Patrick Gallagher. It involved a major critique of the activities of multi-national oil companies, underpinning a strong editorial message that Ireland should refine and market its own oil. Fianna Fáil TDs were the only representatives of major political parties to be interviewed, in a context which demonstrated that the party was deeply split on the issue. Eamonn Smullen of the Workers Party was the only other party political representative interviewed. The programme was highly didactic, and a fine exercise in coat-trailing; but it was also fascinating – and controversial – television. 'I have since seen it stated', the *Irish Press* television critic remarked, 'that this is the policy of Gardiner Street Sinn Féin'.[68] Party line or not, objectors were not mollified by the same critic's suggestion that 'the more openly a point of view is indicated in any programme, the less it may be necessary to restore the balance'. Such was the fuss, in fact, that Seán Dublin Bay Loftus and others succeeded in having a retaliatory programme broadcast, also under the *7 Days* rubric, on 28 November.[69] Not even this was regarded as satisfactory by the interests involved, and a further complaint was made, this time to the Broadcasting Complaints Commission which had been established by Dr O'Brien. As this process was inaugurated, even more extraordinary events came to light. Loftus telephoned RTÉ to ask for copies of the relevant tapes, to be told that RTÉ would not surrender any tapes without a court order. Then, in subsequent discussions with Loftus, *7 Days* personnel got the impression that objectors not only had copies of the programme, but also of the originals from which the programme had been compiled. When staff went to check that the tapes were still

---

66 Combined Divisional and Programme Policy Committee meeting, Minutes, 18 November 1975. **67** Programme transmitted 14 November 1975; RTÉ media library reference TY0120384. **68** Tom O'Dea, *Irish Press*, 22 November 1975, **69** RTÉ media library reference TY0120385.

in Film Dubbing, which was the appropriate repository, they were nowhere to be found.[70]

Institutional nerves were becoming frayed, and not only because of happenings like this. The situation in the North showed no signs of improving and in some respects was deteriorating. A Programme Policy Committee meetings, demands for more resources to report the North had to take account also of increasing viewer resistance to Northern coverage. The country – along with Western economies generally and more seriously than many of them – was still in the grip of the oil price shock created by the decision of the OPEC countries to increase prices dramatically; inflation was now running at around 20%–25% annually. Jobs were being lost wholesale, advertising was sliding, and the prospect of a license fee increase – let alone the investment required for the projected RTÉ2 channel – looked increasingly problematic. Nor were government-RTÉ relationships anything to write home about. Coalition ministers often refused to appear on programmes, especially those dealing with Northern Ireland.[71] The worsening economic situation also affected coverage of other issues – Richie Ryan, Minister for Finance, for example, refused to defend one of his budgets on television – and this sometimes had the effect of banning Fianna Fáil spokesmen as well, or making interviewers feel that they had to interview them with exceptional severity in the absence of a Government voice.[72] At one point, even, the Head of News, Wesley Boyd, was faced with a government demand that he give a written guarantee that, in the event of a hijacked aircraft landing on Irish soil, RTÉ would not cover it as a news story. He refused.[73]

There was a series of bad-tempered turf wars between news and current affairs (and by extension between the NUJ and the WUI) about the coverage of critical political events like the budget and general elections: programmes vied with each other in inviting the same commentators. Discussions involving the three current affairs department heads, Seán Ó Mórdha (television) Mike Burns (News Features) and Michael Littleton (Radio) were only intermittently productive.[74] In March 1976 the NUJ threatened to strike against the termination of the short-term contracts of some of their newsroom members. RTÉ was getting increasing criticism, both from the *Irish Times* and from papers in the *Independent* group, both in relation to the quality of its programming and to allegations of censorship.[75]

Within 7 *Days*, at any rate, no self-doubt was discernible, and indeed four of the original seven people involved in the first 7 *Days* were still on the team. Although financial cut-backs had led to the abandonment of foreign coverage, it

70 PPC Minutes, 13 February 1976. 71 PPC Minutes, 4 March 1976. 72 PPC Minutes, 4 February 1976. 73 Ibid. 74 PPC Minutes, 30 January 1976. 75 e.g. Programme Policy Committee Minutes, 6 May 1976, when some executives suggested that an Nuala Ní Dhomhnaill should be dismissed from RTÉ for having edited, in the *Irish Times* Tuarascail column, an article alleging RTÉ censorship. Cf. also Programme Policy Committee Minutes, 18 September 1975, re criticisms by Independent group newspa-

had, by May 1976, dealt with 129 separate items since the previous autumn. It had also developed a specialism in film documentary (the format which would later provide a career outside RTÉ for Seán Ó Mórdha). Some of its special programmes, however, notably that on the Dublin Bay oil refinery, had prompted controversy about the actual or supposed role of Official Sinn Féin ideology within the team's agenda.[76]

This was the context in which station managers came to consider the autumn schedule for 1976. There was one other feature of the situation which merits mention: this was the fact that there was now a new Authority, the second to be appointed by Dr O'Brien, which took office on 1 June 1976 under the chairmanship of Sheila Conroy (who had been a member of the 1973–6 Authority also). The previous chairman, Dónall Ó Móráin, was not re-appointed a member.

The new Authority held a two-day meeting on Saturday and Sunday, 4 and 5 September at a hotel in County Wicklow, preceded by an ordinary meeting on the Friday evening. In much the same way as the first zephyr from an approaching storm makes its fitful impression on the sea, one member – James McGuire, of the *Western People* – raised the question of a recent 7 *Days* programme on a bank strike which was then current. This in fact was the second such programme. An earlier 7 *Days* decision to run a programme on the same topic, at the end of July, led to rumours that Bill Finlay, an Authority member and a director of the Bank of Ireland, had intervened successfully to prevent it going ahead on the grounds that it might prejudice the negotiations which were then in train.[77] McGuire now argued that the decision to proceed with another item on the dispute meant that there had been a failure in editorial control. He may not have been mollified by the information that a 'strong rebuke' had been issued to those concerned.[78]

By the time the in-depth meeting convened the following morning it was evident that the Director-General had similar concerns. He told Authority members that he was concerned at the present state of the organisation; that inadequate leadership was forthcoming from the controllers; that money was being wasted; and that 'small groups of strategically placed staff exercised inordinate influence'.[79] He then got the Authority's agreement for a number of 'urgent and substantial' changes. Many of these were personnel, and involved sideways moves or altered responsibilities for a number of individuals, including the Assistant Controller of Programmes, Television (Aindrias Ó Gallchóir), and the Controller of Programmes Radio (Seán Mac Réamoinn, who had been a member of the previous Authority). The position of the Controller of Programmes Televi-

pers. **76** John Walsh, '7 Days is a Long Time in Politics' (1976). Walsh points out one additional consistency: ten years after it had first gone on air, the programme was still being produced from a big trailer caravan parked outside the studios. It was, however, a replacement for the original trailer caravan. **77** Tom O'Dea, *Irish Press*, 14 August 1976. **78** RTÉ Authority, Minutes, 3 September 1976. **79** RTÉ Authority Minutes, 4 and 5 September, 1976.

sion, Jack White whose discharge of his responsibilities the Authority now found unsatisfactory, would be reviewed in the following February. Ó Mórdha's contract would not be renewed when it expired in June 1977 and, most pointedly of all, 7 *Days* would be discontinued and replaced by alternative programming with almost immediate effect, i.e. from 1 November 1976. Maloney also indicated that he would, for a limited period, now assume more direct control of programmes on both radio and television.

Most of the people involved in the decisions heard their fate from a news broadcast. In the event, Ó Mórdha did not wait to be sacked but resigned.[80] He had been in London agreeing terms for a contract between 7 *Days* and Mary Holland, and heard the news that the programme was to be discontinued on his return. He was transferred to agricultural programmes. Effective control of current affairs was transferred to Dick Hill, and station executives faced some hostile questions from the print media about the rationale for the changes.

The decision to axe 7 *Days* was initially justified on the grounds that there was a need for newer techniques and formats in current affairs: this rationale faltered as it was pointed out that the techniques and format of the *Late Late Show* were even older.[81] Jack White, loyalty vying with disappointment, noted in an article in the *RTÉ Guide* that 7 *Days* had had a 'long and honourable career', and observed that the members of the team 'will be re-shuffled into a new team which will, we hope, attack this vital area of programme-making with renewed vigour'.[82] Maloney himself went on radio to defend the changes, noting that he personally would be in favour of 'more adventurous and imaginative' current affairs programmes than those presently being made, and held a press conference to defend the timing of the decisions.[83] It was, he suggested, impossible to make them earlier, as the new Authority had only just assumed office and the difficult summer period had intervened: a more sceptical analysis suggests that it was, at the very least, a rush to judgement on the part of a new Authority which was hardly bedded in, or that Maloney felt that the predecessor Authority might not have been as persuadable of the rationale behind his proposed changes.

The current affairs budget was increased by 20%, but this did not noticeably soften the criticism. Donal Foley, in the *Irish Times*, alleged that the changes were now being seen 'as a reflection of the parcel of intimidation that is being parcelled out in Leinster House by a panicky government.'[84] Editorially, Foley's paper was more modest in its criticisms. Although it described the axing of 7 *Days* as something which 'seemed almost to verge on the irresponsible' and called for greater consultation within the station, it underlined the right of the Director-General and Editor-in-Chief to do as he had done.[85]

80 *Irish Times*, 9 September 1976.   **81** *Irish Times*, 9 September 1976.   **82** Jack White, 'Trying out new ideas: favourites return' (1976).   **83** *Irish Times*, 10 and 17 September 1976   **84** *Irish Times*, 14 September 1976.   **85** *Irish Times*, 18 September 1976.

The use of the latter title is in itself interesting. It is not a title that exists in the Broadcasting Act. In the station's earliest days, it was a function exercised indubitably by the Controller of Programmes, Gunnar Rugheimer. A number of developments, however, had in the interim resulted in a power shift within the organisation. One of them was the series of controversies involving government, more especially in the early 1970s, in the course of which the Director-General willy-nilly assumed greater responsibilities. Chief among these controversies was the sacking of the Authority in 1972, and the formalisation of a reference upward system which, although it technically related only to the IRA and Sinn Féin, contributed inevitably to a centralisation of decision-making generally. Another was the division of Controller responsibilities between television and radio as the station grew in size and complexity. Yet another may have been the need to provide adequate promotional opportunities for a number of long-serving station executives. Whatever weight may be ascribed to each of these factors, the outcome – the centralisation of decision-making just noted – had now unmistakeably become, and was to remain for a considerable time, a noticeable feature of the organisation.

The new slate of current affairs programmes was anything but modest in its ambitions. *The Politics Programme*, the first edition of which appeared at the beginning of November 1976, was edited initially by John Kelleher, and set out to deal with 'hard topical issues' on Fridays; *Report*, edited by Niall McCarthy, was to deal with topics in a more reactive or reflective way: it was to go out on Tuesdays. *Survey*, a monthly feature produced by Michael Viney, was to deal with a range of sociological issues, and was to appear for the first time on 7 December. *Next Stop*, edited by Gerry Murray on Wednesdays, was a soft-focus programme about non-metropolitan events (and represented, in all probability, a form of internal exile for its editor). Finally, *Spot On*, on Mondays, was an interview-based current affairs programme largely fronted by Cathal O'Shannon.[86]

Despite a team which included Brian Farrell, Liam Hourican, Mary Holland, and Olivia O'Leary (an arrival from radio, for which she had been working in London and Belfast), the *Politics Programme*, produced by Peter Feeney and Noel Greene (Charlie Bird was the researcher) seemed to fail to catch fire. Hourican actually left for a job with the European Commission at the end of the year. Maloney, stung by newspaper criticism that his excursions into programme-making in his role as Editor-in-Chief were 'frequent and deep'[87] responded that 'RTÉ current affairs staff are not political eunuchs: neither are members of the RTÉ Authority'. He suggested that Tom O'Dea, the author of the criticism, might

---

86 'Hard topical issues', *RTÉ Guide*, 5 November 1976.   **87** *Irish Press*, 5 January 1977.

find it profitable to canvass the views of the vast silent majority of RTÉ staff who are hard-working, totally dedicated, perceptive, and consequently fed up with so much public attention being paid to that tiny minority of their colleagues who trade gossip with the newspapers.[88]

Ripostes like these might have temporarily diverted the flow of criticism, but they did not stem it. Indeed, insofar as it referred specifically to members of the Authority, Maloney's observations indicated that functional changes had been taking place at that level also. Under Hardiman, at least until the sacking of the Authority in late 1972, the role of the Authority had been interpreted primarily as an assessor of the station's implementation of its public service role. Its verdicts were communicated, generally via the Director-General or the Programme Policy Committee, to programme executives, but usually after the event. Post 1972, the tendency for prior involvement of successive Authorities in programme-making seems to have become more marked, partly as an extension of the reference upward systems which had been case-hardened after 1972, and partly because of the continuing interest of successive governments in the detailed operations of the station. An article in *Hibernia* advised viewers: 'Do not adjust your set: interference is normal.'[89]

Not long after the summer 1977 election which returned Jack Lynch and Fianna Fáil with a 20–seat majority, the new Minister for Posts and Telegraphs, Padraig Faulkner, had a meeting with the Authority and the Director-General in which he asked specific questions about programmes being made, what plans RTÉ had, and whether those in charge of the various broadcasting areas were 'nationally minded.'[90] RTÉ NUJ members published a dossier of alleged instances of censorship and interference in their work.; station executives decided that it was beneath official notice as it had the support 'only of small minority of NUJ members'.[91] The same month saw a cameramen's dispute, which blacked out the Horse Show, as well as other events. The Association of Municipal Authorities criticised coverage of provincial affairs, notably in Frank Hall's inventive and iconoclastic programme *Hall's Pictorial Weekly*,[92] and Muintir na Tire launched a campaign against what they described as RTÉ's 'dirty attempt to defile the Christian homes of Ireland.'[93] In the circumstances, it was little consolation that RTÉ turned in a modest profit of £1.5 million for the preceding year (1976). By the end of 1977, Muiris Mac Conghail, whose trajectory from Ceannaire of Raidió na Gaeltachta had included a spell as an assistant to the Director-General, became Controller of RTÉ 1: his Assistant Controllers were Liam Ó Murchú and John Kelleher. In January 1978, two Loyalist organisations

88 *Irish Press*, 10 January 1977.   **89** Jim Keady, *Hibernia* 17 December 1976.   **90** Report by Tom O'Dea, *Irish Press*, 24 September 1977.   **91** *Irish Times*, 1 July 1977.   **92** *Irish Times*, 23 September 1977.   **93** *Irish Times*, 10 November 1977.

were added to the list of those proscribed under the renewed Section 31 directive.

After only three years Oliver Maloney, whose health had not been good, was
coming to the end of his tenure as Director-General. This was in itself unusual:
those who served in this capacity before and after him generally had seven-year
terms. Coincidentally, this was marked by a major controversy about a documentary which was in the process of being prepared by the *Politics Programme*
on the operations of the Irish Sweepstakes. The sweepstakes had been run by
Irish Hospitals Trust Ltd since the 1930s, when they had effectively been given
a monopoly licence to raise money for Irish hospitals and secure substantial
profits for the promoters. The enterprise had been so successful, particularly in
selling tickets to the Irish diaspora, that a number of legislatures – notably those
in Britain, Canada and the United States – had passed laws making the sale of
sweeps tickets in their jurisdictions illegal. This meant, in turn, that the tickets
had to be smuggled into the countries concerned: in effect, a private Irish company whose operations had been sanctioned by the Irish State was breaking the
laws of countries with which Ireland had good, even close diplomatic and trade
relations.

The background to the programme was anything but uncomplicated. The
question of the Sweeps, and their methods of operation, had been raised in a
very public way some years earlier by the journalist Joe MacAnthony, who in an
extraordinary series of revelations in the *Sunday Independent*, had disclosed that
'Irish hospitals are receiving less than 10% of the value of tickets marketed in
their name throughout the world by Hospitals Trust (1940) Ltd.'[94] This had led
to the cancellation of extensive newspaper advertising in the *Independent* group
newspapers by Irish Hospitals Trust for a period of some months and, ultimately, to the departure of MacAnthony for another, successful career as a print and
broadcast journalist in Canada.

In the intervening years, the problem had not gone away, and indeed there
were some suggestions that members of the Government were becoming
increasingly concerned about the negative publicity affecting Ireland which was
being generated in the jurisdictions in which tickets were being illegally sold.
The reporter on the programme, Michael Heney, and the researcher, Charlie
Bird, had actually become aware of a government memorandum which was
highly critical of the sweepstake operation. In 1978, for any media organisation
to have sight of a current government memorandum on any topic was to all
intents and purposes unthinkable. To have it, and to contemplate actually using
it in a television programme, was raising the bar to extraordinary heights – even
though the circumstances in which the memorandum had been made available

94 *Sunday Independent*, 21 January 1973.

(via a senior member of the Authority) suggested strongly that the government was not averse to publicity on this issue, and might even have been happy for RTÉ to raise the issue when it would find it difficult to do so itself.[95]

The initial steps towards developing a programme on this issue had been taken by John Kelleher but, with the re-allocation of responsibilities within the station, the project was transferred to Muiris Mac Conghail. The sensitivity of the topic became apparent at an early stage, and the Hospitals Trust wrote to the Director-General to express its concern. This was an early indication that decisions would be taken at an elevated level. The Programme Policy Committee accordingly decided that

> Given the methodology which it is proposed to use in the production of this programme, Director-General stressed that all material to be used, including the script, would have to have the prior approval of the Director-General if the programme were to go ahead. Controller RTÉ1 [Muiris Mac Conghail] ... noted that a copy of the complete script for the programme was at present with Senior Counsel for examination. The question of transmitting a programme which was likely to damage the Hospitals Trust was one which he considered required attention.[96]

The 'methods' to which Maloney had referred were nothing if not daring. As proposed, they included secret filming of a consignment of Sweeps tickets being inserted into a container due to travel by ship from Dublin Port to the USA. This action, which was generally carried out without the knowledge of the owner of the container or the consignor of the goods involved, was of course illegal. The practice was for accomplices in the United States to retrieve the tickets before the container and its legal contents reached their final destination. This in turn raised the question of whether RTÉ, being aware in advance of a criminal offence which was about to be committed, should notify the Gardaí. Finally, there was the question of the impact of such an exposé on the ordinary people involved. There were two categories of people principally concerned. One category was that of the 'agents' – people to whose private addresses remittances from abroad were sent (in order to conceal the ultimate destination of the money from the postal authorities in the US and Canada) and who were allowed to deduct a percentage of the takings for having allowed themselves to be used as post office boxes for this purpose. These were often old IRA men and others who received an additional income – in some cases substantial – on which they evaded tax. These individuals, however, were less at risk than the 2,000 or so women, many of them of mature years, who worked in the Sweeps headquarters

95 Private source.　**96** PPC Minutes, 17 February 1978.

in Ballsbridge at the menial clerical tasks of preparing and despatching tickets and sorting counterfoils. Many of these, should the Sweeps operation collapse, would find it difficult or even impossible to obtain alternative employment.

Such an explosive cocktail of issues, personalities and interests was potentially lethal. There were even suggestions, possibly even threats, which were seriously entertained by senior executives, to the effect that if the programme went ahead some RTÉ personnel might be in physical danger. Transmission was at first postponed and, despite a brief flurry of publicity,[97] went for re-writing of the script,[98] and then vanished without trace. It was to be broadcast finally, in a re-edited form, many years later, but its suppression in 1978 was as clear an indication of the temper of the times as it is possible to get. The benefit of hindsight, as is frequently said, is that it confers 20/20 vision. Even allowing for this, however, it is difficult to avoid the verdict that this particular episode represented, at the end of the day, a major failure of nerve at senior levels within the organisation. Its causes may have been many, and some of the decisions were undoubtedly taken in good faith; but its implications, also, were many and largely negative. Although he had assumed office on the crest of a wave of goodwill, and on a platform designed to reassure producers and reporters about his commitment to courageous and innovative programming, Maloney's departure was on a more subdued note.

One of the problems about assessing his period as Director-General is that it was so short. His high standing among producers and journalists when he assumed that position was not based on transitory or illusory qualities. He had the ability, and the firm intention, of engaging with all the issues involved in his role – technical as well as journalistic – on a theoretical as well as on a practical level. His premature retirement, in particular, meant that he was not in a position to follow through on the structural changes which he had engineered in current affairs, or to help develop a praxis in this area which might have supported his rationale for the changes. A longer tenure of office might in the end have led to even more significant and long-lasting changes: in the event, his time in charge served largely to underline the extreme difficulty of bringing about change in any large, highly talented and often quarrelsome organisation, especially when some of those who had been initially in favour of change found themselves at the receiving end of particular changes which were not to their liking.

---

97 *Irish Times, 10 March* 1978.　**98** PPC Minutes, 10 March 1978.

CHAPTER 6

The 'Stickies'[1]

George Waters' stewardship of RTÉ as Director-General ran from April 1978 to April 1985: the normal term of office was five years, but he and a number of other occupants of the post generally got two-year extensions to bring their tenure up to seven years. The seven years Waters faced were to be among the most contentious in the station since the early 1970s, with increasing allegations of political bias, notably in current affairs; an intensification of the Northern crisis centred on the hunger strikes; and a shortage of money exacerbated by the launch of additional radio and television channels.[2] Waters' engineering background, on the other hand, ensured that the station was well placed at the end of his period of office for the satellite era that was dawning: he also oversaw the development of mobile community radio, although this, in the end, was not enough to stave off the growing challenge from the pirate radio stations which was to became a major issue in the mid-1980s and thereafter.[3] In organisational terms, the Programme Policy Committee became the Editorial Committee, and its minutes became less expansive: under Maloney's period, concern had been expressed at the extent to which the wide circulation of the minutes was creating problems of confidentiality.

The re-vamped current affairs schedule was slow to get off the ground and slower to impress. David Thornley's death on 18 June 1978 at the tragically early age of forty-two served as a reminder of past glories, even though he had been out of broadcasting and in ill health for a number of years. There was much chopping and changing. A programme called *PM* was introduced on 26 September 1978, then became *Prime Time–PM* and disappeared by Easter 1979. *The Politics Programme*, in particular, failed to make a substantial dent in the ratings, was taken off, and was replaced by *Frontline* on 18 September 1978. There was a dispute between the NUJ and the WUI in November 1978 which blacked

---

1 Non-Irish, or younger readers may be unaware that this word, generally used to describe members of the political movement known originally as Official Sinn Féin, is derived from the fact that at the time of the original Sinn Féin split, adherents of the Official grouping wore small paper Easter Lilies with adhesive backs on each anniversary of the 1916 rising, whereas their counterparts in Provisional Sinn Féin had similar emblems fixed to their lapels with pins.   **2** The first test broadcast of RTÉ2 television was on 24 August 1978; transmission proper was inaugurated – in Cork – on 2 November. Radio 2 was launched on 31 May 1979, although on-going union problems prevented it from broadcasting news until November.   **3** In August 1979 the RTÉ Sales Controller assessed pirate radio as holding 6% to 8% of listenership. Editorial Committee, Minutes, 3 August 1979.

production of current affairs programmes for several weeks, and the participation of NUJ members in *Frontline* continued to generate intermittent problems.

Normal service – in the sense of the sparring match between the station's current affairs programming and Leinster House – was resumed at the end of February 1979 when Jack Lynch's address to his party's Ard Fheis (his last, as it would turn out) was cut off as he overran his allotted time. Party leaders' addresses at Ard Fheiseánna were – and continued to be – a major bone of contention, as few kept to their allotted time and any decision to cut was greeted with howls of protest and allegations of bias. In this particular instance, Lynch accepted the assurances of the Controller of RTÉ 1, Muiris Mac Conghail, that the fade-out had been unavoidable.

There is some evidence, on the other hand, of a closer relationship with government than heretofore. Editorial Committee minutes, for example, occasionally note meetings between senior RTÉ executives, the Authority, and the Minister, but – in contrast to earlier Programme Policy Committee documentation – do not contain any detail of what was discussed. The political situation became more acute in November, as Jack Lynch signalled his intention to resign as Taoiseach and leader of Fianna Fáil, and the jockeying for position as his successor began. As this happened, a *Frontline* programme on the succession was abruptly shelved. The item had originally been agreed between the programme team and the Fianna Fáil Whip in the Dáil, but further contact had taken place on the day of transmission between the offices of the Directorate-General and the Department of Posts and Telegraphs. Mac Conghail, took particular exception to this decision, which he said had been taken 'outside the Controllerate'; Wesley Boyd, the Head of News, noted that such interference by the government 'amounted to editorial control over programme material'. This was met by assurances that the programme had been postponed rather than cancelled; but it left a bad taste.[4]

Section 31 was again becoming a problem, but sometimes for reasons which had in all probability not been fully foreseen when the directives were originally issued. The proscription of the Irish National Liberation Army in July 1979 meant that it, too, now came under the terms of the directive. More complicated was the election of a Sinn Féin councillor as Chairman of Galway County Council in the same month. If the directive was to be interpreted literally, this public representative could not broadcast on any subject, whether related to Northern Ireland or not. The consensus at management level was that the directive should be strictly interpreted, although some managers may have felt that, as the situation became more and more absurd, this would eventually help to force an amendment or even the withdrawal of the directive itself.

---

4 Editorial Committee, Minutes, 23 November 1979.

Elsewhere, initiatives were taking place without fanfares which were a portent of things to come. In 1978 Gemma Hussey, newly elected to the Seanad by the graduates of the National University, wrote an article for the *Irish Broadcasting Review*[5] about the absence of adequate representation of women and women's affairs on radio and television. Clare Duignan then pitched the idea to Michael Littleton of a daily programme by and for women. The outcome was *Women Today*, which began on radio on 31 May 1979, and was allowed to continue into the autumn schedules after it had quickly made a mark. Duignan was the first series producer; Betty Purcell was also a producer, Hilary Orpen a reporter (joined later by Doireann Ní Bhriain), and Marian Finucane the presenter. The programme tapped into a new audience and was described by one commentator as a development which produced 'some wariness upstairs'.[6] He spoke truer than he knew: the direction of radio programmes at this time, under Michael Carroll, was anything but adventurous, and *Women Today* survived in spite of, rather than because of, its success with listeners. An early indication of apprehension was the suggestion that it be transferred from its morning slot to a longer evening slot: this was successfully resisted.[7]

A programme in the series on 21 August which dealt with women's sexual problems raised eyebrows again. Although there was agreement that the topic had been handled 'responsibly', it was argued that the timing was unsuitable because many young children would have been listening during the summer holidays. The team were also spoken to critically by management because of the 'exclusion of the spiritual dimension in their treatment of some religious themes.'[8] The criticisms did not appear to have any noticeable effect: a typical week's programming in November 1979 included items on pre-menstrual tension, rubella and pregnancy, pre-budget submissions to the Minister for Finance by various women's groups, and a regular slot for Nell McCafferty, a contributor whose observations were generally not directed towards the faint-hearted.[9] Jack White, promoted sideways as Director of Broadcasting Resources after incurring the ire of the Director-General and the Authority for his stewardship of current affairs, was one of those who argued successfully against another proposal that it be moved to a late night slot.[10] Later, feathers were further ruffled when the programme team submitted a request to interview Rose Dugdale, accompanied by a letter from her solicitor to the effect that she was not a member of any subversive organisation. The matter was shelved after the Director-

5 Edited by Desmond Fisher, this publication ran for sixteen issues between 1977 and 1983. One issue contained an article by the present author on Section 31. At the time a member of the Parliamentary Labour Party, I was influenced by political rather than journalistic imperatives in reaching the conclusion that the directive was a relatively minor matter. It is not a view I now hold.   6 Gene Kerrigan, 'The Women's Programme' (1983), p. 54.   7 Editorial Committee, Minutes, 6 July 1979.   8 Editorial Committee, Minutes, 16 November 1979.   9 Editorial Committee, Minutes, 23 November 1079.   10 Editorial Committee, Minutes, 31 August 1979. White was to die unexpectedly while in Germany on RTÉ business on 13 April

General observed that such an interview 'would inevitably draw attention to the revolutionary tendencies of the lady'.[11] Women in RTÉ were, however, on the move: the report of a working party not long afterwards drew attention to the fact that only 9% of the station's radio producers were women, 16% were television producers or directors, and only 15% of the news journalists were women. A content analysis also drew attention to the 'virtual non-representation of women' on the main evening television news bulletin on RTÉ 1.[12]

The immediate successor to *Women Today* was *Women Talking*, which was produced by Nuala Ó Faolain and presented by Doireann Ní Bhriain in the summers of 1984 and 1985. Outside of the summer schedules, however, the more successful programme was *The Women's Programme*, which was technically a Features rather than a Current Affairs production. This was produced by Duignan and Ó Faolain, with Marion Finucane and Doireann Ní Bhrian as presenters, and Hilary Orpen as reporter. Nell McCafferty made her goodnight wink the trademark of a remarkable programme.

Radio generally was beginning to flex its muscles, and not just in relation to women's programmes. The series of initiatives launched by Mac Conghail and Littleton in Henry Street in 1971/72 were by no means a flash in the pan. While the News Division in a sense marked time – *Morning Ireland* was not to be established until 1984 – current affairs began moves to fill the vacuum. The vacuum was created, in effect, by the fact that apart from the *This Week* programme on Sundays, the conventions of the news division restricted the depth with which any given topic could be treated. The four-and-a-half minute interview was about as long as a news bulletin item could stretch. Over in current affairs, where John Bowman launched *Day by Day* in the course of 1979, there was much more freedom, and it was a freedom which the programme-makers took with both hands. The agenda it was following had been set, to some degree, by the *Late Late Show*: but it was also a period during which politics was in constant flux. There were three elections in eighteen months in 1981–2; there were the continually attempts to unseat C.J. Haughey as leader of Fianna Fáil; the abortion question, and then divorce, were controversies in which the changes in Irish society were becoming manifest. To anybody involved in current affairs, this was meat and drink, and the constantly large audiences lapped it up.

The resurgence of radio current affairs at this time was facilitated by the degree of flexibility afforded by the technology. In sharp contrast to television, which involved heavy pre-planning and which was producer-driven (producers were the people who controlled the resources essential for such a resource-intensive activity), radio was cheap, flexible, and to a much greater degree presenter-driven. It

1980. **11** Editorial Committee, Minutes, 16 October 1980. **12** RTÉ reference Library, *Working party on women in broadcasting*, April 1981, pp. 9 and 12. **13** *Irish Press*, 15 April 1980. Byrne was a popular pub-

was also, frequently and dramatically, live broadcasting in a way that television could only rarely emulate. This led incrementally to a situation, which to some extent still pertains, in which a current affairs topic on radio could be broached in the early morning news, and given a reprise on *Day by Day* and subsequently on *Today at Five* (after 1984) without in any sense appearing to slake the thirst of a continuously and satisfyingly large radio audience. As if to underline the shift in the radio service's centre of gravity, the Walton's sponsored programme was axed in April 1980, together with its presenter, Leo Maguire, who had been doing this job for twenty-nine years. This was in fact part of a general review (i.e. abandonment) of sponsored programmes which also saw the departure of Frankie Byrne.[13]

Important shifts were also taking place in television. *Frontline* was not working well, or was at least generating unproductive controversy, as in October 1979 when the Authority expressed criticisms of some aspects of a programme on an ESRI report on public attitudes to Northern Ireland.[14] It had to make factual corrections on-air on a number of occasions. As noted above, one programme had been postponed after high-level discussions involving the Department of Posts and Telegraphs. In spite of the fact that it was running before the 9.00 p.m. news bulletin (this created problems for news, which argued that *Frontline* was pre-empting the bulletin in the way in which it treated current affairs) TAM ratings were falling, especially towards the end of 1979. There was a major row about one of its items on the Tralee funeral of John Joe Sheehy, a GAA figure with an IRA past: the item was deferred when it was discovered that part of the film included a long sequence of paramilitaries beside Sheehy's coffin.[15] A *Frontline* programme by Michael Heney in May 1980 on Osgur Breathnach, who spent seventeen months in prison after being convicted by the Special Criminal Court, before his conviction was overturned, evoked mixed reactions. One critic described it as 'public service television in its integrity',[16] but members of the station's Editorial Committee reproached it for allowing Breathnach 'to have the final word on the subject of the Special Criminal Courts even though special instructions had been given that this should be avoided.'[17] The transfer of Mac Aonghusa into the programme, from *Féach*, was not a success. Fianna Fáil was hostile to the programme: Charles Haughey had refused to appear on it at the end of his Ard Fheis in February unless he could designate Proinsias Mac Aonghusa as the interviewer: the programme editor, not unnaturally, declined to bow to his wishes in the matter. Haughey then pointedly agreed to an invitation from Raidió na Gaeltachta instead. Occasional high points, such as a programme on the abortion trail to England on which the presenter was Mary McAleese, tended to disappear amid such recriminations.[18]

lic relations practitioner and a radio 'agony aunt'; she died in 2002. **14** Editorial Committee, Minutes, 19 October 1979. **15** Editorial Committee, Minutes, 1 February 1980. **16** Tom O'Dea, *Irish Press*, 31 May 1980. **17** Editorial Committee, Minutes, 30 May 1980. **18** Information from Charlie Bird, who was the

At this point, the decision was made to change direction. Joe Mulholland, who had had a spell on *Féach* and had also been in charge of the books programme, *Folio*, was asked by Dick Hill and John Kelleher to put together a new current affairs programme. This was to be called *Today Tonight*: nothing if not ambitious, it was to appear four nights a week. The decision was made in order to 'enhance the capacity of the television service to respond to major events in Ireland and abroad and to offer detailed analyses of matters of public interest and concern.'[19] Peter Feeney was placed in charge of special events (notably general election coverage.[20]

The significance that attached to *Today Tonight* virtually from its inception can be traced to a number of different factors. One was the background and personality of Mulholland himself. Born in Donegal in relatively humble circumstances, he had studied at third level in England and had then gone to France, where he acquired his doctorate His political and other sympathies were coloured as much by the realities of small-town life in Donegal, where Protestants and Catholics had perforce learned to live together in amity, as by the wider cultural horizons of mainstream Europe. He was a committed European, pro-EEC as a producer in *Féach* when virtually all the other members of that team would have been hostile to Ireland's entry. He was a tough editor, inaugurating Friday morning post-mortems on the past week's programmes which generated self-criticism far more scathing than anything that appeared in the newspapers. He loved film, and had won awards for two substantial documentaries, although some of his critics suggested acerbically that he operated as if film stock grew on trees. One of his productions, a documentary on the left-wing Irish militant, Frank Ryan, ran for three and a half hours over two different nights. He managed his production team expertly in some areas, moderating the workloads to ensure that screen-time was fairly allocated and not hogged by those hungry for exposure or promotion. On the other hand, he could overlook the effects of critical commentary by himself and others on team members whose egos were more exposed or vulnerable, possibly because he himself always intended such criticisms as professional rather than personal. He could be gregarious, but for some at least the bonhomie was only skin-deep. And he had an intellect as formidable as any in an institution which was not short of gifted programme-makers.

He had worked on *7 Days* under Ó Mórdha, but the relationship did not prosper, so he went to work on *Report*. He was no stranger to the North. In one unplanned episode, he had been working for *Report* on a programme about Bre-

researcher on this programme. MacAleese also featured as an interviewer, e.g. on a *Frontline* programme on the tax marches in January 1980, when she carried out vox pops with the marchers.   **19** RTÉ *Annual Report*, 1980.   **20** He also became joint producer (with Gay Byrne) of the *Late Late Show* for a period, and later made an important series of documentaries on 'The Age of de Valera' to mark the centenary of de Valera's birth in 1982. He stayed in Documentaries and Features until 1986.

ton nationalists who had moved to Ireland after the war and were living in Galway when, on impulse, he decamped with the entire crew to the North and made the documentary *Belfast 72*. It won a Jacob's Award, not least for a memorable sequence in a community hall in the Ardoyne in Belfast featuring an immense circle of women – all of whose menfolk had been interned – singing 'The Men Behind the Wire.'[21] He had also been very active in his union, the WUI, which he had joined in 1974, and worked within that framework to give it more intellectual weight as he felt that it was lacking in leadership from the top. He would certainly have been supported in this by that other WUI activist, Eoghan Harris.

Another, factor in the success of *Today Tonight* was the effect of the financial constraint under which RTÉ was operating, and which was getting worse. The station went into deficit regularily, and its financial situation did not begin to improve until 1989, when it moved again into surplus, however briefly.[22] This, together with the need to devote a continually high level of resources to news, meant that news and current affairs assumed a higher profile as a proportion of home-produced programming generally. In 1980–81, current affairs accounted for 10.3% of total home output, compared with only 5.3% in the previous year.[23] Another casualty of increasing costs was programming in Irish, which shrank from more than 22% of total home production in 1979–80 to 10% in the following year: this also underlined the growing importance of the new current affairs slot. When it is remembered that this larger volume of home produced programming was concentrated in a smaller number of programme titles, the pre-eminence of *Today Tonight* can readily be explained. Running three nights a week initially, and building up later to five, it came to overshadow the news: in a sense, it virtually was the news.[24]

Politically, the North was going from bad to worse, and the deep internal divisions within Fianna Fáil were never far from the surface. This exacerbated the direct and indirect pressures on the station not to do or say anything which might, however innocently, further inflame the situation. The Director-General, George Waters, although he endorsed the proposal for the new programme, was more than aware of the risks. 'Well, Joe', he observed with seeming light-heartedness at one point, 'You're not going to get us into any trouble, are you?'[25] The directives under Section 31 continued in place, and there was evidence of increasing frustration among broadcasters: Gay Byrne made disparaging remarks about it on his morning radio programme, and at one stage in 1981 an entire *Late Late Show* was devoted to the issue.

21 The researcher on this programme was Eithne Viney. 22 RTÉ *Annual Report*, 1990, p 8. 23 RTÉ *Annual Reports*, 1980 and 1981. It is a matter for regret, if not worse, that the publication of detailed programming information which had been a feature, in one way or another, of all annual reports since the late 1940s, was discontinued with effect from 1982. 24 This should not, however, overshadow the impact of another less well-known but also significant programmes like *Public Account*, on which skilful economic journalists like Cliff Taylor and Frank FitzGibbon were involved. 25 Private source.

In evidence to the Joint Committee on State-Sponsored Bodies in 1981, the Head of News, Wesley Boyd, made his opposition to the directive clear,[26] but the situation was confused when P.J. Moriarty, who had been appointed chairman of the Authority in 1979, first appeared to say on *Féach* that he was in favour of the retention of the directive, and then refined his position, saying: 'I know there is a need for the section in its original form but maybe now it [i.e. the directive under the section] should not be so all-embracing as it is.'[27] The situation reached a new level of absurdity in February 1981 when two minutes and 20 seconds of the twelfth episode of a series of programmes by Robert Kee on Irish history, which was a co-production between RTÉ and the BBC, had to be cut because of the directive.

Finally, there was the industrial context. The conflict in the North found an echo within public and voluntary bodies right across the country. The annual conferences of most of the major parties, but especially of Fianna Fáil and Labour, became blood-letting exercises as support for and against a whole range of policy issues was coloured by the degree to which they were seen as having an impact on the Northern situation. Security issues, freedom of information issues, support for dying hunger strikers or sympathy for murdered Unionists, historically-conditioned 'Brits out' sentiments and equally deep-seated rejections of political violence – all of these, and more, became powerful weaponry in a rhetorical battle in which there was, in reality, little (and sometimes no) room for compromise. The prism of Northern Ireland distorted, even as it magnified, the issues involved and the emotions of those engaged in them. The two main RTÉ unions involved were differently affected. The NUJ, because it was a British-based union, could adopt – as it did – a fairly consistent policy opposed to the Section 31 directives, even if there had been in the past, and continued to be, some divided counsels on the issue.[28] The NUJ policies, however, were adopted at their annual delegate meetings which took place for the most part in Britain and had only tangential effect on Irish public affairs, although some policies on matters to do with topics other than Northern Ireland – notably on abortion and on nuclear energy – raised eyebrows early in 1980.[29]

The Workers Union of Ireland, however, was more centrally involved. Its annual general meetings took place in Ireland, as it was an Irish union. It represented most of the non-NUJ production staff in RTÉ with the exception of a small group who were members of Actors' Equity. It regarded itself, with some justification, as a more radical union than the ITGWU, and had indeed come into existence as the result of a split in that union in 1924 and was a glittering prize to be fought over. The combatants were, respectively, those who supported, tolerated, or tended to excuse on political grounds the activities of militant

26 Joint Committee on State-Sponsored Bodies, 18th *Report*, 7 May 1981, p 186. **27** *Irish Press*, 28 March 1981. **28** See *infra*, pp. 122–3. **29** Editorial Committee, Minutes, 21 March 1980.

Republicans on the other side of the Border, and those who regarded paramilitarism as a political cul-de-sac at best, and as a stalking horse for fascism at worst. It was also the union which was most powerfully placed to deliver – or withhold – industrial peace at the station. The corollary of this was that taking disciplinary action against prominent members of the Union – for expressing inappropriate political views, for example – was a high-risk undertaking for management.

The new programme took people from left, right and centre, adding new people to the mix as well. Mary MacAleese came in from *Frontline*, although her new status as a reporter might have been regarded as a demotion from her previous role as presenter. Brian Farrell – whose political sympathies were consistently constitutional nationalist – also joined. Barry Cowan was head-hunted from UTV. Olivia O'Leary, who had left RTÉ for the greener pastures of the *Irish Times*, was lured back, although she retained her *Irish Times* base. There was a problem caused by the shortage of current affairs producer, which led to a raid on a just-ending producers' training course: this yielded up Liam Miller, Tish Barry, Michael Heney and Clare Duignan – by no means a politically homogenous lot. One initial success was to persuade C.J. Haughey to abandon his effective boycott of RTÉ's current affairs output: he appeared on *Today Tonight* for a lengthy interview after Mulholland had talked to him personally, and to such effect that the length of the interview was objected to in the Dáil by Garret FitzGerald. The long interview, as it happened, was essentially part of the Mulholland approach, and allowed interviewees to give a more considered account of themselves in contrast to shorter, more confrontational exchanges.

It was not, or certainly not initially, the kind of mix which would encourage people to believe that it had been taken over by a left-wing conspiracy. As the 1980s progressed, however, this was an analysis which was noised abroad, initially on the gossip circuits ('Already, in the lunch queues in the RTÉ canteen, the mordant wits have been at work on the new current affairs programme that is to replace *Frontline* in the autumn: they are calling it "Stickeyline")[30] and then, more emphatically, in a series of articles in *Magill* in 1982 and, later, in 1988.

The rise in these rumours was accompanied by, and may in some sense have been caused by, the growing electoral success of the party which was presumed to be behind all of this. To understand what was happening it is necessary to revisit the origins of the party concerned.

The split in the Republican movement at the Ard Fheis of Sinn Féin in January 1970 had produced two 'wings': one 'Provisional' and the other 'Official'. The IRA had also split, and each political organisation had its own paramilitary organisation. In 1972, however, the activities of the military wing of the 'Offi-

---

30 Tom O'Dea, *Irish Press*, 2 August 1980.

cials' generated much internal controversy within that organisation, particularly the serious wounding of John Taylor, the Northern Ireland Minister of State for Home Affairs, in February, and the murder of an off-duty, Derry-born British soldier, Ranger Best, in his native city in May. In the latter month Tomás Mac Giolla, the President of the Officials, made a speech in County Tyrone at which he declared that violence in Northern Ireland would lead to a spate of sectarian murders and would ultimately and inevitably frustrate any moves towards unity. This, the party subsequently announced, was 'the beginning of the dissolution of the IRA.'[31] Members who rejected the move towards constitutional politics left or were expelled from the party. Some of them subsequently formed the Irish Republican Socialist Party (with its accompanying military wing the Irish National Liberation Army). In 1975 all three para-military groups organisations engaged in a bloody feud, particularly in Belfast. Séamus Costello, the leader of the IRSP, was eventually murdered in Dublin.

In 1977 the party re-named itself Sinn Féin The Workers Party: by this time it was engaged in an intensive process of internal party education of members in which workshops and residential courses played a large part. Ideologically its views were pro-State development in domestic politics and economics, pro-Soviet in foreign policy. At the general election in June 1981, it returned Joe Sherlock as its first TD in the unlikely (from the point of view of revolutionary socialist ideology) constituency of Cork East. At another election in the following year, Sherlock was joined in the Dáil by Proinsias de Rossa (Dublin North West) and Paddy Gallagher (Waterford): the party changed its name to the Workers Party. At the 1989 election it won seven seats in the Dáil and one in the European Parliament, but six of its deputies left in 1992 to form a new organisation called Democratic Left, which was in turn to amalgamate with the Labour Party in 1998.

The critical aspects of the SFWP/WP history, from the point of view of this work, relate to the organisation's method of working in general, and its attitude to Northern Ireland in particular. In early 1972, according to a journalist who was then a member but who left the organisation in 1976, a number of SFWP members decided to set up an organisation called the Republican Industrial Department, with the specific brief of coordinating the views and activities of party members working in trade unions, particularly in Dublin.[32] In the mid-1970s, one of these activists, Eamon Smullen, who had formerly been a member of the Communist Party in Britain, published a document on the role of such members within the trade union movement generally.[33] According to this document, party strategy involved the creation of 'advisory committees' within trade union sections or branches. These advisory committees would sometimes,

31 www.workers-party.org/wphome.htm   32 Ray McGuigan, 'SFWP 3: The making of a conspiracy', pp. 10–12.   33 Republished as 'Strategy for infiltration', by Eamonn Smullen, *Magill*, May 1982, pp. 18–19.

posing as a party branch, hold an 'open meeting with progressive non-party people.'

> The excuse for the meeting is often to discuss party policy in a certain industry but a part of the time is, as if by accident, given over to discuss a coming union election, rules revision meetings or some other question of policy. At every opportunity every effort is made to recruit new members to the party.[34]

Viewed at this remove in time, this outline of the tactics to be adopted has a quaint, almost antique air to it. This was the era in which Soviet bloc journalism, for example, urged trainees to remember two of the fundamental tasks they had to complete in their work:

> Firstly, to give a relatively detailed presentation of ideological and moral problems that are of general importance to the further development of society; secondly, to provide a coherent description of the programmatic objectives and intentions of the revolutionary party and to unmask reactionary political concepts in a polemical way.[35]

In pursuit of objectives like these, groups were set up within the Workers Union of Ireland and the Irish Transport and General Workers Union, and known as the Ned Stapleton Cumann and the William Thompson Cumann respectively, although whether they were formally units of the party as such remains open to question. Their mode of operation involved, among other things, inviting rising young talent within RTÉ to come to meetings where they would encounter like-minded people: two RTÉ trainees in receipt of such invitations at around this time were Declan Kiberd, now Professor of Anglo-Irish Literature at UCD, and Dermot Keogh, now Professor of Modern Irish History at UCC. Both found the invitations easy to resist. The supposed secrecy of the whole operation was, however, to some extent compromised by the high visibility of some of its members, notably (in the case of RTÉ) Eoghan Harris and (in the case of the ITGWU), Des Geraghty, who was actually appointed a member of the RTÉ Authority by a Fine Gael-led government in 1995. According to one account, Harris was never actually a member of the party himself, although that account features him and another RTÉ employee 'in the audience' at the 1982 SFWP Ard Fheis.[36] According to his own version, however, he had been in the party 'most of my life', and in that capacity organised 'discreet' branches within organisations like RTÉ to promote the party's objectives and ideas.[37]

---

34 *Ibid.*, p 19.   35 Arnold Hoffmann, *How to write a journalistic contribution* (1984), p. 39.   36 Brenda Power, 'Eoghan Harris, Out of The Shadows' (1997), p. 21.   37 RTÉ, *Today Tonight* on the Workers Party (1990), RTÉ Ref. BP20/882 1/7008.

I'm a propagandist, you see. That's what I actually do best, I think. I attempted to push ideas – that's what I did, that's what the industrial sector did in the trade union movement, in the media and in the white-collar unions. So it would be normal for us to have cumainn, to allow people who have a contribution to make.[38]

More colourfully and – like the last quotation, in an interview he did after he parted company with RTÉ – he observed some years later, with his by now characteristic humility:

There was a very heated atmosphere in RTÉ at that time and, to us, the work we were doing was important and principled political work. There was a lot of debate going on, but basically it broke down into supporters of the provos and supporters of the Conor Cruise O'Brien line. There is a retrospective air of manipulation because I was a WP supporter, but I only pulled strings as far as I could pull them verbally, and each case had to be won by debate. And we were better and brighter than the rest, so we got the best jobs. And, if there was a last seat to be filled on a panel debate I'd put on John A. Murphy rather than Tim Pat Coogan, and if it was for a news insert and I wanted someone to interpret a baton charge for me than I wouldn't pick someone who would sound a tribal tone. But if I broke the broadcasting restrictions I never did it in an underhand way [...] I've seen my personnel file in RTÉ and there's a report in it by Michael Garvey where he says that I just wasn't capable of producing an unbalanced programme.[39]

The key Northern issue in 1981 and 1982 was, of course, the hunger strikes by Republicans, all but one of them members of the Provisional IRA, in the H-Blocks of Long Kesh (or The Maze prison as it was also known). One after another, ten men, led by Bobby Sands, starved themselves to death in pursuit of their claim to have 'political status', and certain privileges it embodied, restored to them. It was a protest which drew deeply on one of the most powerful myths in Irish nationalist history, as indeed it was intended to do. The inflexibility of the protest, matched by the inflexibility of Mrs Thatcher, divided nationalist opinion on the island as no issue had done since, perhaps, the Civil War. In 1981–2, as in 1922–3, the hidden debate was, as the political scientist Tom Garvin has aptly analysed it, between those whose nationalist orthodoxy had

38 Ibid.   39 Brenda Power, *Harris*, p. 22. Harris's open involvement in Mary Robinson's presidential election campaign in 1990 created difficulties between him and senior management, who decided that these activities were incompatible with his position as a current affairs producer. After being transferred to less sensitive areas, he resigned.

been enhanced and supported by decades of electoral success and the emergence of a broad consensus opposed to the use of violence for political ends, and those whose alternate sense of nationalist orthodoxy was founded on a sense of moral superiority, of greater fidelity to an ancestral flame, a mythology in which a political majority had no right to flout the natural law of Irish republican politics.[40] In this struggle, as in the hunger strike itself, there had to be one winner, and one loser. There were two sides, and little or no middle ground. And the argument was one perennially powered by levels of emotion, linked to concepts of nation, self and identity which made for bruising personal encounters between protagonists. The fact that it was a war by proxy – the proxy being Northern Ireland as an issue of both politics and identity – did not make the protagonists pull their punches. The wounds left by these exchanges took years to heal: sometimes they did not heal at all. The ferocity of the conflict, additionally, tended to obscure the fact that the views of those engaged in this internecine strife influenced probably only a very small proportion of programmes in the sum total of programming on both news and current affairs areas.

It can be argued, however, that there actually was, by 1980, a broad consensus against the use of violence in Ireland for political ends. Such proto-nationalist sympathies as had been stimulated by Bloody Sunday in 1972 were dampened again quickly by the IRA's Bloody Friday response, and by the continuing carnage, especially among civilians, in the North. A 1979 survey by the Economic and Social Research Institute[41] suggested that no more than 20% of the population of the Republic, or just one in five, retained any sympathy for Republican paramilitarism. Harris, however, in a seminal paper prepared for a conference in London in 1980 on the image of Ireland,[42] argued that for many years, and in the media at least for the preceding decade, Ireland had been (and still was) in the grip of three powerful factors constitutive of political culture – religion, nationalism and land – and that these fundamentally nineteenth-century elements had been revitalised, in a malign form, by the Northern conflict. They now, he argued, constituted the ruling ideology; that ideology was faithfully reproduced by the media, of which it became a prisoner. Then the media, 'denying that it is a prisoner at all, [...] is given the key to its own cell, which it then locks upon the audience.'[43]

He chose the recent visit to Ireland of Pope John Paul, about which RTÉ had been more than usually self-congratulatory, and the election of C.J. Haughey as leader of Fianna Fáil, as case histories to support his argument in which he analysed form and content separately. The domination of these cultural factors, he suggested, could only be ended by challenging the ideology of 'professional-

40 Tom Garvin, *Mythical thinking in political life: reflections on nationalism and social science* (2001), passim. **41** E.E. Davis and R. Sinnott, *Attitudes in the Republic of Ireland relevant to the Northern Ireland problem: Volume* 1 (1979). **42** Eoghan Harris, *The production of the popular image* (1980). **43** Harris, *Image*, p. 8.

ism' and the 'exclusive appropriation of newspaper columns and the airwaves by a small elite, visibly well paid and equally visibly deficient in many of the intellectual and moral requirements that would facilitate political and social change.'[44] Instead, there would have to be access (and appropriate training) for 'the best communicators, the most intelligent and morally committed men and women in our society.'[45] This approach, it has to be said, was rather longer on analysis than on prescription, but its visibility ensured that the topic was kept alive.

Although Harris was not involved in *Today Tonight*, the allegation that WP influence was felt in that programme through those he influenced was advanced most elaborately by Vincent Browne, who addressed it first as early as 1980, when he suggested that RTÉ was now being used by supporters of SFWP (as it then was) for their 'very perverse political motives.'[46] He now charged that the programme had been 'heavy-handed on those issues which are dear to the heart of the party' and that its bias had been most evident in programmes on Northern Ireland, 'where the virulent antipathy to the Provisionals has expressed itself at times in terms of a general anti-nationalist bias'[47] In support of this thesis, Browne argued that *Today Tonight*'s first four programmes on the H-Blocks were all hostile to 'The H-Block cause', and that it had not been until the fifth programme on this topic, on 27 November 1980, that Bernadette McAliskey, 'a supporter of the H-Block cause', was invited to take part.

Two things might be said about this analysis. The first was that there was hardly widespread agreement on what constituted the H-Block 'cause.' This was because it was only incidentally about whether certain prisoners should be treated in certain ways, and was in any case muddied by a widespread human concern about the fate of individuals who had taken such an extreme political stance. It was partly about the morality of the hunger strike itself – and yet even those who felt that it was a wildly disproportionate response to the privations of the prisoners found it difficult not to sympathise with them in their predicament. This sympathy, in turn, was tapped into by those who had a wider political agenda.

The debate was also, at a more fundamental level, about whether the methods of the men who were starving themselves to death (i.e. the methods they had employed before their incarceration, which included killing civilians and members of the security forces in both parts of the island) had any degree of political legitimacy in the Ireland of the late twentieth century. This necessarily brings in the second point, which is that for a decade prior to this, almost all of those who supported the H-Block 'cause' in the sense outlined above, and since 1976 if they were members Sinn Féin or any one of a number of other named organisations, were legally precluded from being interviewed on RTÉ in any shape or form, on this or on any issue.

44 Ibid., p 48   45 Ibid., p 51.   46 *Irish Times*, 18 December 1980.   47 Vincent Browne, 'SFWP 7: The slanting of a programme' (1982), pp. 53–5.

In other words, there were undoubtedly major *lacunae* in current affairs coverage of the North throughout this period: but to locate them in relation to one particular issue, and in one particular programme, needs more evidence than critics of the WP have so far been able to provide. On the other side of the argument, the larger number of complaints about Northern Ireland coverage which reached the Head of Information alleged that RTÉ was 'unbalanced in favour of the Provos.'[48] One high-profile complainant was the Fianna Fáil lord mayor of Cork, Paud Black, who alleged later in the year that RTÉ had been infiltrated by Provisional sympathisers. Questioned about this at a meeting of the European Journalists Association in Dublin, his party leader, Mr Haughey, rejected this as being the view of Fianna Fáil. 'I gladly reaffirm', he added, without any sense of offering hostages to fortune, 'our view of the general integrity and impartiality of RTÉ news and current affairs.'[49]

Browne's analysis in *Magill* was somewhat undermined by his own off-hand comment that WP policies on Northern Ireland were indistinguishable from those of both the Alliance Party and the Unionist Party, a piece of journalistic shorthand that did not do much to enhance his other arguments. It is also noteworthy that, after extensive investigations in the *Today Tonight* office at Mulholland's invitation, his considered opinion on programmes that *Today Tonight* had done about issues in the Republic was that there was bias, but that it attached to 'only a handful of programmes' and involved principally giving air-time to people in a representative capacity whose membership of, or connections with, the Workers Party were not disclosed, and in a treatment of the Workers Party itself which 'bordered on the deferential' in two programmes in 1981 and 1982. If malfeasance was involved, this was probably venial.

Today Tonight made many programmes on many topics in which it would have been difficult to discern any political agenda. One of these was its classic programme made in the aftermath of the Stardust disaster on 14 February 1981, When the team all pulled together, the result was frequently memorable. In the hot-house of RTÉ, however (apart from the other programme areas in which most staff went about their work blissfully unconscious of the conspiracy which was supposed to be fermenting in current affairs) rumour was quick to blossom, and it thrived even in the virtual absence of nutrient, often nourished by personal rivalries and other agendas.

A *Today Tonight* programme on Finglas on 3 December 1981, on which the reporter was Gerry Gregg, evoked allegations of Workers Party influence and local (principally Fianna Fáil) criticism in equal measure. Gregg was transferred to children's programmes some eight months later. The fact that his editor, Mulholland, was simultaneously being given the added responsibility for *Public*

48 Editorial Committee, Minutes, 15 May 1981.   **49** *Irish Times*, 21 November 1981.

Account, a programme formerly on RTÉ2 which was now being promoted to RTÉ1, hardly suggests either that the alleged WP influence was a matter of indifference to station executives, or that Mulholland was in any way associated with it. He was definitively never a member of the organisation, although his own background undoubtedly created an ideological overlap on certain issues.

He summed up his own *modus operandi* as based on the need to create an authoritative current affairs programme with a distinctive style.

> If three big stories break in one day, and each of them could use a programme on its own, we don't do one and hold two for later – we'll do all three that night. So that we must always cram and prune – we can't be long-winded and dull. It's a lot more reactive than any current affairs programme we've done before. It's the news of the day, analysed on the day.[50]

One of his successful hirings, Pat Cox, came to *Today Tonight* with a background that included an unsuccessful attempt to get elected to his local authority in Limerick on the Fianna Fáil ticket. Had Mulholland been successful in hiring other journalists he had his eye on, the story of *Today Tonight* might well have been even more impressive: he unsuccessfully approached, at various times, not only Liam Hourican (from Brussels, Hourican told him that he could not afford the drop in salary), Gerry Barry and Geraldine Kennedy.

Bobby Sands's death on 5 May 1981, after his election to the Westminster parliament while on hunger-strike, was the catalyst for tension that had never been far beneath the surface, and involved principally Mary McAleese and the *Today Tonight* editor, Joe Mulholland. A majority of *Today Tonight* staff were undoubtedly deeply hostile to the provisional IRA. Whether this was because they were in sympathy with the WP's political programme, however, or whether any sympathy they might have had for the WP arose from pre-existing views about the morality of political violence, involves a judgement on the relationship between causes and effects which, at this remove in time, is impossible to make. A Forbes McFaul-presented programme during the first series of hunger-strikes, in which a hunger-striker was interviewed, created a lot of internal controversy among members of the *Today Tonight* Team; a Tish Barry programme on the victims of IRA violence, which won an award, was seen elsewhere as evidence of the programme's allegedly pro-WP leanings. Yet another programme, on Annie Maguire, showed that the programme could endorse a cause which had also been endorsed by the Sinn Féin publicity machine without thereby being tainted.

It was certainly true, as Harris argued, that the nineteenth-century consensus about national political culture was breaking down, not least as the violence in

---

50 John Walsh, 'Today Tonight: where somebody knows practically anything' (1980).

Northern Ireland not only generated horrific slaughter and mayhem, but threatened to spread into the comfortable and somewhat alienated territory south of the Border. The telephone log in RTÉ for 14 August 1981, for example (only three months after Sands's death) exemplified this division: one view, representative of the majority of callers, was that

> There are too many programmes given on RTÉ about Northern Ireland and we also have had too many Northern Ireland presenters that seem to influence the programmes and their content. After all there is plenty happens in the rest of the country to merit some television coverage.[51]

The minority viewpoint was one which attacked Barry Cowan of *Today Tonight* for having described Bobby Sands as a 'convicted terrorist', and for a supposedly harsh interview of C.J. Haughey. Although a very rough and ready yard-stick, the RTÉ callers log suggests that the consensus which Harris was attacking was in fact breaking down faster than he thought. It also suggests the Workers' Party and its adherents or supporters of whatever degree were not by only means the only or even the principal agents in this process, and indeed may have reflected it as much as manipulated it. At the same time, Harris's analysis of the formative role of media in creating the sense of communal myth was – and still is – in the mainstream of media theory, which, as he pointed out, was (and still is) not much understood by practising journalists, or seen by them as relevant to their work.

On the other hand, the fierceness of his prescription – that news should abandon the 'dreary spectre' of C.P. Scott and his dictum about the sacredness of fact – and the unvarnished nature of his assertion that '*Today Tonight* satisfies the public as News never does', to all intents and purposes ignored two other possibilities. One is that news and current affairs outputs, at least in the period under review, have traditionally performed different functions, and that it is often quite difficult to define (or indeed to control) either. It is also arguable that media audiences approach different media outputs in different ways: they expect news to be to a degree flat, unemotional, factual; they look for more depth in current affairs, and are more prepared to be stimulated, and to disagree. The one thing that all media theorists agree on is that media audiences are varied, use media for varied purposes, and respond in ways that can rarely if ever be predicted with any degree of accuracy. Politicians, traditionally, tend to believe the opposite. The freedom which programme-makers like Harris and others found in programme areas is, as has been noted earlier, a necessary component of all large media organisations in any case, but is not, therefore, of itself a guarantee

---

51 RTÉ Print Archives: News Management Meeting 20 August 1981.

that the views of any particular producer or presenter will be replicated in all or any of the viewers or listeners. There is even the possibility that those who had strong feelings about Harris and other producers, whether *pro* or *anti*, tended to take him at his own evaluation of himself, a temptation to which those closer to the action were not always so prone. This tended to magnify, in the eyes of critics and supporters alike, the perceived influence on the station and on programming of a small number of individuals, and even to some extent distracted attention from some of these issues.

The hard-edged ways in which the dividing lines were being drawn on this issue left, as it happened, little room for those nationalists, north or south, who were opposed both to the IRA and to British government policy. These felt – sometimes with good reason – marginalised by the intensity of the arguments, especially at a time when the stakes had been raised to previously incalculable heights, as they were now.[52] At one of the *Today Tonight* post-mortems Mary McAleese argued that *Today Tonight* was so concerned with not being a pawn in the Provisionals' campaign that it was actually having the diametrically opposite effect, and 'instead of alienating the people from the IRA, she claimed, it was alienating the people from RTÉ. Accused of being a 'West Belfast Provo', she stormed angrily out of the meeting.[53]

The same events had their repercussions also in the newsroom. When Bobby Sands became a parliamentary candidate, the NUJ AGM passed a resolution critical of the Section 31 directive on the grounds that it prevented RTÉ from having equal access to all the candidates; this was a form of words specifically designed to conceal internal union divisions by making it impossible for anti-IRA NUJ members in RTÉ to withhold their support.[54]

There were three general elections in the Republic in the space of eighteen months in 1981–82, and instability loomed. Nor was this the only series of problems affecting news and current affairs. A new Authority, with Fred O'Donovan as Chairman, was appointed by an outgoing Fianna Fáil government on 1 June 1981, and politics generally was influenced, almost as much as by events in Northern Ireland as by ongoing arguments about the proposal to insert an anti-abortion clause in the Irish constitution. Fine Gael, followed by Fianna Fáil, had given commitments to anti-abortion campaigners that this would be done, and the broadcast and print media became a battle-ground for both sides. Bishop Comiskey of Ferns was one of a number of clergymen who alleged strongly that RTÉ was failing to be impartial on matters of sexual morality in particular, such

---

52 Editorial Committee, Minutes, 1 May 1981 noted views that 'the hunger strike treatment had concentrated on extreme grounds rather than on middle ground opinion.' **53** Justine McCarthy, *Mary McAleese: An unauthorised biography* (1999), pp. 45–7. **54** Information (September 2001) from Michael Foley, sometime Irish representative on the NUJ NEC, and a union activist during his career as an *Irish Times* journalist. He is currently senior lecturer in journalism at the Dublin Institute of Technology.

as abortion and divorce. From the opposite side of the ideological spectrum, he echoed the critiques of 'objectivity' being advanced by Harris and others.

> The RTÉ radio and television journalist is likely to view any spokesperson for the government or the Catholic Church as handing out propaganda, something in favour of the government or the Catholic Church. The journalist then sees his or her task as that of bringing a note of 'objectivity' into the proceedings.[55]

He was invited onto John Bowman's radio programme, *Day by Day*, in April 1982, but station executives felt he had the best of the argument.[56] There were internal tensions on the same topic. On 30 December 1982 the Chairman of the Authority issued a statement concerning RTÉ policy on coverage of the parliamentary debate and the referendum campaigns on the constitutional amendment on divorce, which gave rise to widespread public discussion. At a meeting of the Editorial Committee the following day, concern was expressed 'over the nature of Authority intervention in programming matters', and almost all the senior executives present, including the controllers of both radio and both television channels, supported a proposal for combined editorial/management committee meeting to be held as a matter of urgency.[57] The minutes thereafter are silent on what, if anything, transpired.

Outside, the controversy continued: the anti-amendment group called for O'Donovan's resignation,[58] and the NUJ complained about the Chairman to the RTÉ group of unions.[59] The Television Producers' Association added its voice to the chorus shortly afterwards.[60] The pressure was such that RTÉ eventually, in an important break with tradition, decided to consider the allocation of free broadcasts under the party political broadcasts rubric to extra-parliamentary pro and anti-abortion interests: this was eventually done.[61] All the interests involved continued to monitor programming closely: Nell McCafferty, who had offered some unsolicited opinions on the amendment on a programme dealing with the Rose of Tralee at the end of August 1983, was banned from radio until after the end of the referendum campaign, and a decision was taken that all future appearances by her on radio would have to be personally sanctioned by the Controller of Radio.[62]

---

55 Brendan Comiskey, 'Should Christians always lose?' (1981), p. 10.   56 Editorial Committee, Minutes, 16 April 1982. In April 1989 Bishop Comiskey made a fresh *démarche* which was highly critical of reports broadcast by RTÉ's then religious affairs correspondent, Kieron Wood, about the succession to the archbishopric of Dublin. The pressure was resisted.   57 Special Editorial Committee Meeting, Minutes, 31 December 1982. Similar criticisms – this time of Authority interference in radio programming – were expressed at an Editorial Committee meeting at the end of 1984: Editorial Committee, Minutes, 30 November 1984.   58 *Irish Times*, 13 January 1983.   59 *Irish Times*, 14 January 1983   60 *Irish Times*, 5 February 1983.   61 Editorial Committee, Minutes, 22 July 1983 and 29 July 1983.   62 Editorial Committee, Minutes, 2 September 1983.

The intricate gavotte between Montrose and Leinster House continued. In January 1982 Liam Hourican, now translated, from poacher to gamekeeper, into the position of Government Press Secretary following his sojourn in Brussels, was in touch with RTÉ to complain about the treatment meted out to the Minister for Justice on a recent radio programme.[63] The rash of elections brought the Section 31 directive back into sharp focus with a vengeance. In the campaign leading up to the election of 18 February 1982 Sinn Féin demanded air time for party political broadcasts. RTÉ, in a rare but welcome display of courage on this issue, concluded that the relevant obligations imposed on it by the Broadcasting Acts overrode Section 31 and required it concede this demand, although it reserved the right to exclude people such as Daithi Ó Conaill who would have been barred from the airwaves by the directive for a reason other than his membership of Sinn Féin. The Government then – as RTÉ had more or less anticipated it would – moved to add party political broadcasts by or on behalf of Sinn Féin to the matters proscribed by the directive.

These events had two obvious implications. One was to underline the fact that the continuing restrictions were imposed by the government rather than by RTÉ. The other was that the fact that the government amended the directive rather than charge RTÉ with being in breach of it demonstrated the objective validity of RTÉ's decision. Sinn Féin then went to the High Court to try and have the government's decision reversed, but went unsuccessfully all the way to the Supreme Court on the issue.

In December of the same year, 1982, Ted Nealon, the former *7 Days* presenter and successor to Muiris Mac Conghail at the Government Information Services in 1975–7, who was now a Fine Gael TD for Sligo-Leitrim and a junior government minister, was given political responsibility for Arts and Culture: on 22 February 1983 he received, in addition, responsibility for broadcasting. This prompted the opposition Dáil spokesman on broadcasting, the Fianna Fáil TD Terry Leyden, to discern immediate evidence of an anti-Fianna Fáil bias on *Today Tonight*, and described him as 'the Goebbels of the Coalition'.[64] Nealon, in reply, called on his own experience to categorically reject the idea that there was someone 'out there burrowing a way in the dark, trying to score on party political issues.' The greatest threat to RTÉ he argued, was 'its own self-censorship, over reaction to criticism.'[65] Fianna Fáil suspicions would have been (quite unfairly) increased by the re-appointment of Muiris Mac Conghail to his old position of Controller of Programmes (Television) in March 1983.

Tetchiness was widespread, across both government and opposition. The Fianna Fáil leader, Mr Haughey, was privately angry about an item on *Day by Day*

---

63 Editorial Committee, Minutes, 22 January 1982. **64** Dáil Debates, 1 March 1983. **65** Dáil Debates, 2 March 1983.

in which John Bowman had interviewed Gerry Barry of the *Sunday Tribune* about the PMPA insurance company, and in the course of which reference had apparently been made to a private conversation he had had earlier with RTÉ executives.[66] The Minister for Communications, Jim Mitchell, who had told the Dáil in 1983 that a minister should intervene in current affairs broadcasting only 'in circumstances where the Authority have failed repeatedly to meet their obligations,'[67] nonetheless felt obliged to reprimand the Authority for broadcasting an interview with the Sinn Féin sympathiser, Martin Galvin, on 28 August 1984.[68]

Feeling ran particularly high among journalists working for RTÉ in Northern Ireland. They had, in May 1983, sent a delegation to Dublin seeking support for 'blacking' broadcasts from constituencies in the anticipated general election in which banned organisations were running candidates. The Dublin broadcasters agreed; Gerry Adams issued a statement congratulating the union; and then, in an atmosphere of some confusion, the Dublin broadcasting branch met again almost immediately to rescind its original decision by 67 votes to 47. Branch officials explained that the later decision had been taken to avoid adding to state censorship and to allow full coverage of the general election. The RTÉ Authority wrote formally at this stage to the government asking for a temporary rescinding of the ban in order to allow full coverage of the Northern election: the outcome might have been predicted.[69]

The position of journalists working for RTÉ in Northern Ireland was, it has to be said, one of unusual difficulty. They had to prepare reports for broadcast in an area in which the entire population had access to transmissions from the BBC and ITV which, although cautious, were not subject to the same restrictions until 1988. Their frustration would have been increased by their lack of success in persuading their Dublin colleagues to take more militant action, allied to the moves away from political abstentionism by Sinn Féin, which would eventually register as a normal political party in October 1985.

These arguments and controversies to some extent overshadowed much of the other programming, notably by *Today Tonight*, and by *Ireland's Eye*, a magazine programme on which Eoghan Harris was now working, and which, although technically coming under the Features department, had developed a strong current affairs sense of identity. There was still caution in some areas: a meeting of the election steering group during the February 1982 general election campaign felt that 'it might be difficult to assure RTÉ control of a [*Today Tonight*] programme in which [Vincent Browne] was a participant.[70] However, the programme went from strength to strength, frequently overrunning its allotted time in a way which alarmed schedulers. Mulholland made a point of

---

66 Editorial Committee, Minutes, 21 October 1983. **67** Dáil Debates, 2 March 1983. **68** RTÉ Archives, Mitchell to O'Donovan, 28 September 1984. **69** Editorial Committee, Minutes, 27 May 1983. **70** Editorial Committee, Minutes, 6 February 1982. In fairness, not all the members of such committees

returning to money-lending on a number of occasions, as if to exorcise the ghosts of 1969;[71] there was a deeply disturbing programme on battered babies – in which one infant was shown with bite marks on its skin – in 1982. A programme in December 1982 on alleged political interference with the Gardaí, featuring the then Minister for Justice, Seán Doherty, produced controversy and positive audience reaction in almost equal quantities, although the Director-General felt that 'more balance' might have been achieved, and expressed concern about the programme concentrating on one Minister and one party.[72] Mary McAleese, still with the programme, was involved in a programme on Darndale in May 1983, a month in which the team also did a fine two-part documentary on drug abuse. On 18 October 1983 Brendan O'Brien presented a documentary on conditions in Dolphin House, a working-class block of flats in the south inner city, which added to *Today Tonight*'s already growing reputation for exploring issues of social deprivation largely neglected by the print media.

One subject was partly off-limits – paradoxically, it was broadcasting, more specifically pirate broadcasting. The problem here was that the Director-General had decided that pirate broadcasters should not be interviewed (a decision which sat a little oddly with RTÉ's request for a suspension of the Section 31 directive).[73] The cancellation of a *Today Tonight* programme on this issue apparently led to a resignation threat by Mulholland, which gives some idea of the sensitivities involved on both sides.[74] A programme in May 1984 dealt, somewhat tentatively but in more detail than had been the practice heretofore, with the provisional IRA: this represented, in a sense, pushing the boat out carefully to see what would happen. The coverage of the Kerry babies Tribunal and its outcome, also in 1984, reflected widespread public concern about the issues involved. Regular programme reporters throughout the 1980s included Brendan O'Brien, whose breathless pursuits of dodgy individuals were at once entertaining and informative;[75] Una Claffey, who interviewed President Ghaddafi in 1986 on the vexed question of whether he provided arms for the IRA ('I have not said that, but we are obliged to support the Northern Ireland cause'); Michael Heney, who did a programme on MI5 in 1987; and Olivia O'Leary, who elicited from the beef baron Larry Goodman the assurance that 'We do not have friends in high places'.[76]

In all of this, there was one issue which had not really gone away: the relationship between news and current affairs. Mulholland himself referred to it in 1984 in a context which suggested that it was never very far from his mind.

---

were as apprehensive.   **71** Cf. Editorial Committee, Minutes, 6 December 1985.   **72** Editorial Committee, Minutes, 10 December 1982.   **73** Editorial Committee, Minutes, 27 May 1983   **74** *Irish Press*, 28 May 1983.   **75** O'Brien also made a courageous protest against the Section 31 directive on the occasion of receiving a Jacobs Award for his television work in 1985.   **76** A number of these programmes feature on the compilation of ten years of *Today Tonight* broadcast on RTÉ1 on 27 August 1992; RTÉ AV Library reference O1DO 1449.

In many stations news and current affairs are combined. People here look on that with suspicion – producers in particular have always fought for a separation of the two, because your current affairs could very easily become just a reporting of facts, which would be very bad. However, in view of our limited resources in RTÉ, I could see a time when news and current affairs would be combined, and there would be a practical pooling of resources – though obviously keeping the two roles distinct.[77]

Although the Workers Party issue had to all intents and purposes subsided, it was to re-appear briefly in 1985, when Dick Spring wrote to RTÉ to allege a pro-Workers' Party bias on a *Today Tonight* programme on 12 June and a *This Week* programme on 16 June.[78] Joe Mulholland, Head of Current Affairs for television, rejected Spring's criticisms as 'outrageous' and said that they 'should be responded to in the strongest possible way'. The Director-General, however, opted for a milder approach, responding in detail to Spring's allegations, and arguing in favour of meeting politicians who objected to programming and discussing their problems rather than simply leaving matters to correspondence.[79] Peculiarly, a markedly different atmosphere was evident some months later, when the Editorial Committee discussed the impression that the station, in its general reporting, gave 'undue weight to the opinions of the Workers Party.'[80] Now, there seemed to be widespread agreement on the Committee that this was the case, although the rationale for such agreement was itself striking: the most likely reason for the publicity the WP received, it was thought, was 'the articulate nature of their comment and their coherent analysis'; although there was, appropriately, also general agreement that because they had excellent public relations did not mean that they should get more air time than anyone else.[81]

Less than a year later, not long before Mulholland left *Today Tonight*, the team did a programme on paramilitary organisations in Northern Ireland.[82] This – ironically in view of the public perceptions of pro-WP bias – led to an immediate complaint to the Broadcasting Complaints Commission by the General Secretary of the Party, Seán Garland. Garland complained that no approach had been made to the party (which featured in the programme by virtue of its associations with the Official IRA) until after the film report had been concluded, edited, and was ready for transmission; that political opponents of the WP were allowed to make serious allegations for which they were not asked to produce evidence; and that an attempt was made by innuendo to suggest that Workers Party Advice Centres in Belfast were financed by illegal activities. In the event, the WP had been given a 14–minute right of reply immediately after the film section.

77 Interview, November 1984.   78 Editorial Committee, Minutes, 21 June 1985.   79 Editorial Committee, Minutes, 21 June 1985.   80 Editorial Committee, Minutes, 1 November 1985.   81 Ibid.   82 5 March 1986.

The Commission's decision did not find the programme unfair. However, it expressed concern at the structure of the programme, the film section of which did not give the Workers Party an opportunity of rebuttal. The Party was given an extended right of reply immediately after the film section. The Commission found the programme, viewed as a whole, fair and the complaint was therefore dismissed.[83]

The period around the end of George Waters' tenure of office as Director-General was notable for one closure, one opening, and one major political controversy. The controversy, although it did not have a direct bearing on news and current affairs, nonetheless created a sense of unease within the station which had a subtle, if indirect effect on morale and possibly also on some programming decisions. This was the decision by the Coalition government, now nearing the end of its term of office, to ask the Authority to suspend the process of appointing a new DG, who was widely reported to be John Sorahan, a member of the station's engineering staff. Jim Mitchell, eating copious mouthfuls of the language about RTÉ's independence that he had uttered when defending the station against Fianna Fáil charges of partiality in 1983, simultaneously announced that he would be instituting an inquiry into the station. The Taoiseach, Garret FitzGerald, defended the government's actions, Sorahan himself denied that he had any Fianna Fáil connections, and – as if to complete the series of political reversals of attitude in progress – Fianna Fáil tabled a motion in the Dáil calling on the government to respect the independence of the Authority.[84] The outcome of this messy business was the appointment of Vincent Finn as Acting Director-General in April 1985; he was confirmed in that position in November of the same year.

Joe Mulholland was appointed as Controller of Television Productions in March 1986, ending his association with *Today Tonight* and with current affairs broadcasting generally. There were two candidates to succeed him – Michael Heney and Eugene Murray. The latter was appointed, but the new generation of *Today Tonight* lacked some of the impact of its predecessor.

The departure of *Féach* from the schedules in 1985 marked the end of a different kind of era. It had been some eighteen years on air, in one form or another, since its first broadcast on 16 July 1967. Its first editor, John Ross, had given a flavour of his approach at that time: 'Let's shoot the hairs of an interesting nose rather than the whole of a dull face.'[85] It was never a programme about Irish, or a programme to help people to learn the language: initially, its linguistic stance was as uncompromising as its political one. It was not immune from criticism (its presenters Proinsías Mac Aonghusa and Breandán O hEithir were continually in

83 Broadcasting Complaints Commission, *Report 1987*, pp. 3–4.   **84** *Irish Times*, 4, 5, 6, 7, 8, 13 and 14 March 1985.   **85** Quoted by David Hanly in 'Féach!'

hot water, usually for their non-RTÉ journalism). There was fresh controversy in 1973 caused by an extended interview with the poet Seán Ó Riordáin, in the course of which he had expressed pro-IRA views. The heavily-edited interview gave rise to a flurry of commentary in the newspapers, and both Ó Mórdha and Mac Aonghusa were told that their published comments were 'quite unacceptable from people working in current affairs programming'.[86] A programme in April 1977, in the opinion of Oliver Maloney, had 'broken every rule in the book' and had been heavily biased in favour of the Labour Party (although Proinsías Mac Aonghusa's description of Brendan Halligan, on the same programme, as a 'carpet-bagger' suggested that this bias was not entirely unqualified).[87]

It was edited for a period after September 1980 by Mac Aonghusa which was in itself unusual in that Mac Aonghusa was a journalist: the normal thing would have been to have an RTÉ staff producer act as editor. Its decline was partly related to the success of Mulholland with *Today Tonight*, and because of scheduling: in the autumn 1980 schedules it clashed directly with the main evening news of Raidió na Gaeltachta. There was also a difficulty in finding public figures with sufficient command of Irish who could be interviewed on current affairs topics. This led to an increasing use of English on the programme (although the same tendency had been noted as early as 1969). One of its final producers on RTÉ1, before it was transferred to RTÉ2 in the autumn of 1982, was Nuala Ó Faolain. Muiris Mac Conghail, who assumed overall responsibility for the programme in the summer of 1983 when he was re-appointed as Controller of Programmes on RTÉ 1, felt that Irish language programming – in common with other areas – was in need of fresh blood,[88] but the station's increasingly parlous financial condition precluded this. Critical elements of the decision to close it down were the increasing use of English, and the fact that although its team was Dublin-based, much of its programming was recorded in, and based on, Gaeltacht events and personalities, resulting in an exceptionally heavy drain on already scarce resources. Although the Workers' Party issued a call for the programme to be retained[89] it had, by now, become a lost cause.

As the star of *Féach* set, another rose. This was *Morning Ireland*, which was broadcast for the first time on 5 November 1984. It had had a long gestation. Mike Burns, in a long and varied career in both radio and television, had first presented news segments on the Mike Murphy programme *Morning Call*: he had pressed, around 1970, for a full-scale morning news programme, but the weight of opinion within the station was against him.[90] In March 1982 Shane

86 PPC, Minutes, 14 December 1973. **87** PPC, Minutes, 7 April 1977. The same week was also noted for Deirdre Purcell's appearance as RTÉ's first woman newsreader. **88** Profile (unsigned) of Muiris Mac Conghail, *Sunday Tribune*, 8 May 1983. **89** *Irish Times*, 8 August 1985. **90** For much of the information in this section I am indebted to my former MA in Journalism student, Eoin Licken, and his valuable term paper on 'History and Structure of *Morning Ireland*'.

Kenny, a member of the News Features staff since the mid-1970s, was given the brief to prepare a morning programme; there was to be a matching programme from 5 to 6 p.m. each evening. A provisional launch date of 18 October was chosen, but the programme never went ahead: the lack of adequate facilities was a major factor. Kenny, promoted to head of News Features in early 1983, re-commenced planning; additional staff were hired, bringing the number at News Features to twelve, and *Morning Ireland* (the name was chosen by Kenny himself) went on air for the first time on 5 November 1984, replacing Mike Murphy's morning show, which had included only a short news bulletin at 8 a.m. The first major news story was the assassination of Indira Gandhi; only eight days later, the journalists involved found themselves reporting on the death of some of their colleagues in the Eastbourne air crash on 13 November: this was, in effect, its first major domestic news story, and the expertise with which it was treated attracted much favourable attention. Resources, however, were always a problem in the early days. Out of approximately eight interviews per programme. In its first incarnation, rarely more than three were live, and much of the show had to be recorded the previous evening. Much of the credit for the programme's initial success can be ascribed to the work of Tom Savage, who had presented *What It Says in the Papers* as a free-lance, and who edited *Morning Ireland* from within a few months of its inception until 1986.

The programme's first presenters were David Davin Power and David Hanly. It is hard to imagine it now, but it had a distinctly shaky beginning. This was partly because of inadequate technical resources, but it was also because of divided views within the station. The Chairman of the Authority, Fred O'Donovan, who favoured light entertainment over talk radio, described it after only six weeks on air as an experiment. It received much criticism at the first Editorial Committee meeting after it went on air, when it was put on probation for three months, together with the new *Today at Five* programme, presented by Pat Kenny.[91] The increased amount of talk radio prompted turf wars with its parent, the News Division, and there were some disputes between presenters. The first indications of good ratings, however, were evident as early as December 1984, when Cathal Mac Coille and Gerry Reynolds sampled opinion on Dublin streets and came back to the station with good news. It was just in time to off-set a long 'list of criticisms' of the programme submitted in a letter to the Director-General from the gifted and combative Fine Gael TD, John Kelly, who in his own unique way thus signalled his appreciation of its potential.[92]

---

91 Editorial Committee, Minutes, 9 November 1984.   92 Editorial Committee, Minutes, 30 November 1984.

CHAPTER 7

Into new territory

Vincent Finn's appointment as Director-General was ratified in November 1985 by a different Authority from the one that had appointed him as Acting DG earlier in the year. The new Authority, under the businessman Jim Culliton, was the first non-Fianna Fáil Authority to be appointed in almost a decade, and included two journalists – Pat Kenny and Mary Leland. The Authority's term of office, however, was now five years (as compared with the three for which its predecessors had served) which at least presented the possibility of a longer-term view of programming and its needs, and even the possibility of radical review. In the event, not a great deal happened until just before the end of the Authority's term of office in May 1990. Financial and personnel problems were as chronic as ever. Joe Mulholland left *Today Tonight*, to be succeeded by Eugene Murray, in March 1986. The resignation of Muiris Mac Conghail from RTÉ, in June 1986, deprived the organisation of a rare talent. Although these two events were not connected, the degree to which, in the period leading up to these changes, Mac Conghail's control over station resources had been reduced, and Mulholland's enhanced, provided plenty of food for station gossips.

The situation was complicated by the fact that pirate radio stations were becoming ever more numerous, and sometimes extremely profitable (not least because they tended to regard themselves as exempt from the normal requirement to pay royalties and other fees). RTÉ management's response had been to put forward a plan whose chief element was a proposal that there should be no national rival to RTÉ radio (as in fact was, and remained the position in Britain for a number of years after the introduction of commercial radio). It also proposed the allocation to RTÉ of at least one new local station in Dublin and a number of other stations outside the capital. This created a total stalemate within government: the minority Labour partner, which had a close relationship with the RTÉ Trade Union Group, refused to accept any compromise, and the RTÉ unions were in any case not prepared to allow their own management any room to manoeuvre.

Despite the appointment of an informal Commission[1] to examine the problem, it dragged on, unsolved. The significance of this factor for RTÉ and its

---

1 The Interim Radio Commission 1985–87, under the chairmanship of Dr Colm Ó hEocha, president of University College, Galway. The Commission, of which the present author was a member, produced a report, which was never published.

news and current affairs services, was that radio audiences were now becoming ever more volatile. The station, conscious of this, commissioned audience research in 1985 which showed that 57% of respondents said that RTÉ was very important to the life of the country, while a further 30% said it was fairly important. These percentages were somewhat inverted in relation to another question, in relation to which 28% said they were very proud of RTÉ, some 47% said they were fairly proud of it. The Director-General, Vincent Finn, commented that 'while the Irish public may not be head over heels in love with us, they do hold us in a certain regard.'[2]

More significantly in the medium term, the then Fianna Fáil opposition was now moving rapidly towards a pro-deregulation position, not least because of its by now case-hardened perception that RTÉ news and current affairs (particularly the latter) contained strong, and ineradicable, pockets of anti-Fianna Fáil bias. Mr Haughey, touchy as ever, was annoyed by a *This Week* interview on 20 April 1986, just after his Ard Fheis, because a divorce question had been sprung on him: he believed that this should not have formed part of the interview agenda because his party had not yet taken a decision on it.[3] On the face of it, this was a somewhat flimsy excuse for a protest. The party had, however, at least circumstantial evidence of Workers' Party influence – if not control – in some programming areas, although its concern would have been magnified by the paranoia affecting politicians of all parties in relation to the media..

At a lesser level of significance, the pirate radio issue featured one of RTÉ's former star performers, Mary McAleese. McAleese. After leaving *Today Tonight*, McAleese had basically gone back to her career as a law lecturer in Trinity, until the *Irish Times* journalist (and later its editor) Conor Brady, persuaded her to come back to television and co-present with him a magazine programme called *Europa*.[4] She then moved to Pat Kenny's morning radio programme at the invitation of its producer, Ed Mulhall, and established an excellent reputation as a reporter whose legal training enabled her to be more adventurous than others in broadcasting about courts: her reporting of the McArthur case in 1983 was a case in point. She subsequently moved to *Studio 10*, the fore-runner of *Today at Five* (but only on a weekly basis). Early in 1984, however, after she appeared as a member of the Catholic hierarchy's team when it made a submission to the Forum on Northern Ireland on 9 February 1984, her membership of the NUJ was suspended, ostensibly on the grounds that her full-time occupation was not in journalism but as a lecturer in law. Her supporters felt that – given the NUJ's traditionally watery attitude towards double-jobbing elsewhere – this was no more than an excuse. The circumstantial evidence strongly supports this inter-

2 *Irish Times*, 15 January 1986.   3 Editorial Committee, Minutes, 24 April 1986.   4 McCarthy, *Outsider*, pp. 60–7 for a detailed and colourful account of this period of McAleese's career.

pretation: the union did not appoint a committee to investigate double-jobbing until after her membership was finally terminated in February 1986, and took no visible initiatives in this area thereafter. Now, only a few months after her exit from the station, she was heard broadcasting on pirate radio, and was sent a 'strong letter' by the Director-General, to which she declined to reply.[5]

The continuing controversies about major social issues such as divorce and abortion created pressures on the organisation from conservative religious sources, and the increased tension in Northern Ireland as a result of the 1985 Anglo-Irish agreement had exposed RTÉ crews to increased risks from loyalists.[6] The annual renewal of the Section 31 directive led to discussions about a work stoppage by the NUJ in the station, in spite of assurances given to the union by the Director-General that it had been making unavailing efforts to have the directive suspended for appropriate broadcasts. The effectiveness of these requests, both on government and as a means of assuaging journalistic opinion, was considerably diminished by the fact that, up to October 1987, they were made in private, and because station executives generally decided not to participate in radio or television broadcast discussions on the ban.[7]

Sinn Féin maintained the pressure, but with only minimal effect: a letter from Gerry Adams enquiring why the party's Irish-language publication had not been featured on the newsroom programme, *Na hIrisí Gaeilge*, was treated with caution: perhaps luckily, the publication in question had not been sent in to the station.[8] Adams complained again about a *Today Tonight* programme on the British general election from which Sinn Féin had been excluded: station managers concluded gloomily that the BBC's treatment of the provisional IRA in the context of the general election raised 'major questions' for RTÉ: the standards of BBC interviewing were regarded as 'very bad and, in contrast, Mr Gerry Adams was a highly competent performer.'[9]

NUJ militancy on this issue had in fact become increasingly evident, and reflected more widespread tensions within the station evoked by the sharply critical attitude towards Republicanism adopted by the *Today Tonight* team. This was also partly related to events in Britain, where action taken by BBC management to censor a 'Real Lives' documentary on Northern Ireland led BBC and ITV union chapels to vote in favour of a 24–hour strike in August 1985. This coincided with a particular RTÉ ban, on 9 August, on a proposed interview with Martin Galvin, an Irish-American official of the Noraid organisation which was

5 Editorial Committee, Minutes, 20 June 1986. Another letter was sent to Professor William Binchy, whose voice had also been heard on pirate radio: he replied, dissociating himself completely from what had been a misuse of a taped interview. 6 Editorial Committee, Minutes, 10 January 1986. 7 Cf. *Irish Press*, 19 October 1987, when the Authority issued a public statement observing that 60% of the households in the State now had access to broadcast services which were not affected by any such directives. On non-participation in programme discussions, see e.g. Editorial Committee, Minutes, 9 January 1987. 8 Editorial Committee, Minutes, 5 September 1986. 9 Editorial Board, Minutes, 5 June 1987.

believed by the Government to be a conduit for North American funds for the IRA. This provoked a second stoppage by RTÉ journalists, this time for 24 hours, but it was not an uncomplicated decision. The events in Britain were in the forefront of everyone's mind: the journalist Mary Holland, referring to the UK strike, suggested that the UK journalists' action 'makes the silence of RTÉ's journalists all the more disturbing'.[10] At a meeting of the union's Republic of Ireland Industrial Council (RIIC) on 9 August, a motion calling for an NUJ campaign against section 31 was passed, and an amendment sponsored by RTÉ journalists opposing any industrial action was defeated.[11] Despite this, the Broadcasting Branch, at its meeting on 10 August, voted for a mandatory branch meeting from 7 p.m. on that day until midnight on the following day (in effect a strike, since journalists have to attend such meetings under threat of expulsion from their union and are therefore unavailable for work). Gene Kerrigan, in a sharp contemporary micro-analysis of this tempestuous episode, quoted an unnamed RTÉ journalist as observing: 'It would never have happened if we weren't shamed into it by the BBC.'[12]

Prompted by events on the other side of the Irish Sea or not, this contributed to a new climate of militancy on the part of union officials coming up to the date, in the following January, when the ministerial directive would be renewed for the following year. At its meeting on 25 November 1985, the union's RIIC called on all chapels to declare their support for a one-day strike on the renewal date for the directive in January 1986 Less than a month later, on 6 December, the same body noted that 'it was already obvious in some areas that members would not agree to the stoppage'. The *Irish Times* chapel officers notified the union on 22 December that the proposal for a stoppage had been defeated on a chapel vote. By 10 January 1986, the Council was facing the fact that every unit of the organisation had set its face against industrial action, with the exception of RTÉ, where a two-hour stoppage had been agreed. Nonetheless, it circularised all branches and chapels on 14 January with a compromise wording, telling them that although 'it was clear [...] that a one-day strike was not a tenable proposition', all journalists were urged to attend a demonstration outside the Dáil on 22 January, 'and if necessary to leave work to do so'.

The situation was suddenly complicated by unilateral action by the FWUI, which decided on a 24–hour work stoppage on the same day. Taken in conjunction with the two-hour stoppage by NUJ members in the station, this protest blacked out the main news bulletins and a number of other current affairs programmes, and drew some adverse newspaper comment. The *Irish Times*,

---

10 *Irish Times*, 7 August 1985.   11 Gene Kerrigan, 'Two weeks in the life of the media', *Magill* 8 (18), (September 1985), p. 28. For a detailed discussion of some of the issues involved, see Horgan, *Censorship*, which is also the source for references in this section which are not otherwise specified.   12 Kerrigan, 'Weeks', p. 32.

although it described the ban itself as 'a pointless bit of window-dressing by the politicians', commented: 'Those involved in the protest are perpetrating an offence which is very similar to that of which they accuse Mr Mitchell [Minister for Posts and Telegraphs]. Are there not other ways in which their point might be put across?'[13] One casualty of the continuing ban was Phil Flynn, general secretary of the Local Government and Public Services Union, who wrote to Finn in May 1986 inquiring about his non-participation in radio or television programmes. The Director-General's view was that Flynn should take his complaint to the government, not to RTÉ.[14]

This particular renewal date, as it happened, was the only occasion on which a political initiative aimed at preventing the re-imposition of the ban was taken. The terms of the SFWP motion, however, were eloquent of that party's internal difficulties on the issue.[15]

At its meeting on 14 February 1986, the NUJ's RIIC reviewed the protest, which had been attended by some 200 people, about half of them journalists (it will be remembered that NUJ membership in the Republic at this stage amounted to about 2600). One RTÉ member, Patrick Kinsella, 'reported difficulties experienced within the ranks of FWUI in RTÉ on the question of support for a stoppage. He suggested that over militant methods had landed them in trouble with their members.' Although the union's AGM in the same year passed a resolution congratulating the RTÉ journalists on their action, it declined to accept a motion which would have committed it to paying £5000 to support the campaign.[16] The following two years, as it happened, were to see a substantial change of tactics by the NUJ and – paradoxically – a sharp deterioration in relationships between the union's central organisation in Ireland and NUJ members in RTÉ itself.

The size of the mountain that had to be climbed was clearly illustrated by a survey carried out in 1986 which disclosed that 38% of a sample of Dubliners were completely unaware that there was a law preventing RTÉ from interviewing certain groups on its news and current affairs programmes and that, of the 62% who were aware, 16% were unable to say what the law was about or what it was called.[17] Equally noticeably, the North was becoming a boring subject for many viewers.[18] The general difficulties of dealing with the North were exemplified by a *Today Tonight* programme on racketeering in March 1986. The programme, although generally praised, was bedevilled by the difficulties of finding people who were willing to appear on camera on this topic. More ominously, the *Today Tonight* team who travelled North on this assignment, encountered increasingly sinister forms of harassment (including the trashing of a hotel room) and

13 *Irish Times*, 22 January 1986.   14 Editorial Committee, Minutes, 16 May 1986.   15 Cf. supra, pp. 143–4.   16 *The Journalist*, May-June 1986.   17 Jane Horgan and Niall Meehan, op. cit., p. 29.   18 Editorial Committee Meeting, Minutes, 18 July 1986.

were eventually advised by security force sources to return to Dublin early, and by a specific route, in order to escape further harassment, or worse.[19]

The difficulties attaching to the making of documentary current affairs programmes – and of course their expense – prompted a fresh look at other formulae. Peter Feeney, who returned from a sojourn in documentaries and features in 1986 to work under Eugene Murray in current affairs, established and edited two new models: *Questions and Answers*, and *Marketplace*. The first, although undeniably a borrowing from the similar BBC formula, was broadcast for the first time in the autumn of 1986. Its first chairperson was Olivia O'Leary, who was succeeded after two years by John Bowman. Despite – or perhaps because of – its somewhat predictable format, it rapidly achieved a substantial audience, and is still an established and valuable component of the station's current affairs scheduling after almost two decades. *Marketplace*, which was also first broadcast in autumn 1986, bespoke a renewed interest in economics, which was in turn to underpin more and more of RTÉ's current affairs programming in the early and middle 1990s.

Implementation of the Section 31 guidelines was becoming somewhat haphazard: apparently part of the problem was that the guidelines were not issued to new reporters; nor were such reporters briefed on their implications.[20] Government were watching: the Government Press Secretary, P.J. Mara, alleging in particular that Sinn Féin was being allowed to plant its supporters in the audience for *Questions and Answers*.[21] Fianna Fáil effectively boycotted the programme for a period thereafter, which created considerable problems, not least because it was the only television current affairs programme on air from Thursday to Tuesday.[22] Fianna Fáil was not alone: Fine Gael's Gemma Hussey called for the programme to be taken off the air until RTÉ put its house in order – in other words, implemented the Section 31 directive. Olivia O'Leary later departed as presenter of *Questions and Answers*, in part because of the way this issue was being handled.

The impending election – it was to take place on 17 February 1987 – generated visible nervousness about news and current affairs programming, especially as it had begun to seem as if Fianna Fáil might come out in favour of removing the Section 31 directive. *Morning Ireland* was criticised for an interview with Nicky Kelly because Kelly, who had claimed the right to free speech, had not been 'probed on the right to life', and David Hanly and Brian Farrell both came under notice for 'aggressive' interviewing.[23] A newspaper article which identified Eoghan Harris as the author of the Workers' Party party political broadcast also came under notice,[24] raising again the old (and still evidently unsolved) question

19 Private source. 20 Editorial Board, Minutes, 4 September 1987. 21 Editorial Board, Minutes, 17 September 1987. 22 Editorial Board, Minutes, 4 December 1987. 23 Editorial Committee, Minutes, 22 January 1987. 24 Editorial Committee, Minutes, 6 March 1987.

of the involvement of staff in political activities. Both before and after the election, Fianna Fáil ministers felt that RTÉ was harping on the health issue, to the detriment of their party.[25]

There was also nervousness on other issues, notably bad language, and programmes dealing with sexual matters. A *Liveline* item on child sexual abuse on 28 May 1987 prompted regret that it had been broadcast on a Holy Day when children were at home, and an evidently lengthy discussion about the need for a better balance between 'good' and 'bad' news. Views were more or less evenly balanced about the quality of RTÉ output in this regard, but one senior executive alleged that RTÉ was 'painting a distressing and distorted picture of society which was not a realistic presentation of the views of the vast majority'.[26] Related issues included a *This Week* interview with the victim of a rape in County Cavan, and a *Pat Kenny Show* interview with an American male prostitute, which was not deemed any more acceptable by virtue of the fact that it had been used to fill a gap created by the withdrawal – at the request of the Editorial Committee – of an item on massage parlours.[27] A clearly exasperated Director-General noted that it now appeared to him that 'there were no limits to what some producers felt they could use on either radio or television' and, while this view did not command universal acceptance, there was evidently increasing concern that the Editorial Committee was proving little more than a talking shop to which programme-makers were paying little or no attention.[28] There was a sense of the wagons being circled: producers were criticised for using too many *Irish Times* journalists, and external journalists in general.[29] Eyebrows were raised when Fintan O'Toole, who had written critically about RTÉ in *Magill*, was interviewed (about drama).

Today Tonight was also in the wars, but not only for aggressive interviewing. Eugene Murray, its editor, was spoken to 'in very strong terms' after a controversial programme on a Garda security leak in connection with a holiday by the British ambassador in Co. Kerry: station management felt that the programme had, inadvertently, been 'set up' by the IRA as part of a propaganda coup.[30] Within three months, the Enniskillen bombing, on 8 November 1987, generated an even sharper reaction. A policy decision was taken that any proposal to use Nell McCafferty – who had expressed strongly Republican views in a radio interview shortly afterwards – as a programme contributor should be referred upwards for approval; she was prevented from going on a *Liveline* programme, despite union protests.[31] This inaugurated a period of growing tension, which

25 A complaint by Ray McSharry, in particular, is noted: Editorial Committee, Minutes, 3 July 1987. 26 Editorial Committee, Minutes, 28 May 1987 and 5 June 1987. 27 Editorial Committee, Minutes, 5 June 1987. The massage parlour item was broadcast some time later in a considerably truncated version. 28 Ibid. 29 Editorial Board, Minutes, 7 August 1987. The Supreme Court decision, upholding the earlier High Court decision, can be found at *O'Toole v Radio Telefís Éireann* (1993) ILRM 458. 30 Editorial Board, Minutes, 14 August 1987. 31 Editorial Board, Minutes, 20 November 1987.

reached new heights with the Gibraltar killing of IRA personnel by the British SAS early the following year. The nervousness was, it appeared, to a degree even-handed: the approach being adopted by Eoghan Harris in a recent train-ing course for producers, in which he had mounted a dramatic critique of Republican ideology, and of what he considered to be the responsibility of RTÉ to expose and challenge this ideology,[32] also evoked criticism, and was discussed not only by the Editorial Board, but by the management committee and by the Authority.[33]

This training course, based on a series of role-playing exercises, was the ori-gin of a paper which Harris (at this time editor of the Irish-language current affairs programme *Cursai*) wrote in 1987 on 'Television and Terrorism'.[34] The political context was the Enniskillen bombing, in the aftermath of which he had resigned from the Federated Workers' Union of Ireland because of what he described as 'their continually ambivalent attitude to the provisional IRA cam-paign'. This paper involved a passionate denunciation of 'hush puppy broad-casters' and 'liberals' for being soft on the IRA.[35] It is not difficult, even a quar-ter of a century after the event, to envisage the effect his polemical and highly charged style, and his recourse to stereotyping, would have had on his oppo-nents, some of whom still believe that he was the single worst thing ever to have happened to the station. 'Television and Terrorism' also involved a detailed exploration of the notion of consensus: more significantly, perhaps, it challenged the traditional notions of 'impartiality' and 'objectivity' ('What kind of a repor-ter, except a psychopath, could be objective about Enniskillen?'),[36] and argued that such antediluvian notions had been banished from RTÉ Programmes Divi-sion by Lelia Doolan and himself, 'which is why *Today Tonight* is so good and why the public trust it.'[37]

Television, he argued, was not about thought but about emotion, not about facts but about truth – and 'professionalism' ideologically excluded both. *Today Tonight*, he argued, 'does not see the interview as a voyage of discovery, or as a cross-examination or as an arid exercise in finding out the facts as if that were an exercise in finding out the truth. What it does is find the answers first and then makes the whole programme one huge question to an answer it already knows. Stating the question on film in a dramatically intelligible way is what makes it a moral drama and not a trivial pursuit full of useless answers to useless ques-tions.'[38] This document, as sent to senior executives, was accompanied by a 20–point programming plan to explain protestant fears and accelerate change in the Southern consensus against terrorism on a sectarian basis. His covering let-ter noted:

---

32 Cf supra, p. 18.   33 Editorial Board, Minutes, 4 December 1987.   34 Eoghan Harris, *Television and terrorism*, Reference Library, RTÉ (mimeo) 1987.   35 Harris, *Terrorism*, p. 2.   36 Ibid., p. 12.   37 Ibid. 38 Ibid., p. 23.

There will be those who will attempt to discount it on the basis that I am an open supporter of the Workers' Party. This charge deserves attention: I support that Party for it's [*sic*] unflinching stand against sectarian terror: a stand which arouses support from quarters as diverse as Lord Fitt, John Taylor, Paddy Devlin, Conor Cruise O'Brien and the Belfast Telegraph, who treat charges of fraud against past or present members of the party as sometimes mediated by provo media, sometimes true, and if so, on a very different moral plane to mass murder. Lord Fitt and Paddy Devlin support the Workers Party for one reason: from a ghetto it speaks peace.[39]

The intensity of Harris's attack on the 'consensus' begged the question of whether what was involved was, at another level, an attempt to replace one consensus (assuming such existed) with another. Bob Quinn, one of his erstwhile allies in the days of *Sit Down and Be Counted*, observed later[40] that it was 'surprising how many talented professionals capitulated to this second-hand idea that news and current affairs must adopt the techniques of "drama".'

These skirmishes were placed in a new context by the major controversy that erupted within a few months in the wake of the shooting of three IRA members – two men and one woman – by British forces in Gibraltar in March 1988. The bodies of the three were flown back to Dublin, and were taken northwards from Dublin by road on 14 March. A radio report on this by a young RTÉ contract reporter, Jennie McGeever, was broadcast on a morning news programme on 15 March 1988. Although the report did not contain an interview with any banned person, the voice of Martin McGuinness – then as now a prominent member of Sinn Féin, who was to admit later that he had been, at least in 1972, a member of the IRA in Derry – was heard explaining to anyone who chose to listen that the RUC would not allow the coffins across the Border because they were draped with the Irish national flag.

Ray Burke, the Cabinet minister responsible for Communications, immediately issued a public statement attacking RTÉ. McGeever was suspended by the station on the same day because her package was 'in breach of the Broadcasting Act'.[41] Her contract was terminated on 22 March.

The Authority's action was not without its supporters, and among some journalists at that. 'This section 31 rule', one national newspaper editorialised, 'is not an interference with the freedom of the air, but has everything to do with ensuring that subversives, and those of like mind, do not cynically make use of a State broadcasting system to advocate views which tend to undermine the State.'[42]

39 Harris to Bob Collins and others, 17 November 1987.   **40** Quinn, *Maverick*, p 204. Quinn added that Harris 'appears never to have forgiven the organisation for not carrying out his varying instructions to the letter'.   **41** NUJ: Assistant Personnel Manager to McGeever, 15 March 1988.   **42** *Irish Independent*, 16

Insofar as the NUJ and RTÉ were concerned, however, the stage was set for a long and divisive dispute. Officials from the NUJ's Irish Council wanted to fight the McGeever sacking as an issue of press freedom. McGeever's colleagues in the broadcasting branch of the union, however, were decidedly unenthusiastic and, after a lengthy discussion, declined to fight her case on the issue of freedom of speech. Her case was probably not helped by the fact that she had not, at the material time, become a member of the broadcasting branch of the union: she had earlier been working for a pirate radio station, and was a member of the union's Press and PR branch, the only branch which would accept pirate radio journalists into membership.

The gulf between union and branch was now quite substantial: the branch was prepared to accept that there had been a breach of the directive, but would argue that this had been merely a technical breach, and that the case should be dealt with either through a rights commissioner, the employment appeals tribunal, or both. A difficulty with this, as RTÉ's own industrial correspondent pointed out to his union colleagues at a heated branch meeting, was that for technical reasons McGeever was not entitled to utilise these mechanisms, because she could claim the protection of the relevant legislation only if she had been employed by RTÉ for a period longer than that provided for in her contract. Ignoring these apparently substantial warnings, the branch maintained its position.[43] The union's officers, on the other hand, while they would have preferred to fight it as a freedom of speech issue, were prepared to compromise to the extent of arguing that it was primarily an industrial relations problem, in that any error in the broadcast report had been caused by RTÉ's unwillingness to recruit sufficient staff to cover the demanding Northern Ireland situation (McGeever had been up all night before filing her report, and told NUJ officials later that she had submitted it to the station with a warning that it needed editing.)[44] A compromise suggested by the NUJ officials – that McGeever should serve out the term of her contract without anticipating re-appointment – was rejected by management, and union officials involved suspected strongly that government sources were putting pressure on the station to scapegoat the reporter concerned.[45]

Despite this attempt at a compromise, relations between branch and union soured to the point where branch officials withdrew from a meeting between union officials and RTÉ management. Matters became even more complicated when RTÉ summoned the programme's two editorial executives, who had overall responsibility for the content of the programme to a disciplinary meeting, and the RTÉ journalists immediately threatened a 48–hour strike if disciplinary

---

March 1988. **43** Information from Michael Foley. **44** Information from Jim Eadie, NUJ Irish organiser at all material times during this period, September 2001). **45** Information from Michael Foley, who participated in the negotiations.

action was taken against either of them.[46] The significance of this was not lost on the union's national organiser, Jim Eadie, who prepared a report for *The Journalist* on 23 March, noting that this 'seemed to put the Branch in a position of applying different standards of protection to the three members'.

The RTÉ branch then organised a ballot on the action to be taken in relation to McGeever, but this was suspended while McGeever took a High Court action seeking a judicial review of her dismissal. At the same time, the chairman of the RTÉ NUJ branch, Charlie Bird, expressed his disagreement with his own union publicly: 'The NUJ adopted a position on Section 31 which we oppose. This policy affected only our branch, and we think it is ludicrous that other branches are adopting a policy which we have to implement. We opposed that resolution at last year's annual conference.' Eadie, plainly nettled, replied: 'Members in RTÉ are governed by union authority. Do Charlie Bird and his members want to defy us?'[47]McGeever, who was supported financially by the union throughout the dispute, eventually settled her action against RTÉ out of court and moved to a job on an American magazine. No disciplinary action was taken against her supervisors.

The RTÉ branch of the union was now, it seemed, in the unenviable position of being opposed to the directive issued under Section 31, but unable, not least because of its internal divisions, to determine a coherent political or industrial strategy by which they could express their opposition, and unwilling to accept a strategy determined by their own union. If nothing else, this neatly, if rather embarrassingly, summarised and exemplified a deep strategic weakness on the part of the union faced with a key set of political and media issues. The ideological split within the union, in particular, was sharply exposed at the end of the year when the NUJ decided to take an action against the government's Section 31 directive as a test case at the European Commission of Human Rights. Despite the fact that this course of action was official NUJ policy, the Union could not find any member of the NUJ working at RTÉ prepared to lend their name to the proceedings, as was required. The case was eventually brought jointly with the FWUI, some of whose producer members signed, and by Seosamh Ó Cuaigh, an NUJ member working for Raidió na Gaeltachta.[48]

The response of RTÉ management, too, raised a number of important questions. The differential treatment of McGeever and her editorial supervisors suggested strongly that the station was operating on the basis of a number of institutional imperatives related directly to what had happened in 1972. The sharp political criticism from Ray Burke which followed the broadcast was a warning

46 *Irish Independent*, 23 March 1988. **47** *Irish Times*, 27 March 1988. **48** Horgan, *Censorship*, pp. 389–90. This decision by the NUJ prompted a threat – not subsequently carried out – by the Chairman of the Union's broadcasting branch, Charlie Bird, to resign from the NUJ on the grounds that his branch had not been consulted.

shot that could not be ignored. In particular, the fact that the failure in 1972 to do more than reprimand editorial staff for an 'error of judgement' had led directly to the sacking of the entire Authority, suggested that at least one head should roll on this occasion. The decision to sack McGeever, in these circumstances, smacked of scapegoating. At the very least, McGeever's dismissal was *pour encourager les autres*. It is certainly difficult to see how what she did was a sackable offence, even given the existence of the directive: but she, like others, and to a degree irrespective of her own political views, whatever they may have been, was caught in the cross-fire of a proxy war, like others before her. As the Assistant Director-General, John Sorahan, pointed out shortly afterwards,

> recent events had ensured that nobody was in any doubt as to the gravity of breaches of Section 31 [*sic*] and the consequences that would flow from such breaches to the people concerned. It must be very clear that breaches, whether technical or deliberate, would have implications for the people concerned and that individuals who were associated with a number of technical breaches would face disciplinary action.[49]

This particular comment is notable for two things. One was the virtual equation of 'technical' or 'deliberate' breaches. Another is that a known Sinn Féin candidate had been interviewed on *Morning Ireland* some six months earlier, without any disciplinary action being taken: RTÉ executives commented on that occasion only that they felt journalists, faced with this sort of issue, 'should be more alert in the future.'[50] Finally, the fact that RTÉ eventually settled out of court the legal action brought against the station by McGeever argues that the station felt itself to be on shaky ground. There was also one other factor: as in 1971 and 1972, external political reaction had been crucial. The difference was that in 1971 and 1972 that political reaction had been to a degree discounted: RTÉ, it seemed, was not going to make the same mistake three times.

Today Tonight was spreading its wings: in 1989 Michael Heney went to Hanoi, Una Claffey to Moscow. But in the following year there was a changing of the guard. Eugene Murray resigned in January 1990 as editor of *Today Tonight* and head of current affairs. Both roles were now taken by Peter Feeney, who reported to Clare Duignan, now Head of Features and Current Affairs.

Looking back over the history of *Today Tonight*, and of current affairs generally in RTÉ up to this point, some significant formative factors can be isolated. One of them is that, in a small (by international standards, and particularly by the standards of the BBC and ITV with which it competes for audience share) public service broadcasting station, the critical decision to be made is whether there

---

49 Editorial Board, Minutes, 25 March 1988.   **50** Editorial Board, Minutes, 4 September 1987.

should be one flagship current affairs programme, or whether the current affairs brief should be spread across a number of different programme areas. The history of what happened in RTÉ tends to suggest that the station's reputation is built primarily, not just on the authenticity of its news coverage, but on the impact made by a flagship current affairs programme. This is for a number of reasons. One of the more obvious is that a flagship current affairs programme, like 7 *Days* or *Today Tonight*, makes its long-term reputation as much on investigative and documentary material as it does on its studio-based treatment of the issues of the day. If its documentary function is removed or minimised, good documentary makers within the station will want to migrate to whichever area promises them the best outlet for their talents: there will be a programming equivalent of 'white flight'. This suggests in turn that if a flagship current affairs programme is not doing well, for whatever reason, the most appropriate response is to work out what is wrong, and remedy it – not to split it up and distribute its resources across a number of different programming areas. At the same time, political or managerial imperatives aimed at maximising domestic production, combined with an accountancy-led approach to the unit cost issue, can suggest that more programmes with smaller budgets are better than fewer programmes with larger ones. This, however, begs the all-important question of content and – above all – impact. If the station's impact on its main target audience is dissipated, so, in turn, will the audience be. Finally, there is the difficulty – more understandable in a way – that very good programmes, including good current affairs programmes, tend to act as 'seed' programmes: their individual editors, directors, producers and presenters can be rewarded by allowing them to depart from the team and head up their own programme idea or area. This is a trend which can be justified on promotional or motivational grounds, but can, if overdone, lead similarly to a weakening of core current affairs activity.

The political climate was becoming harsher: in particular, a cap imposed on RTÉ's advertising revenues by the Minister for Communications, Ray Burke, in 1990 was eating into the station's finances: the popular wisdom was that Fianna Fáil, now in a position to wreak its revenge, was deliberately curtailing RTÉ financing in order to force the station to cut back particularly on the kind of investigative programmes on which RTÉ in general, and *Today Tonight* in particular, had based its reputation.[51] Some of them had begun to focus on issues in which the links between politics and business, in particular, had been closely examined. One of these was a programme about the property developer Patrick Gallagher, which had been prepared for transmission in November 1989, was

---

51 Cf. Mary Holland, 'Tackling unpopular issues at RTÉ', *Irish Times*, 10 January 1990. An instructive source of documentation and information on the relationship between Mr Burke and RTÉ at this time can be found in the Tribunal of Inquiry into Certain Planning Matters, Transcript of Proceedings on Tuesday 18 July 2000, No. 169 (Doyle Court Reporters, 2 Arran Quay, Dublin 7).

withdrawn on that occasion following representations from the Director of Public Prosecutions, and later broadcast in a slightly different form.[52] Morale in RTÉ was hardly improved when John Sorahan, who had been rejected as a nominated Director-General by a Fine Gael Minister for Communications in 1985, was now appointed by the Fianna Fáil/PD Government as Chairman of the new Authority which took up office in June 1990.

Under Feeney, current affairs was being re-structured. The frequency with which *Today Tonight* had been able to broadcast the programme had been declining in any case, but now its specifically documentary function was to be transposed to a new *Wednesday Report* slot: the *Today Tonight* programme itself would now appear twice a week, on Tuesdays and Thursdays. Feeney was frank about the difficulties it faced. One of them was the political consensus which had existed in the Dáil since the Fine Gael leader, Alan Dukes, had brought his party – broadly speaking – in behind the economic policies of the Fianna Fáil/PD government. This decision by Dukes, named the 'Tallaght Strategy' after the location of the speech in which he announced it – inevitably meant that current affairs producers looking for political opposition had to look to the political Left – thus increasing the suspicion, particularly in government, that a political agenda was at work within the station.

A second difficulty was the ageing profile of the station: one critic, John Waters, described it as 'the same old faces pawing around the same old succession of evasive, colourless and largely irrelevant politicians'.[53] A third was that, in Feeney's view,

> One of the functions of the media is to unearth hypocrisy, dishonesty and crookedness, but that is getting increasingly difficult. My experience is that there is a growing cynicism and a belief that these things aren't the function of journalism. As a profession in Ireland we're not actually good investigative journalists. We don't have any strong tradition and I think that it is a reflection of Irish political culture. There's no moral outrage at misbehaviour. We are tolerant of abuse, and that in turn impacts enormously on our journalism.[54]

Not long after Feeney took over, an old controversy returned, as the programme ran an item on the Workers Party, triggered by the resignation from the party of Eoghan Harris and Eamon Smullen after they had published a document, 'The Wealth of the Nation', advocating a significant change in the party's direction.[55] This programme featured interviews with one of the station's

52 *Irish Times*, 30 November 1989. Gallagher had at this stage pleaded guilty in a Belfast court to false accounting and company theft charges.   **53** John Waters, 'Prevailing winds blow cold on current affairs', *Irish Times*, 20 October 1990.   **54** Ibid.   **55** Mark Brennock, 'Harris quits WP in row on article', *Irish*

senior journalists, Gerry Barry, and with Eoghan Harris himself, who now spoke on air for the first time about his political involvement.[56] Barry voiced his concern, in particular, at the fact that membership of that party was concealed by its members within RTÉ, and claimed that 'within RTÉ the area within which the Workers' Party exercised most control was the Workers' Union of Ireland, of which Eoghan Harris and a lot of people involved in the television current affairs production were involved, and that's the level at which the Workers' Party had most influence.' The reporter's voiceover went on to suggest that 'Harris's attempts to push his ideas within RTÉ were resisted. He lost that battle.' The programme, however, re-kindled an old controversy, because Harris was an RTÉ employee, and station executives felt that although the programme had been fair, his contribution 'highlighted the need for an urgent review of policy on staff involvement in politics as there was an element of vagueness about it'.[57]

Almost immediately, an interview with Proinsias de Rossa, in which he had agreed that not all members of his party openly admitted their membership, and acknowledged the existence of certain 'special' branches, led to an intensified study of this area by the directors of the three output areas and the Director of Personnel.[58] It is not clear what, if anything, was done further to clarify station policy: when Harris resigned from RTÉ on 28 November 1990, it was in the context of his role in Mary Robinson's election campaign, and did not appear to have been related to his open acknowledgement of his party activities. The reaction of station executives can best be judged from a request by the Director-General, T.V. Finn, that if Harris were invited to participate in future programmes care should be taken to identify him as a 'former' RTÉ producer.[59]

Given that the station's policy on the political activities of staff in sensitive positions had been initially devised a decade before the Workers' Party was formed, and that the public perception of RTÉ as being unduly influenced by that party had been current for most of the decade up to 1990, this is indicative either of lethargy on the part of station management, of skilful footwork by staff members who may have had a party political agenda, or some combination of both. As it happened, the spectre of Workers' Party involvement had effectively disappeared by the mid-1980s: nonetheless, the sensitivity remained, not least because the widespread public perception of inappropriate influence had proved difficult to eradicate, and because those perceptions were most vividly entertained by politicians in general, and by Fianna Fáil politicians in particular. These suspicions were also very programme-specific. John Caden, another

Times, 12 March 1990. **56** RTÉ Ref. No. BP20/882 1/7008. Eoghan Harris's contribution has been quoted supra, at pp. 164–71. Harris had acknowledged his party membership before, in print, in an interview in *Comhar* in 1988. Some time after leaving RTÉ, Harris wrote to the Director-General to accuse RTÉ broadcasters of 'settling old scores against him on various programmes': Editorial Board, Minutes, 7 June 1991. **57** Editorial Board, Minutes, 27 April 1990. **58** Editorial Board, Minutes, 4 May 1990. **59** Editorial Board, Minutes, 29 November 1990.

Workers' Party supporter and an ally of Harris in their internal struggles in the FWUI, was originally an accounts clerk who became a gifted radio producer. One of his most significant contributions to broadcasting was as producer of the *Gay Byrne Hour* on RTÉ Radio One. This programme, which generated some quite extraordinary listenership for some dramatic and innovative programming (Byrne's reading of listeners' letters following the death of the pregnant Anne Lovett in Granard is a case in point) was accused over the years of many things, but never of WP sympathies.

On the other hand, Fianna Fáil was not alone in its complaints. Fine Gael went so far as to register a protest with the Broadcasting Complaints Commission against a *Today Tonight* programme on 24 January 1990 (the complaint was not upheld).[60] In the same month as Harris resigned both Garret FitzGerald and Alan Dukes complained, this time with more success, that Gay Byrne was 'allowing his political views to appear too prominently.' On this occasion the Director of Radio Programming spoke to the presenter and 'there had been no recurrence.'[61] There were other complaints about Byrne, too, but on an even more sensitive topic: an item which included a long interview and graphic detail of child sexual abuse occasioned some anxiety when it was re-broadcast on *Playback*. In its defence, it was pointed out that this particular item had also evoked a response from a large number of people who had been victims in similar circumstances.[62] Not for the first time, RTÉ was exploring issues which would become much more prominent later on, and in circumstances which often led viewers and listeners to form the erroneous impression that RTÉ had avoided these subjects and that they were not properly addressed until British television stations had featured them in programming. There had in fact been an even earlier programme on child abuse in 1985, reporter Gerry O'Callaghan did programmes on the meat exporting scandals well before Susan O'Keeffe's programmes on Granada in 1991, and RTÉ also did a programme in 1995 on the home at Monageer where child abuse had occurred.

The re-shuffle of current affairs that had taken place with Eugene Murray's departure had been operating for little more than two years when it came under renewed pressure. This time the pressure came, not from the outside, but from the office of the Director of News, Joe Mulholland. Like his predecessor Wesley Boyd, Mulholland had found occasion to complain that news material was being accessed all too readily by programmes personnel, leading to the overlapping of agendas and, occasionally, to poor editorial calls in the programme area that would not have been made by more experienced journalists.[63] The difference between Boyd and Mulholland, however, was that whereas the former's criticisms could be discounted as a traditional newsroom gripe (Boyd's back-

---

60 Editorial Board, Minutes, 23 March 1990. **61** Editorial Board, Minutes, 2 November 1990. **62** Editorial Board, Minutes, 23 November 1990. **63** Editorial Board, Minutes, 8 March 1991.

ground was entirely in journalism), Mulholland, as a programmes man of considerable standing, was in a stronger position to throw a bridge over the divide. He now argued trenchantly that the time was ripe for a reappraisal of RTÉ's current affairs policy, wondering whether there wasn't 'a certain lack of editorial courage and loss of will.'[64] His criticisms were rejected with the argument that the main problem had not been loss of will, but the malign influence of litigation which had become ever more oppressive, but there was evidence, at least from the TAM ratings, that something was slipping. In its heyday, *Today Tonight* had won a place in the top half-dozen programmes, reaching some 60% of the available audience as late as 1987. It was now further down the list, coming in at between 15th and 20th. Legal problems, as already noted, were also mounting. The Taoiseach, who sent RTÉ a solicitor's letter seeking an apology and compensation for remarks which had been made about him by Senator John A. Murphy,[65] was only one name in the queue: no doubt partly for the same reason, *Today Tonight* was having more and more difficulty in persuading ministers to come and be interviewed.[66]

It was, of course, also operating in a different environment. Part of that was external – the competition from other channels. Part of it, however, was internal, notably the re-vamping of news under Mulholland. Mulholland's move to news had in fact been made partly at the prompting of some staff members within that division, who felt that there were a range of problems which needed attention. Training needed to be upgraded, and there were apparently recurrent difficulties with presentation and production and design values. With Ed Mulhall, who had come into news from radio and who was to be Mulholland's successor, the whole news operation began to undergo radical change. The *6.01* news, filling an entire hour since its launch in 1988, was only the most visible example of the division's new sense of importance and mission. Rounding up the news from thirty minutes to a broadcast hour required a certain nerve: it was done by initially expanding the feature-style reports, such as those emanating from regional correspondents. These formed the soft underbelly of the programme, which could expand or contract as the need arose. Later, with improved resourcing, the hard news element of the programme expanded, and the softer news shrank, concertina-like, to make way for it. Even as reorganisation approached, two of the most talked-about moments on television belonged not to current affairs, but to news, and specifically to *6.01*.

The first was Seán Duignan's interview with Brian Lenihan in the middle of the 1990 Presidential election campaign, when Lenihan sought to retract, on 'mature reflection' a statement he had made some time earlier to an academic

---

64 Editorial Board, Minutes, 17 May 1991.   65 Editorial Board, Minutes, 19 June 1992. Mr Reynolds's immediate predecessor, Mr Haughey, had earlier suggested that RTÉ had been 'trawling' for opponents to his leadership of Fianna Fáil: Editorial Board, Minutes, 13 December 1990.   66 Editorial Board, Minutes, 3 July 1992.

researcher, Jim Duffy, about his role in an earlier incident involving President Hillery. Lenihan's recantation, and his overt appeal to the electorate as he turned away from the interviewer and addressed the camera directly, was one of the most dramatic moments of the entire campaign. Then in 1991, as Charles J. Haughey resigned from the leadership of Fianna Fáil, another Duignan interview on *6.01* sent an electric current through the party and the general public alike. A senior Fianna Fáil minister, Gerry Collins (who had overseen both the issuing of the original Section 31 directive in 1971 and the sacking of the Authority in 1972), went on the programme. Ostensibly speaking in order to avoid a damaging split in the party, but in all probability trying to advance his own cause as a potential successor to Haughey, he appealed to Albert Reynolds, the immediate front-runner, not to 'burst up' the party. Like Lenihan earlier, he chose to do this by way of an emotional appeal made directly to the camera. Outside his field of vision, and out of camera-shot, Duignan was using his hands to give the 'str-e-e-e-tch' signal to the director, as if to say: 'pay out more rope: this is going well'. At the end of the interview, all he had to do was to thank Collins: it was undoubtedly one of the great moments on Irish television.[67] Both appearances underlined the fact that, whatever the risks, senior politicians increasingly preferred short and sharp exposure on *6.01* to more thorough, and potentially difficult, inquisition by broadcasters like Olivia O'Leary on *Today Tonight*. As well as all this, other programmes were nibbling away at the formerly closely guarded current affairs brief. The most dramatic example of this was an episode of *Nighthawks* in January 1992, when the former Minister for Justice, Seán Doherty, went on air to talk about his relationship with Mr Haughey in an interview which inaugurated the final stages in Mr Haughey's loss of political power. RTÉ's editorial committee, commenting on this 'bizarre' episode (and quite under-estimating its significance) noted that the *Evening Press* had been able to reveal the programme's contents 48 hours prior to its transmission, despite the fact that neither RTÉ's News Division nor the RTÉ Press Office had been given any information.[68]

With the new, aggressive, top-of-the-agenda approach by news went a more conscious programme-making style, in which news bulletins were looked on less as a sequence of events related to each other only by virtue of their descending order of magnitude, and more as a programme conceived as a whole, with a beginning, middle and end. New technology – satellite broadcasting in particular – was beginning to come into its own (even though old technology was more difficult to dislodge because of strong union views, and was at the centre of a dis-

---

67 Duignan later accepted an offer from Reynolds to be Government Press Secretary, which he filled with some distinction until Reynolds's displacement by Bertie Ahern, at which point he wrote a hilarious and revealing book about his experiences, *One spin on the merry-go-round* (1998). He later returned to work in RTÉ before retiring in 2002.   **68** Editorial Board, Minutes, 17 January 1992.

astrous six-weeks strike in 1995 in which the NUJ was also involved). Many of the specialist correspondents had been in post for a considerable time: Mulholland re-shuffled them frequently and energetically, rarely winning friends as he did so. Young journalists who applied for jobs were not just interviewed, but taken on for a weekend so that they could show their paces in real-time situations.

More regional offices were opened and, on 1 October 1995, Mark Little took up an appointment as RTÉ's first Washington correspondent. In one way or another, news was coming of age. The early evening bulletin, in particular, now frequently notched up higher audience ratings than the 9.00 p.m. bulletin, which had originally been regarded as the premier bulletin, but which had to face particularly fierce prime-time competition from other channels. In common with other programme areas, it tended to consume resources at a rate greater than anyone could provide them. One member of the News Division team, Katie Kahn-Karl, was regularly despatched to London at Christmas time with bottles of Irish whiskey for BBC executives whose help to Dublin had often exceeded what could legitimately been expected, and which could not be remunerated at normal rates.

The impact on current affairs was inevitable and, on 1 April 1992, a new current affairs schedule was announced for the autumn – one which would not, for the first time, include *Today Tonight*, its 1500 previous programmes notwithstanding. The *Today Tonight* reporter, Brendan O'Brien, expressed his strong opposition to the move on both radio and television programmes on 2 April. In the administration building they waited for the storm to blow over.

Although subsequent reports suggested that the reorganisation of current affairs which was now to take place had been the occasion of sharp internal disagreements, and objections in particular from Peter Feeney,[69] there was an impressive show of unity when the re-organised programme structure was finally disclosed.[70] The revised schedule, for which the new head of programmes on RTÉ1, Bob Collins, was largely responsible, adopted a model that was not dissimilar from that which took the place of *7 Days* in 1976. Instead of one flagship programme, there would now be a whole clutch of them. John Bowman's *Questions and Answers*, produced by Betty Purcell on Monday nights (which had shown impressive audience growth) was one. *Tuesday File*, to be presented by Emily O'Reilly of the *Irish Press* (although difficulties subsequently arose about her dual role as presenter on this, and commentator on other RTÉ programmes) would be the second, and a slot for major documentaries. *Marketplace*, an economics programme formerly running on RTÉ2, would be transferred to RTÉ 1 on Wednesday nights, and fronted by Miriam O'Callaghan, another returnee from the BBC. *Prime Time* would be presented on Thursdays by, among others,

69 Andy Pollak, 'RTÉ offers few prime cuts as state of current affairs worsens', *Irish Times*, 16 July 1994.
70 Brendan Glacken, 'The night they buried "TT"', *Irish Times*, 29 August 1992.

Olivia O'Leary, no stranger to RTÉ, who passed up an opportunity to present the BBC's *Newsnight* in order to come back to Dublin. Brian Farrell would take his unique combination of gravitas and waspishness to *Farrell*, an interview programme on Sunday evenings, described by one insider as 'Walden with an audience.'[71] There would be six new staffers in current affairs generally, slightly larger budgets, and a determined attempt to slew the television audience away from its dangerous reliance on the over-40 age group and towards a younger group of viewers from a wider range of social classes.

This re-organisation was faced with much the same set of problems as that involving *7 Days* had encountered. There was the danger that dissipating the resources (even given a somewhat larger budget) over a greater number of programmes would result in a loss of depth; there was the difficulty of establishing a new flagship programme (*Frontline* had demonstrably failed to do this). There was the problem of which programme, or programmes, would react to a major breaking news event, and in what way. There was the problem of overcoming the suspicion that current affairs were being squeezed financially because they were an embarrassment in the station's perennial need to negotiate increases in the licence fee, determined as always by governments that was hostile at worst, suspicious at best. On the positive side, there was the fact that a conspicuous array of broadcasting talent was involved, much of it female. Apart from Olivia O'Leary, Emily O'Reilly – who had done work on *Today Tonight* earlier – and Mary McAleese on *7 Days*, current affairs had been largely a male preserve, and Olivia had achieved the added distinction of being the only woman presenter in the first twenty-five years of the Sunday radio programme, *This Week*. Noel Curran, who came to *Marketplace* from *Business and Finance*, was to move rapidly up the RTÉ hierarchy. Another *Marketplace* contributor, George Lee, migrated successfully from Riada stockbrokers into broadcasting. Kevin Dawson, who also joined *Tuesday File*, was to progress to an important commissioning role in relation to the independent sector. Others in the mix included reporter/presenters Brendan O'Brien, Carolyn Fisher and Ingrid Miley, and editors and producers such as John Masterson and Neasa Ni Chinneide.

As *Today Tonight* moved towards its final broadcast on 27 August 1992, Section 31 raised its awkward head again. This time, it was in the shape of a High Court case at the end of July in which a Sinn Féin member who was also a member of a trade union which was involved in an industrial dispute in 1990 at the Gateaux bakery company was seeking a declaration that RTÉ's refusal to interview him at that time under the terms of the directive was not legal. In the High Court on 31 July, Mr Justice O'Hanlon found in favour of the applicant, Larry

---

71 Michael Foley, '"Today Tonight" will soon be part of yesterday's news', *Irish Times*, 27 August 1992. Brian Walden's Sunday morning highbrow political interview programme on Britain's Channel Four was legendary for its minuscule audience share.

O'Toole, on the grounds that the Authority's decision to refuse 'on arbitrary grounds to allow the views of the workers concerned in a major industrial dispute which was arousing widespread public attention to be put forward on their behalf by the person they had appointed their spokesman' was in fact a breach of the Authority's statutory duty to observe rules of fairness and impartiality in broadcasting news and current affairs.[72] This, however, instead of making things easier for RTÉ, actually made things more difficult. This was because clearance to interview Sinn Féin members or supporters in certain circumstances did not invalidate RTÉ's further obligations under Section 18 (i) of the Broadcasting Act, which prevented the airwaves being used by anyone who might incite violence or 'undermine the authority of the state': the Court decision, in effect, would account for only one of three categories covered by the statutory order, and the others would still apply. An appeal was therefore lodged – not because RTÉ disagreed with the decision, but because they needed it to be clarified.[73]

There was, in the meantime, a change of Director-General, as Joe Barry succeeded Vincent Finn in November 1992. Programme-makers, as was customary, threw their collective hands into the air at the prospect of yet another DG from the technical side of the house (Barry's previous position had been as director of production facilities). Despite this apprehension, Barry's easy manner and wide familiarity with personnel at all levels in the organisation were to stand him in good stead, but the organisation's problems – notably the lack of resources caused by a failure to increase the license fee – persisted. Unsuccessful applicants were reported to have included Mulholland, Kevin Healy (Director of Radio Programming), Liam Miller (Controller of Television Production and Resources), Bob Collins (Director of Television Programmes) and Eugene Murray.[74] This was a drama which was to be re-enacted in less than five years' time.

The Supreme Court ratified the High Court decision on the Section 31 directive in a judgement delivered on 30 March 1993. As the year wore on, the ambiguities continued to surface: Seán Mac Stiofáin was interviewed on radio on 14 September, but even though he had given up IRA membership, his interview was felt to be largely a defence of his actions and those of the organisation when he had been a member.[75] Later in the year, Raidió na Gaeltachta looked for permission to interview him again, and similar anxieties were expressed.[76]

In the middle of all this *Sturm und Drang*, radio marked two notable anniversaries in November 1993. The first was the tenth anniversary of *Morning Ireland*, the younger sibling of *This Week* and *The News at One* (which had changed from the *News at One-Thirty* in October 1989). *Morning Ireland* itself had moved from a thirty-minute slot to an hour-long one in 1985, and was now a 90-minute slot

72 *Irish Times*, 1 August 1992.   **73** Editorial Board, Minutes, 7 August 1992.   **74** Joe Carroll, 'Old feud revived in RTÉ over appointment of new DG', *Irish Times*, 22 July 1992.   **75** Editorial Board, Minutes, 17 September 1992.   **76** Editorial Board, Minutes, 18 December 1992.

starting at 7.30. One commentator noted that the birthday party was attended by 'a line up of cars not seen since the last great Mafia funeral', and observed prophetically that 'when it starts broadcasting at 7 a.m., we'll know we've really joined the European Union.'[77] One of the black limousines had conveyed the Taoiseach, Albert Reynolds, who jovially reminded the party that one of the programme's first controversies, in November 1984, had involved an item about the then Taoiseach, Garret FitzGerald's decision to accept a lift back from Indira Ghandi's funeral in Mrs Thatcher's British government jet. Some stories just keep coming back.

The same month marked the twenty-fifth anniversary of *This Week*, whose first broadcast had been on Sunday, 3 November 1968. Originally a thirty-minute programme, it had been successfully extended to an hour. The Sunday lunch-time slot, with extended interviews of political and other figures, had helped to embed it in the popular consciousness: it had been edited since 1990 by Seán O'Rourke. As already noted, it had been the programme on which Kevin O'Kelly's report on his interviews with IRA leaders, in 1972, led indirectly to the sacking of the entire Authority; but it had also been responsible for other, equally memorable interviews. In one of them, an embattled Mr Haughey had advised his critics to 'go dance on someone else's grave'. In another, an over-confident Jack Lynch had suggested that any Taoiseach who presided over an unemployment figure in excess of 100,000 should resign. Nor were politics the only milestones: Malcolm McArthur's mother revealed, in one spine-chilling interview, how her son had hatched a plan to electrocute her by re-wiring the electrical kettle. Mike Burns, one of the programme's founders, told a celebratory party at RTÉ on 9 November that there had for a time been a slogan on the wall of the *This Week* studio which noted, with elegant simplicity: 'When there is nothing more to be said – some fool always says it.'[78]

The future was beckoning, as well as the past. In early November the RTÉ Authority sent Michael D. Higgins draft guidelines which, they said, would be put in place if the Section 31 directive was not renewed. Although technically these guidelines did not need to be approved by the Minister, they would to a degree have strengthened his hand. When the directive was finally allowed to lapse on 19 January 1994, Higgins having secured Cabinet approval for this course of action, the revised guidelines were issued within 24 hours. They emphasised the continuing role of Section 18, although it was clear that there would be a learning process for all broadcast reporters who had had to work for years under the earlier guidelines and directives.[79] The stage was set for the first

---

77 Frank McNally, 'Schoolmaster marks a decade of parading duff students', *Irish Times*, 3 November 1994. The programme now starts at 7.00 a.m. **78** Leo Enright, 'Recalling all that doom, gloom and boom', *Irish Times*, 10 November 1993. This article misplaces the Kevin O'Kelly interview in December 1972: it took place in November. One of those attending the function was Kevin O'Kelly, who was to die in September 1994.

major RTÉ interview with Gerry Adams (who had already, as it happened, been interviewed by Classic Hits 98 FM on the occasion of the banning, by RTÉ, of an advertisement for his book of short stories in October 1993). *Prime Time* asked for the first interview, but RTÉ's editorial committee decided that it should go, instead, to David Davin Power, RTÉ's then Northern Editor.[80] This was to indicate that the interview would take place within the context of regular editorial news judgement, rather than as a high-profile television interview by a current affairs interviewer such as Olivia O'Leary or Brian Farrell.[81]

There was a certain circularity in all of this. The original directive had been imposed at a time of acute political sensitivity, and had been intended largely to ease the task of the politicians (as the politicians themselves defined that task) in controlling a difficult political situation. Its abolition at this point was not due in any way to a sudden access of respect for freedom of expression on the part of the successors of those who had imposed it in 1971 (no doubt with the exception of Higgins, who had always held strong views on the matter). It was due primarily to the fact that the Taoiseach, Albert Reynolds, believed – correctly as it turned out – that it would be an important confidence-building measure in the wary and tentative approach to a new IRA ceasefire. The British ban on interviews with Sinn Féin or IRA members or supporters, which had been imposed in 1988, was lifted shortly afterwards by a somewhat annoyed Mrs Thatcher, who felt that she had no alternative in the circumstances.[82]

One of the more unexpected outcomes of this government decision was the tabling of a motion by the Progressive Democrats, then in opposition, calling on the government to re-institute the ban. Moving the motion, their justice spokesman, Michael McDowell, charged:

> The IRA is the controlling element in the Provisional movement. Sinn Féin is not an independent political force. It is controlled and supervised by the leaders of the IRA at every level [...] It is our thesis and fixed conviction in the Progressive Democrats that allowing Sinn Féin access to the airwaves is allowing the IRA to use the airwaves [...] The net effect of access of Sinn Féin to the airwaves in the last fortnight is that they are becoming part of the legitimate establishment of this country while holding on to the right to blow out someone's brains or blow up children when it suits them.[83]

---

79 A *Prime Time* interview of Ruairí Ó Brádaigh in June 1995 raised concerns about an apparent breach of Section 18, for example. See Editorial Board, Minutes, 30 June 1995. **80** Editorial Board, Minutes, 14 January 1994. **81** Michael Foley, 'RTÉ staff given a small bite of the forbidden fruit', *Irish Times*, 13 January 1994. **82** Personal information from Michael D. Higgins. The UK ban, it is worth noting, allowed for the use of actors to repeat the words of those being interviewed, which the Section 31 directive did not. The UK ban was also relaxed for election campaigns. **83** Dáil Debates, 1 February 1994.

He was supported by his fellow PD TD Bobby Molloy, who charged Higgins with asking the Dáil 'to welcome to the airwaves members of a subversive revolutionary movement who, day in day out, use murder as part of its stock in trade'. A number of Fine Gael speakers also opposed the lifting of the ban, notably Frances FitzGerald, who warned of the danger that the removal of the ban would lead to 'a steady erosion of this State'; Jim O'Keeffe, who argued that it 'damages the peace process'; Alan Shatter, who said that Gerry Adams was now being treated as the 'Kevin Costner of Irish politics'; and Austin Currie, who argued that 'those whose relatives have been murdered by the IRA are outraged and the morale of IRA activists and supporters has been increased.'

The evolution of the attitude of Democratic Left from its former incarnation as Sinn Féin The Workers Party and the Workers' Party was encapsulated by its leader, Proinsias de Rossa, who noted that DL had tabled a Bill which would have required every directive issued under Section 31 to be the subject of a mandatory debate in the Dáil. He added:

> Last November I suggested lifting the order, for a trial period, to see how then broadcasters would deal with the situation. Public attitudes in the Republic to Northern Ireland have changed dramatically since the order was first activated in 1972 [*sic*]. More than 20 years of the most extreme viciousness has removed in all but the most fanatical minority any notions of some romantic liberation struggle in Northern Ireland and the majority of people, including broadcasters, see the paramilitaries for the sordid sectarian gangs they are.[84]

Rejecting the Fine Gael and PD arguments, the minister, Michael D. Higgins, also criticised what he described as 'the deterministic view of television', argued for the public's capacity to draw distinctions, and drew attention to the 'existing corpus of statutory restraints that continue in force for broadcasters.'[85] It had been the first full-scale debate on the directive since it was first introduced in 1971, and there was a sense of pent-up emotion being released, as well it might have been. The peculiar circumstances in which the policy was changed – the first Fianna Fáil-Labour coalition pitted against a Fine Gael/Progressive Democrat opposition, with Democratic Left stranded on a traffic island in the middle – added to the piquancy of the occasion. At the end of the day, it is difficult to see that it would have been lifted by this or any government if the political environment had not been at a particularly delicate juncture. In almost a decade since that debate took place, not a single politician has proposed its reintroduction.

84 Ibid.   **85** Ibid.

As Section 31 and its directives began to fade into the background, a new political scene began to unfold, which also involved RTÉ in the final act of a drama which had been played out over the preceding summer, and which involved RTÉ more directly. This concerned the long-running tribunal of enquiry which had been set up early in 1991 under Mr Justice Hamilton to investigate allegations of fraud and political corruption connected to the export of meat from Ireland, principally to Iraq. The tribunal's report had been published in the summer of 1994, under circumstances which nearly provoked a terminal breach between the government partners as Reynolds refused to let Spring see the advance copy of the report until after he had prepared his own commentary on it.

The significance of all of this for RTÉ, and indeed for *Morning Ireland*, went back almost five years. On 1 February 1989 the normally innocuous *Farm Diary* programme stated that a leading Irish meat company was involved in a meat fraud investigation in the Middle East. The following day, *Morning Ireland* and other news programmes repeated the allegation. In the background, the Goodman Group moved swiftly into action, and writs were threatened. Within less than a week, RTÉ was forced to broadcast on its news bulletins a 'comprehensive and substantial' apology.[86]

It is difficult to recall any apology issued by any media organisation in relation to any other matter which was more extensive, detailed, and specific. It stated that RTÉ now accepted that the matters broadcast were completely false and without any foundation in fact; that no irregularity of any kind had been carried out by the company in question; that no fraud investigation whatsoever was being carried out in relation to the company; that there had been no question of export credit facilities being abused in any way; and that no attempt had been made by the company to misrepresent the age and quality of the meat it had exported. It ended:

> RTÉ would like to express its sincerest apologies to the Irish meat company concerned which it recognises has been the major meat supplier to Iraq, having started and developed the market for Irish meat exports. RTÉ sincerely regrets the damage that has been caused by the untrue statements broadcast.[87]

The length and detail of this apology provoked, as might have been expected, press criticism of RTÉ standards, prompting the Managing Editor of Television News, Ed Mulhall, to defend his record: in the previous 100 days, he

---

86 Editorial Committee, Minutes, 10 February 1989.   87 Text in Fintan O'Toole, 'A Draft Apology to the Media', *Irish Times*, 5 August 1994.

argued, the station had broadcast a total of 2,000 news items, with only three acknowledged errors – two minor and one (presumably the Goodman one) serious.[88] If anyone felt that the subject matter of the broadcast merited further investigation, they kept their counsel: in any event, the subsequent establishment of the tribunal to look into the issues concerned effectively transferred the whole area out of journalism and into politics and law.

Between the establishment of the tribunal and the publication of its report, the tortuous and complex evidential trail tended to baffle all but the most dedicated and persistent analysts. The protagonists, however, were keeping as close an eye on the media coverage as on what was happening in the witness box in Dublin castle. As early as July 1992, Goodman objected to the use of Fintan O'Toole as a commentator, on *Today Tonight*, on the evidence being given at the Beef Tribunal, in which he figured.[89] In July 1993, the Fianna Fáil Minister Michael O'Kennedy threatened to sue both *Morning Ireland* and O'Toole.[90] In November of the same year, a report by O'Toole on the Tribunal forced RTÉ to make a public apology for a suggestion that the Fianna Fáil minister Ray McSharry had made a sworn statement to the Tribunal in advance of giving evidence.

The Tribunal Report, when it was published, concluded among other things that Goodman International was perpetrating a 'substantial abuse' of export credit insurance by including large quantities of beef which had been sourced outside the State in its exports to Iraq. It also concluded that irregularities were being carried out in a number of the company's Irish plants, and that a fraud investigation had been launched into two of these (although not in relation to any of its Middle East operations). It also found that the age and quality of much of the meat that had been exported to Iraq were not as stated on the contracts between the companies and the Iraquis.

This gave rise to two separate issues. The first related to the constant use of O'Toole as a commentator during the course of the tribunal. Station executives were divided on this, some feeling that he had been used to a degree that implied that RTÉ had endorsed his judgements, others maintaining that he had complemented the more bread-and-butter reporting of Cathy O'Halloran, Una O'Hagan and Carole Coleman, the station's regular tribunal team.[91] The second, arguably more serious, related to the action taken by RTÉ at the time of the original apology. At that time, the Head of Agricultural Programmes, Joe Murray, had been held responsible, and had been disciplined. He appealed his penalty – the loss of a salary increment – to the Labour Court, which ruled in his favour after a hearing in which the sub-text was an unsuccessful attempt to discover whether there had been any ministerial fingerprints on the original decision to punish him.

88 Editorial Board, Minutes, 6 November 1992.   **89** Editorial Board, Minutes, 3 July 1992.   **90** Editorial Board, Minutes, 9 July 1993.   **91** Editorial Board, Minutes, 5 August 1994.

Now two years in operation, the revised current affairs schedule was again coming under scrutiny. Some of the *Tuesday File* documentaries were being externally sourced, and this generated reservations about the maintenance of programme standards. An independent production documentary for the same slot – '50,000 Secret Journeys' – which dealt with women travelling to England for abortions, was withdrawn in March 1994 on the grounds that it would have breached RTÉ's statutory obligations.[92] It was eventually transmitted in October. The same month featured Charlie Bird's news interview with Emmett Stagg after the then junior minister had become embroiled in publicity about his private life: the orgy of media coverage on this matter, on RTÉ and elsewhere, was in marked contrast to the lack of media coverage for politicians' private lives in earlier years. Child sexual abuse, not least since the fall of the government, was cropping up on programmes of every kind. In July, Olivia O'Leary left *Prime Time*: almost simultaneously, the Chairman of the Authority, John Sorahan, was unsuccessfully urging an Oireachtas Committee for a 21% increase in the license fee. The Director of News, Joe Mulholland, was urging that 'current affairs programming should be the backbone of our scheduling, and must be given priority before tackling drama, documentary, or any other type of programming.'

Outside, the political scene was changing. On 16 November, Albert Reynolds resigned as Taoiseach in the wake of a controversy involving a paedophile priest, the role played by his Attorney-General in the prosecution of that priest, and the filling of a vacancy for president of the High Court. Reynolds's loss of power was the occasion for a bravura performance on *Prime Time* by his ministerial colleague, Brian Cowen.[93] There was now a new government, in which the only continuity was provided by the Labour Party, now in coalition with Fine Gael and Democratic Left, and without an intervening general election.

This government appointed a new RTÉ Authority on 1 June 1995. Under the chairmanship of Professor Farrel Corcoran of Dublin City University, it now included two producers. One of them, unusually, was Bob Quinn, who had resigned from RTÉ in tempestuous circumstances in 1969 during the 'Sit Down and Be Counted' controversy; the other was Betty Purcell. The new Authority was also noteworthy for the inclusion of a former Fine Gael Taoiseach, Dr Garret FitzGerald.

Media generally were – not least because of the circumstances in which the Labour/Fianna Fáil coalition led by Albert Reynolds had collapsed – developing a new and sharper focus on the topic of child sexual abuse. The report of the Beef Tribunal had also kindled a renewed interest in questions of political corruption. The lifting of the Section 31 directive, and the rapid evolution of polit-

92 Editorial Board, Minutes, 31 March 1994.   **93** Seán Duignan, *One spin on the merry-go-round*, p. 163. Duignan notes that after his *Prime Time* appearance Cowen returned to the wake in Government Buildings and burst into tears.

ical developments in Northern Ireland as a result of the IRA ceasefire which succeeded – and was partly related to – the lifting of that ban, also created a fresh
media dynamic in which the Northern political parties and the British and Irish
governments were all deeply involved. There was also increasing competition in
the broadcast sector. Although TV3 was not yet up and running, its arrival was
thought to be imminent, and radio competition was taking audiences from the
only place possible – the RTÉ audience.

The new Authority, in a series of meetings with staff, set about encouraging the
creation of a climate in which risks would be taken. The underlying message was
that mistakes would inevitably be made, but they would not be followed by witch-
hunts or dismissals. Independence from government was also stressed. At one
level, this might seem remarkable, given the presence on the Authority of a former Taoiseach whose party was now the majority partner in government.
FitzGerald, however, has always been to some degree a law unto himself, and his
views on broadcasting, and indeed on many other subjects, were occasionally het-
erodox insofar as his Fine Gael party were concerned. He had also had the experience, probably uniquely among fellow-members of the Authority, of being asked
politely to leave the RTÉ newsroom. This had happened many years earlier
when, as Leader of Fine Gael, then in opposition, he had gained access to the
newsroom and was using a desk there as he drafted a statement for publication.
His crime had been compounded by his request to see a copy of the statement
which had been issued earlier (but not yet broadcast) by the Taoiseach, C.J.
Haughey, so that he could better frame the terms of his reply. Poacher now turned
gamekeeper, he assumed his new responsibilities with his customary relish.

In the relatively brief period between the appointment of the new Authority
and the retirement of Joe Barry as Director-General in April 1997,[94] there were
a number of major controversies which underlined the salience of these areas of
investigation for current affairs programmes. One was in October 1995, when
solicitors for the Catholic archbishop of Dublin, Dr Connell, wrote to the
Attorney-General about a forthcoming *Prime Time* programme dealing with
child abuse and, in particular, a decision by the Dublin archdiocese to make a
loan to Fr Ivan Payne, a priest later found guilty of this offence. The Attorney-
General wrote to the new Chairman of the RTÉ Authority, Professor Corcoran,
in terms which suggested that the broadcast of this programme might prejudice
ongoing Garda investigations. The intervention was fruitless: the episode
marked yet another milestone in the relationahip between RTÉ and powerful
institutional forces outside it. Another was the *Prime Time* programme in which
Ursula Halligan interviewed someone who claimed to have been the recipient
of payments from a senior political figure; a third was the *Dear Daughter* docu-

94 At the author's suggestion, April 1997 has been agreed by RTÉ as the most appropriate end-date for
this study.

mentary by Louis Lentin which focused on allegations of physical abuse of children at an orphanage run by the Sisters of Mercy at Goldenbridge in Dublin.

The *Prime Time* programme, broadcast on 2 November 1995, had been heavily scrutinised by the station's legal experts before transmission, largely to ensure that there would be no possibility of identifying the figure who was supposed to have made payments to the programme's informant, a Mr Patrick Tuffy. On the following day's *Morning Ireland*, the Democratic Left TD, Eric Byrne, had mentioned the name of Michael Lowry, the then Fine Gael Minister for Communications, in connection with the story: the radio programme had also interviewed Halligan. The government had been in session until 2 a.m. on the night of the programme, and now Lowry himself effectively identified himself as the person involved, and made no secret of his intention to seek redress. A full and complete apology to Lowry was broadcast on the 9.00 p.m. television and radio news bulletins on 6 November. The situation, however, was complicated by the fact that – as a result of legal advice that it might erode the value of the apology – RTÉ itself did not supply a spokesman for that evening's news bulletin or for the following day's *Morning Ireland* programme, on which David Hanly interviewed one of Lowry's ministerial colleagues, Michael Noonan. This gave the public (and, more damagingly, the politicians) the idea that RTÉ was either unwilling or unable to give an account of itself in such circumstances.[95] Embarrassing though this episode was at the time, it nonetheless served to underline the authenticity of the new approach: the investigation of sensitive areas involving government (including a government party which had formerly been led by a member of the Authority itself) was not off limits; and there would be no retribution for honest mistakes, as long as they were not the result of unbridled incompetence. In point of fact, there were mixed views on the editorial committee about the credibility of the programme's chief witness, even on the morning after transmission; but the thrust of programming remained unimpaired.

The *Dear Daughter* programme, which had been some eighteen months in preparation, was transmitted on 22 February 1996, and secured an audience of just under a million. Made by the independent film-maker, Louis Lentin, it was a drama documentary which featured principally Christine Buckley, a woman who had been a resident of the Goldenbridge orphanage as a child, and who made very serious allegations of ill-treatment against its staff, and against one staff member in particular. It was seen in some respects as a programme which recovered some of the ground in relation to investigative programming that had been surrendered as a result of the apology over the Tuffy programme, and interest in it had been heightened by a major publicity campaign which saw substantial news stories in the *Irish Times*, *Irish Independent* and *Star*. Interestingly, it

95 Editorial Board, Minutes, 3 November 1995.

was not the first time that Christine Buckley had been interviewed: Gay Byrne had spoken to her on his radio programme in 1993. What had happened in between was a climatic change in which topics like these had suddenly leaped onto every front page. In the circumstances, *Dear Daughter* was followed by a fresh wave of media publicity, in most of which 'the media were content to repeat the allegations in the film and concern themselves with finding more such horror stories' despite the fact that 'from the beginning other voices tried to be heard, but were never given an airing'.[96]

Programme format was at least partly responsible for these difficulties. *Dear Daughter* was a drama documentary, with actors, reconstructions, and other dramatic elements combined with factual reportage and interviews. It was not, in the strict sense of the word, broadcast journalism, although many of those who watched it might well not have been aware of the distinction. And it underlined a central problem, echoing Eoghan Harris's remarks about Enniskillen: how can the media be 'impartial' about something which is objectively offensive? Was RTÉ being required, like the Canon in Honor Tracy's famous novel, to 'walk the narrow path between good and evil'? It also raised numerous other issues. These included the question of whether those named in the programme had been given an adequate opportunity to respond, in the programme itself, to allegations made. Overall, however, it probably raised another, equally serious issue, and one which had nothing to do with the content of the programme itself. This was the issue of whether the process of running down RTÉ's own programme-making facilities, and the necessary involvement of a greater range of outsourced productions, had implications for editorial control.

This was in fact becoming of ever greater importance. RTÉ had been given a license increase in 1994, the first in a decade, but this did little more than compensate for the simultaneous decision to require the station to furnish a certain amount of programming to the new Irish television station, Telefís na Gaeilge (later TG4). Legislation had also obliged the station to allocate a certain amount of money to independent film and programme producers, in an effort to boost the independent sector in Ireland.

The latter policy had a number of side-effects, not all of which, evidently, had been foreseen. One was that the amount, originally fixed as a percentage of the RTÉ budget, was later changed into a fixed amount to be increased by an inflation index in each successive year. As the revenue from the licence fee remained unchanged until 2002, it followed inevitably that this amount grew as a percentage of RTÉ's total budget, leaving even less money for in-house programme-making. The second major consequence of this decision was that the money for the independent sector was not confined – as small independent com-

---

96 Michael Foley, 'Lack of Balance in Coverage of "Dear Daughter"', *Irish Times*, 19 March 1996.

panies had perhaps unwisely supposed it might be – to high quality public service programmes in the areas of arts, culture and current affairs, but spread across a whole range of programming, including variety programmes, gardening and quiz shows.

Only time will tell whether the new licence fee policy adopted by the government in the wake of the report of the Forum on Broadcasting in 2002 will help to re-generate RTÉ's domestic programme-making capacity to the desired extent. In 1996, however, the financial stringencies were cutting ever deeper. A group of RTÉ producers, in an independent response to the Government's Green Paper on Broadcasting, angrily described their own station's schedule as 'a series of low-cost, formula programmes, many of them merely imitating what has been commercially successful elsewhere…with success or failure measured primarily in terms of output and market share.'[97] This verdict encapsulated the problem neatly, but if anything under-estimated the central problem, which was that, in the continuing squeeze on resources, the options open to RTÉ if it was to maintain an audience of any size were pitifully few.

The third major area to pre-occupy the Director-General in his last two years of office was the question of the North and para-militarism. Here too there was a learning curve. A *Prime Time* programme on 11 April 1996 on a feud within the Irish National Liberation Army involved interviews with members of an illegal organisation, including some individuals who had absconded from bail and had weapons on a table in front of them (although the interviews were broadcast sub-titled, without a sound track). There were also problems arising from the fact that the ban had been in force for so many years – principally the use, and over-use, of an IRA propaganda video to illustrate items about Republican tactics and activities, in the absence of any suitable news or current affairs film within RTÉ's own audio-visual archives. There was concern, too, at the degree to which – as Loyalist violence erupted each August – RTÉ coverage was coming across as 'from our people, for our people'.[98]

The Authority, as well as divisional heads, was concerned at the extent to which Sinn Féin interviewees, in particular, appeared to have mastered interview techniques inasmuch as they rarely seemed to be under pressure or at a disadvantage when being interviewed on RTÉ, and were able to evade, or refuse to reply to, embarrassing questions with relative impunity. They were eventually enlightened, although hardly re-assured, by accounts of how Sinn Féin and IRA members had been trained to resist interrogation by members of the British and Northern Ireland security forces – training which put them generally at a dis-

97 Quoted in Quinn, *Maverick*, p. 91.

tinct advantage when dealing with broadcasters, however incisive or detailed their interview technique might be.[99]

Finally, at one of the last meetings of the Editorial Board before his retirement, Joe Barry must have wondered if, after so many years in the organisation, anything had really changed: there had been, he reported, an increasing volume of correspondence to his office, complaining that the station through its programming was damaging the moral fibre of the country – particularly in relation to marriage. In other words, RTÉ was at it again.

Bob Collins, immediately on his appointment as Director-General, served notice that he proposed to review the operation and composition of the Editorial Board, which he regarded as 'one of the most significant parts of organisational activity.'[100] It is not clear, in fact, that it had been anything like that in recent years. It is not within the brief of this particular book to review any changes or developments subsequent to his appointment, but one at least can be identified, if only because it signalled, finally, the end of a long-running battle which had been joined within the organisation some thirty years earlier with the transfer of 7 *Days* into the News Division. This was the decision to amalgamate news and current affairs finally within a single division under Ed Mulhall. This was accompanied by a lack of controversy which, given the experiences of earlier attempts at merger, was truly remarkable. In a sense, it probably reflected not only the overall stature of the people involved, but the final acknowledgement that the cultural, professional and organisational changes which had been moving news and current affairs closer and closer, particularly over the preceding decade, had now reached the point at which their appropriate institutional and structural expression had become inevitable.

98 Bob Collins, Editorial Board, Minutes, 9 August 1996. **99** Private source. **100** Editorial Board, Minutes, 24 April 1997.

Epilogue

The history of news and current affairs in RTÉ came full circle in 2002 when both activities were united in a new division headed by Ed Mulhall. This organisational development marked a definitive stage in a process which had been put in train in the autumn of 1968, when *Seven Days* was transferred, with considerable controversy, from the Programmes Division to the News Division.

The thirty-five intervening years had seen multiple battles being fought over the same terrain, not least because of the intense interest in these areas of broadcasting on the part of political and other elites. Throughout this period, a number of different factors have combined, not always in the same way, to make the task of the public service broadcast journalist at best hazardous, and sometimes worse. These include: the fact that a large part of the income of Irish public service broadcasting is derived from a licence fee which is determined by the political elite; the dismissal of the RTÉ Authority in 1972 and the resultant chilling effect; the changing role of both the Authority and the Director-General over the years; and the emergence of competition in both radio and television. The successive directives under Section 31 of the Broadcasting Act had the additional effect of transferring a measure of editorial control back to government, in sharp contrast to the spirit (if not the letter) of the Act which established the national broadcaster in 1961.

The attitudes of the political elites to the national broadcaster, and particularly towards its news and current affairs components, went through a number of different phases during this period. Initially there was bafflement, tinged with querulousness. How dare they! This was to be succeeded, as the Northern crisis gathered momentum, by a renewed sense of the political imperatives of government, culminating in the dismissal of the Authority in 1972. The inevitable consequence of this, insofar as a number of succeeding Authorities were concerned, was the development of a consciousness that they had been put in place to mind the shop rather than to develop and protect public service broadcasting. This tendency was if anything exacerbated by the way in which the station's financial problems became endemic as the licence fee was effectively eroded and costs escalated.

The two principal attempts to put manners on the unruly child were the disciplinary transfer of *Seven Days* to the News Division in 1968, and the closure of that programme in 1976. There were other, minor strategies, such as the inter-

212

mittent cold-shouldering of programmes – particularly current affairs programmes – by angry politicians. These strategies were, however, only partially
successful in meeting their somewhat different objectives: journalism, like water,
tends to find its own level. And this was the context in which the de-regulation
of broadcasting assumed a new significance in the late 1980s. It was going to
happen anyway, in one way or another: but the way in which it happened provides strong evidence for one commentator's view that 'the political goal of
establishing a source of television news outside the control of RTÉ remains the
primary function of the1988 Radio and Television Act.'[1]

There were, of course, two modes of journalism involved. In the area of news,
broadcast journalism was considerably hampered, for quite some time, by being
in thrall to the culture of print, and by the cumbersome nature of early broadcast technology. And all of this was overlaid, after 1968, by the Northern crisis.
The extent to which RTÉ news nevertheless succeeded, during this period, in
displeasing many powerful (and sometimes opposed) interests is an index of a
modest degree of success. In making attempts, right from the beginning, to provide space for points of view other than (and sometimes indeed hostile to) those
of traditional nationalism, it was swimming against a powerful tide that was not
only political but communitarian. The ease and frequency with which Northern
Unionist politicians and their British counterparts now find the time to con-
tribute to RTÉ radio and television programmes is at one level a measure of the
kind of authority that the station has acquired: at another, it serves to obscure
the historical reality that the early development and defence of this policy was
attended by very real difficulties. Almost two decades after the government of
which he was a member dismissed the RTÉ Authority, the Minister most closely involved, Gerry Collins, was to express his evidently still profoundly held
belief that at that time IRA leaders had a 'hot-line into the newsroom', and that
RTÉ journalists had 'glamourised' their activities.[2]

In the area of current affairs, the culture was initially quite different. Indeed,
the exuberant questioning of dominant values and ideas by a new generation of
young programme-makers had more than a touch of P.G. Wodehouse's journalistic hero, Psmith, about it. As Psmith told his editor, on the eve of assuming
responsibility for the innocuous journal, *Cosy Moments*, he planned a makeover:

> My idea is that *Cosy Moments* should become red-hot stuff. I could wish
> its tone to be such that the public will wonder why we do not print it on
> asbestos. Above all, we must be the guardian of the People's rights. We
> must be a search-light, showing up the dark spot in the souls of those who

---

1 Richard Barbrook, 'Broadcasting and national identity in Ireland' (1992), p. 217. **2** RTÉ1, *Forty years of news*, 20 December 2002.

would endeavour in any way to do the PEOPLE in the eye. We must detect the wrong-doer, and deliver him such a series of resentful biffs, that he will abandon his little games and become a model citizen.[3]

The problem about this, of course, is that a Chinese wall has traditionally been erected, by legislation, between public service broadcasting and advocacy journalism. The bricks in this wall are the concepts of impartiality and balance, enshrined and refined in our broadcasting legislation since 1960.They are concepts which provide a useful praxis for broadcasters, who generally invoke them in a non-reflective, highly operationalised manner, and they are in fact often a useful defence against criticism by special interests. They have been incorporated into the professional culture of both news and current affairs. They have also, in a positive sense, contributed substantially to the overall credibility of news and current affairs on the broadcast media, particularly on television, an area in which they have traditionally been given statutory effect, at least on this side of the Atlantic. Journalists – taken as an undifferentiated group – tend to rank poorly in public opinion surveys in terms of their general credibility and authority: a 2001 poll taken for the European Commission (the Eurobarometer) suggested that journalists came eighth out of ten different professional groups in terms of public esteem, equal to businessmen, and outranking only politicians (14% to 7%). On the other hand, a more recent UK poll suggested strongly that when journalists are broken down into disparate categories, journalists in ITV News, BBC News and Channel Four News came out among the most trusted groups, with 81% saying that they trusted them a great deal or a fair amount. Figures for journalists on broadsheet papers were lower, but similar (65% in both categories combined), whereas the 'trust' figures for red-top or tabloid journalists sank into substantial minus categories (-69%).[4]

There are multiple paradoxes at the heart of both the theory and practice of news and current affairs in both broadcast and print media, and one of them is that the professional culture of objectivity, impartiality and balance, which is almost certainly at the root of the high credibility rating given to legislatively-controlled electronic media, can also become a Trojan horse. As has been noted:

> Despite the unmistakable gains in reliable factual information and in openness, objectivity does not provide reporters with the political authority they need to accomplish their democratic mission. It does not protect news workers as they ask the hard questions and probe democracy's unpleasant issues. Rather, objectivity renders the press weak in the face of pressures from the market, the public, or the political elite.[5]

3 P.G. Wodehouse, *Psmith, journalist*, p. 33.   4 Ian Mayes, 'Trust me, I'm a journalist', *Guardian*, 15 March 2003.   5 Richard L. Kaplan, *Politics and the American press: the rise of objectivity, 1865-1920*, p. 194.

In the early days of RTÉ, university-educated programme makers were increasingly aware of these limitations, and fought against them. The classic academic case against them was expounded most articulately by one of the most influential of them, Jack Dowling, as far back as 1973.[6] What many of them, on the other hand, failed to recognise at the time is that the checks and balances that were placed on their exuberance within the station were not all (although some undoubtedly were) the reaction of a cautious broadcasting establishment which did not want to rock the boat. They were, in at least some cases, the reaction of managers to the prospect that, if things got out of hand, there would not in the end even be a boat left to rock. The broadcasters' criticism of these limited, and sometimes ambiguous, concepts undoubtedly on occasion made the task of senior station managers, fighting against powerful forces of whose existence and methods the broadcasters were only dimly and intermittently aware, objectively more difficult. The space that was finally created was limited: but it was, and remains, a space.

In the intervening years, subtlety, sophistication and professionalism have taken the place of bluff, bluster and power-plays. In the political and social environment within which news and current affairs broadcasting must operate, the legislative hammer-blow, the ukase, and the intimidatory phone call have given way to the pseudo-event, the sound-byte and the spin. The nature of the problem for public service broadcasters in current affairs has, accordingly, changed. As the difficulties connected with censorship recede, those connected with dangers of co-option by powerful political and economic interests assume a greater significance. Sophisticated political and economic elites, with their retinues of media consultants and advisers, have long since learnt that confrontation is not a recipe for good media coverage, and have learned to disguise or internalise their (no doubt frequent) belief that they are being mistreated or maligned. The risk in all of this is that broadcasters, intent as ever on ensuring that the powerful forces with which they deal continue to play by the rules, may overlook the possibility that the goalposts are being gradually moved.

As part of the same process, the cultural differences between news and current affairs have been elided, although not to the point of disappearance. There is a sense that they are two dialects of the same tongue, rather than mutually incomprehensible gibberish. This too has its problematic aspect. There is a sense in which the need for news to maintain its own distinctive dialect can be threatened by factors which can affect news values themselves: the culture of the celebrity reporter or presenter, for instance; and the extent to which news, which is essentially an information business, can find itself tempted (in an era of powerful competition from other networks with enormous resources) by the electronic media's enormous potential for entertainment.

6 Jack Dowling, 'Broadcasting: an exercise in deception?', *Aquarius*, pp. 123–33.

These factors pose new challenges to broadcasters in both areas. One of the few academic studies of broadcast content noted, specifically in relation to its study of the coverage of the divorce referendum campaign on RTÉ in November 1995:

> How we conduct our political television obviously has major ramifications for how we conduct our politics. Tendencies towards greater concision, and reliance on soundbites, on the one hand, and case histories and personalisation on the other, have important implications for how we discuss and make decisions about our future. If a programme dwells on research findings and statistics, it may alienate and bore, if it attempts to personalise a story, it may become superficial, and if it tries to present information in a lively and attention-grabbing style, it may only contribute further to the creation of a soundbite culture.[7]

The whole post-modern culture in which broadcasting now takes place, and in which the somewhat Victorian concepts of balance and impartiality become increasingly problematic, raises new questions for broadcasters and researchers alike. The amount of academic material related to RTÉ and its news and current affairs output is still pitifully small. *Media Audiences in Ireland*, already cited, deals with some important questions, but there are many more. A more recent work, *Challenging Perspectives: the majority world on Irish television*,[8] contains valuable suggestions for other forms of social and cultural research into the output of the national station in the area of international politics and development. In this context, news and current affairs broadcasters should take heart from the regard in which they are held by the public; but they should also ask themselves continually: do we deserve it? Is the public regard a recipe for complacency, or a guarantee of support for risk-taking? How can public service broadcasters 'ask the hard questions and probe democracy's unpleasant issues' without assuming the garb of a public prosecutor, which has the potential simultaneously to erode their credibility and threaten the always fragile relationship with political elites? How can they reflect the whole of society, and not only its most articulate or powerful components, without ceding all-important audience share to rival broadcasting systems which are not encumbered by any such democratic or public service notions?

In all of this they have, even in an age of globalisation, at least one powerful weapon. It is that the news and current affairs components of an indigenous

---

7 Stephen Ryan, 'Divorce Referendum coverage', in Mary J. Kelly and Barbara O'Connor (eds), *Media audiences in Ireland* (1997), p. 209. It is symptomatic of the problems of media analysis that this academic article features audience responses to only three RTÉ television clips. 8 Dierka Grießhaber (Comhlamh: Cork, 1997).

public service broadcasting system, for as long as they are accepted as authentic and authoritative by their audience, are at one and the same time their best protection against political and economic interference, and their best justification for that continuing support from the taxpayer without which theoretical and practical questions alike will melt into thin air.

Appendices

Appendix 1: Text of broadcast report by Kevin O'Kelly on *This Week**

Script of broadcast made by RTÉ between 1 p.m. and 2 p.m. on Sunday, 19 November 1972, as taken down from the tape supplied by RTÉ at the Department's request.

Earlier today I talked to David O'Connell, the Vice-President of Sinn Fein and I put to him the large question – <u>What right has the provisional I.R.A. to wage war on behalf of the Irish people or any section of them.</u> He said there were 2 <u>justifications,</u> the first arising from the right to defence against attacks – attacks specifically by Stormont <u>and the second justification he asserted was that the provisional I.R.A. would contend that they were pursuing the historic claims of the Irish people to self-determination without interference from Britain</u> – <u>a right written in the proclamation of 1916 and</u> – he said – <u>asserted on 5 occasions in this century.</u> Also earlier today I talked to Sean MacStiofain. I asked him first of all in a lengthy interview which we have condensed, did he think that anything Mr. Heath had said or did or the British Government had said or done recently had changed his attitude. <u>And he said if by our attitude you mean determination to continue the armed struggle until demands have been met then no.</u> They have said nothing and they have done nothing – he meant the British Government – which had changed this attitude. I asked him, therefore, if he thought there was any realistic chance of making the British change their mind. <u>I put it to him that the bombing campaign in the North had been declining recently. He said you get ebb and flow in every war and certainly in every guerrilla campaign.</u> But he said I can say with confidence that <u>we can</u> escalate at will and if we were not in that position we would be out of business. I asked him then if it was in the long term that they wished to drive the British out and he said when we met Whitelaw and Co. during the Summer we suggested a date I think January 1975 and we also feel, he said, if I might add, at this point, the declarations we

---

*The text of the broadcast is as contained in the National Archives files: all misspellings and emphases have been reproduced.

demanded from the British Government would have the effect of bringing many Unionist people in the North to grips with reality. They would realise that the British have used them for years, that they were gong to jettison them and they had no further use for them. Sean MacStiofain said that in a conference with unionists he believed they could achieve a solution based on the Proclamation of Easter week which guaranteed equal rights and equal opportunities.

I put it to him that the very breath of the notion that the British were about to leave had had the very reverse affect. It had formed the U.D.A., U.V.F., L.A.W. Mr. Craig had come to the fore and his reply – well I think this very splintering of the Unionist population shows confusion among their ranks and it arises from the suspension of Stormont. We feel that this disunity among them and the confusion which is among them at the present moment will help us to achieve our full objectives. But apart from the confusion I suggested it has also engendered militancy and he said it is well to keep in mind that quite a number of killings have been carried out by under cover British army agents and under cover British army personnel. Did he then discount the U.D.A., U.V.F. and tartan gangs and so forth as a militant force. And he said certainly not; only a fool would do that. But he said let me say this we hope that common sense will prevail with the leaders of these organisations, that they will realise the same as <u>we the leadership of the republican movement</u> realise that a bloody sectarian civil war would benefit no one. And if I can do anything he said with this interview, if I get that point across, we will have achieved something.

I am quite sure, he went on, that due to the circumstances of history a number of people, quite an appreciable number of people, that we have been talking about would have been antagonistic towards us and our ideas even without the campaign of armed struggle. For example look at the reaction that the peaceful demonstrations provoked several years ago. He said the impression I want to give is this that we are hoping civil war can be avoided. H said I am not saying we are confident it can be avoided. I am saying we are hoping that it will be avoided. We are hoping that even at this late hour those who are moving towards a civil war position will have second thoughts in the matter. But I asked what grounds for this hope have you given, that you intend apparently to continue a bombing campaign which has already engendered some violence on the other side and if continued would shortly engender more. He said well now lets get our facts right it has, I suppose it is correct to say, engendered some violence but this is because our motives have been misunderstood and because many of our actions have been deliberately misrepresented. <u>He said we have never directed any of our operations against people on account of their religion. Our operations have been directed against British Army personnel, U.D.R. personnel, R.U.C. personnel, and against economic targets and administrative targets.</u> But I put it to him that this was a euphemism and he said that he directed activity against economic targets. It means I said you blow up buildings where people work; when the buildings are blown up the people have no work. He said there is always a very good reason for any factory that was attached and if you check the records you will find that very few factories were in fact attacked and that those that were attacked had notorious records as far as sectarian discrimination in employment was concerned. Now turning to the political scene as he saw it, he once again demanded that the British Government recognise the rights of the Irish people as a whole, acting as a single unit, to decide the future of Ireland. The British he says have made up their minds as to the type of solution they intend to impose on the Irish people and I think we have got to look at things in that light. Whatever solution the British intend to impose they will not be imposing it on the people in the North alone: they will be imposing a solution on the Irish people as a whole to be given the opportunity to find their own solution that this is where we clash head on with the British. We will not accept a British imposed solution. Some time ago we called for an all Ireland conference so that the Irish people themselves could come up with a solution to what is the Irish problem. And we feel that this conference should be held as soon as possible. That means that there has got to be a bit of give and take among the various groupings, but it means that if the conference is held we can come up with a solution that can be presented to the British as the Irish people's alternative to the proposals that they would impose on the people again. Obviously, he went on, the republican movement will play a leading part in the conference but all involved Northern groupings would also participate. Such a conference without meaningful protestant or unionist representation would be meaningless.

Mr. MacStiofain asserted that he believed that the British Government's determination to impose a solution would disappear if the conference came up with an acceptable Irish solution and we asked him what kind of solution.

He said we would be pushing our own proposals and we would hope to have the opportunity of explaining them in detail. We have said many times that we would welcome and do welcome dialogue with any Protestant organisation in the North. I do not want to use the term Protestant he said but it is unavoidable. We feel that we have a lot in common with any organisation that genuinely represents ordinary people. Were they, therefore, willing to negotiate on their proposals? They are a basis for discussion he said. We would obviously scrap them not scrap them or alter them radically but there is room within the frame work of the proposals for a fair bit of manoeuvre. We can assure the Protestants that their rights would be safeguarded. Well and Protestants that have been killed by the I.R.A. have been killed because they have been serving in one or other of the British occupation forces, so he asserted. The facts are these he said that the origins of all the violence in Ireland, all the responsibility for the violence in Ireland rests fairly and squarely on the British Government. Did he therefore contend that there was no way out but violence and he said we believe that by armed struggle alone can we achieve our objectives. Do you see any basis at all for dialogue with those who think differently, for instance in the recent talk about negotiated independence which John Taylor has talked about and various other people. And he said we would like to know rather more about what Mr. Taylor means by negotiated independence, what the object of this negotiated independence would be. For example he said a negotiated independence cold lead to the establishment of a permanent totalitarian regime in the North in which the minority within the 6 county area would be very badly treated by the people in power there, the same as is happening in Rhodesia. What we would like to see he said is to see Mr. Taylor and his friends taking an interest in our proposals particularly in our Regional Government proposals in Dail Uladh. If he and his friends got down to a serious study of them that might possibly lead to a basis of dialogue between people who think like Mr. Taylor and people who think like us. Then with the plebescites and the local elections coming up in the North, was there any possibility I asked him that politically the Sinn Fein movement, of which he represented the military arm, might find it profitable to engage in politics, at least for the moment the battle being lulled.

Well he said there are all kinds of obstacles in the way of republicans fighting a political fight in the North. Sinn Fein is banned; there are all kinds of republicans contesting local elections and the new proposals for local government could be seen as the thin end of the wedge leading to a reconstructed Stormont and we would have to move very warily he said in that direction. Also there are all kinds of difficulties regarding oaths and declarations. Well supposing some means were found to allow them, or they were enabled somehow to contest the Northern elections, would you think as the military mind of the republican movement that it would be worthwhile trying this in principle. That any participation in local elections would be a collective decision between the combined leadership, the leadership of the republican movement to decide but he thought at the moment it was very much pie in the sky. But one noted that they had not contested elections the Republic. There was no Sinn Fein candidate in the mid-Cork by-election. Were they reluctant to put their ideals to the test? Under present circumstances he said we see no point in contesting the odd by-election. The odds he said were loaded in favour of what he called professional political parties in by-elections and he felt that the time was not opportune to contest general elections either. Of course they would have to take into consideration the circumstances that existed whenever a general election was called. If a general election was called in the near future, for example he said I doubt very much if the republican movement would contest it. The Sinn Fein organisation have stated that they intend to contest the local elections in the 26 counties next year and this is regarded as a step in the right direction if we are to have, he said, suitable candidates in the right organisations in certain other countries – certain other conditions. <u>We believe that by</u> <u>armed struggle alone he said again we can</u> <u>achieve our objectives.</u> Now that was the substance on an interview I had with Sean MacStiofain. It was in fact in the early hours of this morning.

Appendix 2: RTÉ Policy on Current / Public Affairs Broadcasting (1970)

1. Article 40 of the Constitution guarantees liberty, subject to public order and morality, for the exercise of the right of citizens to express freely their convictions and opinions. The same article goes on to state 'that the education of public opinion being, however, a matter of such grave import to the common good, the State shall endeavour to ensure that organs of public opinion, such as the radio, the press, the cinema, while preserving their rightful liberty of expression, including criticism of Government policy, shall not be used to undermine public order or morality or the authority of the state'.

   Article 10 of the 1948 European Convention for the Protection of Human Rights and Fundamental Freedoms, to which Ireland is a signatory, states that 'everyone has the right to freedom of expression. This right shall include freedom to hold opinions and to receive and impart information and ideas without interference by public authority and regardless of frontiers'.

   As a corollary to these expressions, the communications media carry a serious duty in the provision of information. As a foremost medium of communications and as a public service organisation, RTÉ accepts this responsibility in full. In doing so it operates on behalf of the community as a whole.

2. A basic information service is provided in news bulletins, in which the public is given facts, selected and presented in accordance with responsible news criteria.

3. But the right of the public to information extends beyond this. To be properly understood, news developments and matters of concern to the public must be placed in a context. This is achieved by means of current/public affairs programming which examines the background of events and public affairs, explaining the relevant factors and what the consequential effects may be. In this way, the public is helped to understand and assess the significance of events and issues.

4. Broadcasting is not just a channel for any and all opinions, nor can it be neutral in its basic philosophy and attitudes. It should seek to widen and deepen the knowledge of the audience. At the same time, it must generally reflect the mores and respect the values of the society in which it operates. In this

context, it has an obligation to respect standards of taste, decency and justice; it must be impartial and it must observe the law. This does not, however, preclude the broadcasting media from making such critical examination of public issues as are considered necessary to fulfil the needs of impartial and objective enquiry.

It is recognised that the selection of material for broadcasting is inescapably bound up with the standards of the programme-maker. The process of selection should be carried out with the intention of fully informing society and not with the intention of giving expression to the views of the individual programme maker.

5. Section 18 (1) of the Broadcasting Authority Act contains a specific provision as follows:–

'It shall be the duty of the Authority to secure that, when it broadcasts and information, news or feature which relates to matters of public controversy or is the subject of current political debate, the information, news or feature is presented objectively and impartially and without any expression of the Authority's own views'.

6. This requirement is interpreted in RTÉ in the light of the following considerations:

   (a) The Authority, in this context, is taken to include all its staff and all those who may reasonably be seen by the public to be speaking on behalf of RTÉ.

   (b) The obligation to objectivity is seen as requiring broadcasting staff to apply normal programming criteria in their selection and presentation of programmes without allowing personal leanings to influence their judgement in a manner inconsistent with those criteria. In this context, the presentation of programmes includes all the visual and other techniques used in programme making.

   (c) The obligation to impartiality is seen as requiring broadcasting staff to acquire the relevant background knowledge on the subject matter being treated of, to present, either directly or through participants, the relevant information correctly and to achieve fair balance in representation.

   (d) It is recognised that, especially in 'live' programmes, the achievement of objectivity and impartiality can be judged only after transmission.

7. The following considerations are to be regarded as a framework of reference for current practice:–

    (i) The general approach must be positive and no arbitrary limitation should be placed on the scope of current/public affairs programming. In the range of output the programmes deal with trends and changes in political, economic, social and cultural affairs and matters of public controversy should be fully reflected.

    (ii) The Provision of information, skilled analysis, informed comment and open discussion are accepted as essential elements of current/public affairs programming. The purpose is to provide the public with the information and knowledge on which it can make up its mind on the question at issue.

    (iii) There is a primary obligation to be fair to all interests, public or private, involved in the issues which are treated in broadcast programmes. Care should be taken to avoid unfairness to those who, for any reason, are unable to present their own case, and to those who are unorganised or inarticulate. Programme-makers should ensure that their own concern does not result in a one-sided or incomplete presentation of an issue.

    (iv) In seeking balance in current/public affairs programming, it is accepted that all significant view-points should be represented. It is recognised, however, that in the treatment of issues which are or are likely to be of continuing public interest, this may not always be practicable in every single programme; in that case the duty of impartiality will be regarded as discharged if a balance is maintained between different viewpoints, taking one programme with another, over a reasonable period of time.

    (v) In approaching any programme, the programme-makers should judge what information is relevant within the context of the programme. Sometimes they may decide to concentrate a programme on one segment or aspect of a subject. In such cases, it should be the practice to make clear to the public the precise limits of the treatment selected.

    (vi) All who appear on radio or television are regarded as agreeing to face penetrating questions, but are entitled to courtesy and fair play. RTÉ does not assume any right to place any person on trial before the nation by aggressive questioning or otherwise.

    (vii) RTÉ accepts that any person, whether in private or in public life, has a right to decline an invitation to appear in a programme without giving any reasons and that conclusions must not be drawn by the programme makers from such refusal. Only in rate and exceptional cases are programme makers regarded as justified in informing the public that an invitation to take part in a broadcast has been issued and refused.

(viii) Where certain parties or interests involved in public issues have been invited to take part in a programme but one or some of them refuse, RTÉ does not regard itself as being thereby precluded from going ahead with the programme. The attitude is that cancellation of a programme because any particular party or interest refuses participation would be equivalent to granting this party or interest a veto over the particular subject. Such a veto would be seen as inconsistent with RTÉ's duty to deal with important issues. RTÉ reserves its right to use its own discretion in fulfilling its obligations in such a situation.

T.P. Hardiman
Director-General

8th May 1970

Sources

Archival sources
Desmond Fisher papers
Dublin Diocesan Archives (DDA)
National Archives of Ireland (NA)
National Union of Journalists (NUJ)
Radio Telefis Éireann Archives
    RTÉ Reference Library
    RTÉ Audio-visual Library
    RTÉ Written Archives
    RTÉ Authority Minutes
    RTÉ Programme Policy Committee Minutes (PPC)
    RTÉ Editorial Board Minutes
    RTÉ Annual Reports
    Radio Éireann Handbook
Seán Lemass papers
United States National Archives (USNA)
University College, Dublin, Archives Dept: C.S. Andrews papers (UCD)

Public sources
Debates, Dáil Éireann
Debates, Seanad Éireann

Newspapers and periodicals
Cork Examiner/Examiner
Hibernia
Irish Broadcasting Review
Irish Independent
Irish Press
Irish Times
Leader

Magill
Sunday Tribune
RTV Guide/RTÉ Guide
The Journalist
Sunday Independent
Sunday Review
Sunday Press

Books and articles

Andrews, C.S., *Dublin made me* (Dublin: Mercier Press, 1979).

Atton, Chris, 'News cultures and new social movements: radical journalism and the mainstream media', *Journalism Studies*, 3:4 (November 2002), pp. 491–505.

Barbrook, Richard, 'Broadcasting and national identity in Ireland', *Media, Culture and Society*, 14 (1992).

Broadcasting Review Committee, *Report 1974* (Dublin: Government Publications Sale Office, 1974)

Browne, Vincent, 'SFWP 7: The slanting of a programme', *Magill* (May 1982).

Byrne, Gay, *To whom it concerns* (Dublin: Gill and Macmillan, 1972).

Carr, Bunny, *The instant tree* (Cork: Mercier Press, 1975).

Collins, Pan, *It started on the Late Late Show* (Dublin: Ward River Press, 1981).

Comiskey, Rev. Brendan, 'Should Christians always lose?', *Irish Broadcasting Review* (12) (Autumn/Winter 1981).

Cooney, John, *John Charles McQuaid: ruler of Catholic Ireland* (Dublin: O'Brien Press, 1999)

Curtis, Liz, *Ireland: the propaganda war* (London: Pluto, 1984).

Davis, E.E., and Sinnott, R., *Attitudes in the republic relevant to the Northern Ireland problem: Volume 1: descriptive analysis and some comparisons with attitudes in Northern Ireland and Great Britain* (Dublin: Economic and Social Research Institute, paper No. 97. 1979).

Doolan, Lelia, Dowling, Jack, and Quinn, Bob, *Sit down and be counted: the cultural evolution of a television station* (Dublin: Waterloo Publications, 1969).

Dowling, Jack, 'Broadcasting: An Exercise in Deception', *Aquarius*, 3 (1973).

Duignan, Seán, *One spin on the merry-go-round* (Dublin: Blackwater, 1998).

Dunn, Joseph, *TV and politics* (Dublin: The Catholic Communications Institute, 1971).

Feeney, Peter, 'Censorship and RTÉ', *The Crane Bag*, 8:2 (1984).

Fisher, Desmond, *Broadcasting in Ireland* (London: Routledge, 1978).

Fuller, Louise, *Irish Catholicism since 1950: the undoing of a culture* (Dublin: Gill and Macmillan, 2002).

Garvin, Tom, *Mythical thinking in political life: reflections on nationalism and social science* (Dublin: Maunsel and Company, 2001).

Gorham, Maurice, *Forty years of Irish broadcasting* (Dublin: The Talbot Press, 1967).

Griesshaber, Dierka, *Challenging perspectives: the majority world on Irish television* (Cork: Comhlamh, 1997)

Hanly, David, 'Féach!', *RTÉ Guide*, 11 December 1970.

Harris, Eoghan, *The production of the popular image* (1980), photocopy. RTÉ Reference Library.

——, *Television and terrorism*, 1987, mimeo. RTÉ reference library.

Hofffman, Arnold, *How to write a journalistic contribution* (Prague: International Organisation of Journalists, 1984).

Horgan, Jane, and Meehan, Niall, *Survey on attitudes of Dublin population to Section 31 of the broadcasting act* (Dublin: National Institute for Higher Education, 1987).

Horgan, John, *Lemass: The enigmatic patriot* (Dublin: Gill and Macmillan, 1997).

——, *Irish media: a critical history since 1922* (London, Routledge, 2001).

——, 'Journalists and Censorship: A Case History of the NUJ in Ireland and the Broadcasting Ban 1971–94', *Journalism studies*, 3:3. (2002).

Irvine, John, 'Broadcasting and the Public Trust' (Thomas Davis Lecture, 1976), mimeo.

Joint Committee on State-Sponsored Bodies, *18th Report: Radio Telefís Éireann* (7 May 1981).

Kaplan, Richard, *Politics and the American press: the rise of objectivity 1865–1920* (New York: Cambridge University Press, 2002).

Kealy, Alacoque, *Irish radio data 1926–1980* (Dublin: RTÉ, May 1981)

Kelly, J.M., 'The Constitutional Position of RTÉ', *Administration*, 15:3 (Autumn 1967).

Kelly, Mary J., and O'Connor, B., *Media audiences in Ireland: power and cultural identity* (Dublin: University College Dublin Press, 1997).

Keogh, Dermot, 'Ireland and "Emergency Culture": between Civil War and Normalcy, 1922–1961', *Ireland: a journal of history and society*, 1:1 (1995).

Kerrigan, Gene, 'The Women's Programme', *Magill* (November 1983).

McCaffrey, Colm, 'Political communication and broadcasting: theory, practice and reform', PhD thesis (University College, Dublin, 1991).

McCarthy, Justine, *Mary McAleese: An unauthorised biography* (Dublin: Blackwater, 1999).

Mac Conghail, Muiris, 'Politics by wireless: news and current affairs on radio 1926–2001' (Thomas Davis Lecture, 30 April 2001), mimeo.

McDermott, Linda, 'The political censorship of the Irish broadcast media 1960–1994', MA Thesis, Department of Communications and Theatre, Notre Dame University, Indiana, 1996.

McGuigan, Ray, 'SFWP 3: The making of a conspiracy', *Magill* (May 1982).

McGuinness, James, 'News broadcasting', *Administration*, 15:3 (Autumn 1967).

Mitchel, Charles, 'Stepping into the News', *RTÉ Guide* (31 October 1971).

O'Connor, Ulick, *The Ulick O'Connor Diaries 1970–81: a cavalier Irishman* (London: John Murray, 2001)

O Drisceoil, Donal, *Censorship in Ireland 1939–45* (Cork: Cork University Press, 1996).

Ó Móráin, Donal, 'The Irish Experience', *Irish broadcasting review*, 10 (Spring 1981)

Philo, Greg, *Really bad news* (Glasgow: Writers and Readers, 1982).

Pine, Richard, *2RN and the origins of Irish radio* (Dublin: Four Courts Press, 2002).

Power, Brenda, 'Eoghan Harris: out of the shadows', *Magill* (November 1997).

Quinn, Bob, *Maverick: a dissident view of broadcasting today* (Brandon: Dingle, 2001)

Ross, John, 'Looking back', *RTV Guide* (8 December 1961).

Savage, Robert, *Irish television: the political and social origins* (Cork: Cork University Press, 1996).

Thornley, David, *Ireland – the end of an era?* (Dublin: Tuairim, 1965).

——, 'Television and politics', *Administration*, 15:3 (Autumn 1967).

Tóibín, Niall, *Smile and be a villain* (Dublin: Town and Country House, 1995).

Walsh, John, 'Seven days is a long time in politics', *RTÉ Guide* (7 May 1976).

——, '"Today Tonight": where somebody knows practically anything', *RTÉ Guide* (14 November 1980).

White, Jack, 'Inquiry, discussion, controversy', *RTÉ Guide* (31 December 1971).

——, 'Trying out new ideas: favourites return', *RTÉ Guide* (24 September 1976).

Williams, Raymond, 'Base and superstructure in Marxist cultural history', in *Problems in materialism and culture* (London: Verso, 1980).

Wodehouse, P.G., *Psmith, journalist* (London: A. & C. Black, 1923).

Index